From Net Neutrality to ICT Neutrality

Patrick Maillé • Bruno Tuffin

From
Net Neutrality
to
ICT Neutrality

 Springer

Patrick Maillé
IMT Atlantique
Rennes, France

Bruno Tuffin 🆔
Centre Inria de l'Université de Rennes
Rennes, France

ISBN 978-3-031-06270-4   ISBN 978-3-031-06271-1   (eBook)
https://doi.org/10.1007/978-3-031-06271-1

This Springer imprint is published by the registered company Springer Nature Switzerland AG
The registered company address is: Gewerbestrasse 11, 6330 Cham, Switzerland

Preface

ICT (for *Information and Communication Technology*) is omnipresent in our modern society, and the economy has gone beyond the industrial economy to the Internet and ICT economy. Thanks to hyper-connectivity, there are now lots of opportunities for innovation. As of January 2022, the top 3 most valuable companies worldwide are all ICT companies (Apple Inc., Microsoft, Alphabet Inc.), and three other ICT companies (Amazon Inc., Facebook, Tencent) appear in the top 10.[1] Internet Service Providers (ISPs), Content Delivery Networks (CDNs) and cloud providers, and social network actors, all services and content providers are among actors researching a business model as profitable as possible.

But the success of ICT is often coined to be linked to the open and free Internet, fostering participation and innovation. With numerous actors willing to design and implement business models to increase their revenue, the impact on the whole network outcome can be significant. That issue has been highlighted when ISPs started claiming that some big content providers, representing an important part of the traffic flowing through their network, should participate to the network infrastructure upgrading costs, with the threat of being blocked or slowed down in case of refusal. This launched the *network neutrality debate*. Basically, net neutrality means that Internet providers should treat all Internet packets the same way, regardless of their type, content, origin, or destination. Network (non-)neutrality has become a very hot topic in the past few years, at the same time from political, economic, and daily life points of view, because it may refashion the Internet business model and in general the telecommunications vision and future. Our purpose is to review the debate and discuss arguments and regulation passed worldwide. We also aim at providing a balance between mathematical theory and practical discussion.

Another issue is that while the network neutrality issue has been the polarizing on ISPs' role, the Internet has changed from the simple content-ISP-users delivery chain to a more complicated ecosystem with numerous intermediaries between content and users and players affecting the online experience. The book aims at

---

[1] https://fxssi.com/top-10-most-valuable-companies-in-the-world.

highlighting the role of those other actors (CDNs, search engines, "structuring platforms," social networks, etc.) and the impact of their possibly non-neutral behavior, which can bypass the general neutrality principles without violating the (packet-based) rules currently evoked in the debate. A typical example is the ranking algorithms of search engines being suspected of voluntarily putting in a higher position their own businesses or their "relations" and lowering the position of competitors, leading to the so-called *search neutrality debate*. One of our goals is open the reader to the complications of limiting the neutrality debate to ISPs, potentially requiring to extend the neutrality framework to a general definition encompassing all actors and clarifying the rules. That issue leads to a debate on the transparency of algorithms, expected by regulatory bodies, that we hint in the last chapters.

We hope that the text will open the readers' mind to the issues of fairness, freedom, and economic efficiency, among others, and illustrate the complexity of confronting those high-level considerations with the constantly evolving ICT technical realities.

Rennes, France   Patrick Maillé
                                                                                Bruno Tuffin

Acknowledgments

We, the authors, would like to thank the editors, in particular Ralf Gerstner, for their assistance, encouragement, and patience during the preparation of this book. Any mistake, error of judgement, or treatment imbalance in the book is our sole responsibility.

Contents

About the Authors

Patrick Maillé graduated from Ecole Polytechnique and Telecom Paris, France, in 2000 and 2002, respectively. He has been with IMT Atlantique (formerly Telecom Bretagne) since 2002, where he obtained his PhD in applied mathematics in 2005 and his habilitation (Rennes 1 university) in 2015. He has held visiting scholar appointments at Columbia University (June–December 2006) and UC Berkeley (academic year 2014–2015). His research interests are in all economic aspects of telecommunication networks, from pricing schemes at the user level to auctions for spectrum and regulatory issues. He currently serves as an Associate Editor for *Electronic Commerce Research and Applications* (Elsevier) and *IEEE Open Journal of the Communications Society*. He has authored or co-authored more than 150 papers on those topics and is along with Bruno Tuffin the author of *Telecommunication Network Economics: From Theory to Applications* published by Cambridge University Press in 2014.

Bruno Tuffin received his PhD degree in applied mathematics from the University of Rennes 1 (France) in 1997. Since then, he has been with Inria in Rennes and has been the leader of the team called ERMINE since January 2022. He spent 8 months as a postdoc at Duke University in 1999. His research interests include developing Monte Carlo and quasi-Monte Carlo simulation techniques for the performance evaluation of telecommunication systems and developing new Internet-pricing schemes and telecommunication-related economic models. He has published close to 200 papers on those issues. He has also led or participated into several French and European projects and co-organized several conferences. He is currently Area Editor for *INFORMS Journal on Computing* and Associate Editor for *ACM Transactions on Modeling and Computer Simulation* and *Queuing Systems: Theory and Applications* and was formerly Associate Editor for *Mathematical Methods of Operations Research* and *INFORMS Journal on Computing*. He has written or co-written three books: *Rare Event Simulation Using Monte Carlo Methods* published by John Wiley & Sons in 2009, *La simulation de Monte Carlo* (in French) published by Hermes Editions in 2010, and *Telecommunication Network Economics: From Theory to Applications* published by Cambridge University Press in 2014, also co-authored with Patrick Maillé.

Acronyms

ADSL	Asymmetric Digital Subscriber Line
AI	Artificial intelligence
API	Application Programming Interface
ARCEP	Autorité de régulation des communications électroniques, des postes et de la distribution de la presse
ARPA	Advanced Research Projects Agency
BEREC	Body of European Regulators for Electronic Communications
BT	British Telecommunications
CDN	Content delivery network
CERN	European Organization for Nuclear Research
CP	Content provider
CRTC	Canadian Radio-television and Telecommunications Commission
CTR	Click-through rate
DNS	Denial of service
DPI	Deep packet inspection
DSL	Digital subscriber line
EU	European Union
FCC	Federal Communications Commission
FTC	Federal Trade Commission
FTTH	Fiber to the home
GAFAM	Google, Apple, Facebook, Amazon, and Microsoft
ICT	Information and Communication Technology
IoT	Internet of Things
IP	Internet Protocol
ISP	Internet service provider
NIST	National Institute of Standards and Technology
NPT	Norwegian Post and Telecommunications Authority
OECD	Organisation for Economic Co-operation and Development
OS	Operating system
OSI	Open System Interconnection
P2P	Peer to peer

QoE	Quality of experience
QoS	Quality of service
RFC	Request for Comments
SE	Search engine
TCP	Transmission Control Protocol
TRAI	Telecom Regulatory Authority of India
UDP	User Datagram Protocol
VoIP	Voice over Internet Protocol

Chapter 1
Introduction: A Bit of History

1.1 The Advent of the Digital Economy and the Need for Regulation

ICT (for *Information and Communication Technology*) is an acronym that designates the field integrating all technologies dealing with communications, computing, and information processing. ICT is the extension of IT, for *Information Technology*, which was coined for the first time around the Second World War (particularly in Los Alamos for nuclear research) for the development of computers. The extension to ICT was to encompass electronic communications. ICT concerns the design, development, and analysis of hardware and software in computer and information systems, including networking, data management, etc. It has become omnipresent in our daily life and changed the way we live and work. ICT tools assist us at each step of our activities: we use computers and smartphones to communicate, even with people far way, through voice calls, emails, videoconferences, and social networks; we can access any information and buy everything online; ICT enables new education means, including virtual reality, interactive multimedia, and distance courses; it simplifies entertainment, thanks to online and on-demand television and video gaming; it simplifies healthcare with tele-health and distant monitoring; it also helps companies in their activities; it is key in the development of robots to perform many tasks, etc.

The impact and weight of ICT in the worldwide economy keeps increasing. Many types of figures can be given, and the reader is advised to look for example at the Web page maintained by OECD (Organisation for Economic Co-operation and Development) with some key ICT indicators http://www.oecd.org/internet/broadband/oecdkeyictindicators.htm, or at [79]. To illustrate the increasing impact of ICT in our lives, let us focus on e-commerce (i.e., buying things online). Updating data published in [104], e-commerce sale have increased from US$1.34 in 2014 to US$3.53 trillion in 2019 and $4.9 trillion in 2021 (an average 20% growth, almost unaffected by the COVID-19 crisis); they are projected to reach US$6.4

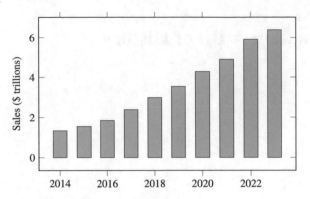

Fig. 1.1 Evolution of e-commerce sales (Statista data). Values from 2014 to 2020 are real data, 2021 and later projected values

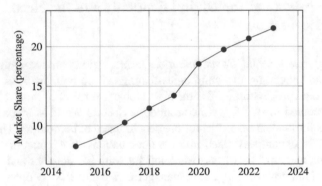

Fig. 1.2 Evolution of e-commerce market share. Values from 2015 to 2020 are real data, 2021 and later projected values

trillion in 2023. Figure 1.1 details this evolution of worldwide sales with values per year. Not only sales value increases: the e-commerce share of total global retail industry also keeps increasing, and that trend is expected to continue as shown in Fig. 1.2.[1] Another notable indicator of ICT predominance can be found on the businesses' side: as of January 2022, the top three most valuable companies worldwide are all ICT companies (Apple Inc., Microsoft, Alphabet Inc.), and three other ICT companies (Amazon Inc., Facebook, Tencent) appear in the top ten.[2] Finally, Fig. 1.3 plots the volume of Internet traffic year by year from 1990 to 2017, with predictions at the time we got figures for 2018 and later. It illustrates the growth and increasing importance of Internet traffic in our modern society and the associated technological challenges we are facing if we want to ensure a sufficient

---

[1] For data, see https://www.shopify.com/enterprise/the-future-of-ecommerce or https://www.emarketer.com/content/global-ecommerce-2020.

[2] https://fxssi.com/top-10-most-valuable-companies-in-the-world

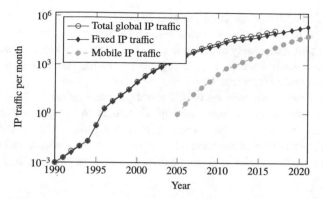

Fig. 1.3 IP traffic evolution in petabytes per month, logarithmic scale (Cisco data)

quality of service to all users: new technological concepts need to be created to ease the load on the network, wired (e.g., with caching), and/or wireless (with the evolution from 3G to 4G and now the advent of 5G).

But all the advances to ease our life and business are also accompanied with many fears and threats. First, it is often argued that ICT impacts physical activity[3] and therefore impacts health, due to the increasing time spent in front of screens and the less physically demanding tasks we tend to do. Another complaint is that ICT reduces physical social interactions and therefore somewhat counterintuitively favors isolation. A third raised concerns the easiness of disseminating fake news enabled by ICT, which has become a major concern for public education: the news were before managed by professionals (journalists) checking facts in most cases; now any individual can propagate false information without control. Moreover, all those new ICT activities have also brought a new type of criminality, named cybercriminality. The new types of offenses include[4] (i) phishing, using fake email messages to get personal information (email account, data, bank account, credit card number), (ii) hacking a network or a Web site, and (iii) distributing hate or pornography. Consequences include identity theft, cyber-extorsion (e.g., ransomware), cryptojacking, or cyberespionage. Finally, there is an increasing concern about the environmental impact of ICT, in terms of greenhouse gas emissions and power consumption (it is expected that billions of IT Internet-connected devices will produce 14% of global emissions by 2040, and the communications industry could use 20% of all the world's electricity by 2025[5]).

In summary, ICT brings a lot of positive externalities to society, eases life, and offers opportunities and new interactions but naturally comes with some issues

---

[3] https://medicalnewsbulletin.com/technology-physical-activity-levels-students/

[4] See among others https://www.government.nl/topics/cybercrime/forms-of-cybercrime.

[5] https://www.climatechangenews.com/2017/12/11/tsunami-data-consume-one-fifth-global-electricity-2025/

and worries. ICT keeps evolving, and as it involves several types of interacting commercial actors, behaving in most cases selfishly to maximize their profits, it seems important that society checks the impact of those behaviors on social welfare to prevent a potential harm. This is typically why regulatory bodies have been introduced: to ensure a fair use of ICT.

One of the most vivid debates in ICT about potential behaviors harming welfare regards what occurs in the Internet "pipes": that is the so-called Net neutrality debate, which we detail, develop, and extend in this book. The next section recalls some historical events and explains why the debate has become a major issue. We will next discuss how and why it can be extended to all domains of ICT.

1.2   The Internet: Worries About the Lack of Neutrality

The central element of the ICT economy is probably the Internet network. The principle of the Internet started in the early 1960s (even by Feb. 7 of 1958, when the Advanced Research Projects Agency (ARPA) was launched in the USA, starting research on the topic). The basic idea was to be able to connect computers in order to share information and resources for research, but also in order to provide a robust network to the US military during the Cold War. At that time, the USA was worried about the scientific advances from the Soviet Union, in particular their success with the Sputnik satellite in 1957, igniting fears about the impact it could have on the US long-distance communication network. The project, led by J.C.R. Licklider, was the inception of what we now know as the Internet. The concept was (and still is) to transmit data by cutting information into so-called *packets* sent independently one after the other and re-ordered at the received end. In contrast to the traditional telephone network transmission method, called *circuit-switching* because a *circuit* (a set of resources necessary for the communication along the whole path) is built and reserved for the communication, there is no need to reserve resources here: packets can be sent one after the other and re-sent in case of any problem, making the communication more robust. A packet is easily built and is made of two parts: the *payload* containing the slice of data to be sent and the *header* containing information such as source, destination, and any other useful detail used for routing among other things [84, 174]. The first connection between two computers was effective in 1965, between the Massachusetts Institute of Technology and California, followed by the "ARPAnet" network and connecting universities and research organizations in contract with the US Defense Department. That network was implementing applications, routing, and addressing protocols still in use nowadays. Many other networks of universities were then created using the same protocols and were therefore able to interoperate with ARPAnet. The Internet was officially created in 1983, when ARPAnet was separated from the military network, connecting universities across the USA. The transmission control protocol (TCP) was adopted, facilitating transmissions between computers and boosting the network development. Internet communications knew major progresses with the creation and standardization of the hypertext transfer protocol (http) at the European Organization for Nuclear Research (CERN), allowing to access Internet sites, and with the creation of the Mosaic Web browser in 1993. Due to its success and the new opportunities it opened for the society, the network was then opened to support commerce and industry in the early 1990s, with Internet providers building their own networks linked to the Internet backbone at access points and selling access to end users or companies themselves offering services or content to customers.

The Internet has thus evolved, from a network connecting universities to a global network actively used by 4.88 billion people worldwide as of October 2021, connecting 62% of the global population. The network has evolved fast in 60 years and for sure keeps evolving. Due to the essence of the Internet as a non-commercial network between universities, cooperation between entities was the main functioning principle of the network; with the introduction of for-profit organization, it is not the case anymore, and commercial agreements have to be settled between all parties. Users' perception of what the Internet should be remains, for many, an open and in some respect a "cost-free" network. Hence the perceived notion of "neutrality" (to be better defined later on), probably due to what the network was at its origin: the network is expected to not filter anybody, nor any application or service. But over time, several instances of such (non-neutral) behaviors have been observed, leading to worries and initiating the *debate on net neutrality*. Here is a chronological list of such historic events, non-exhaustive but illustrative of the reasons of the debate; see also among others [67]:

- The concerns about a philosophy change in the Internet particularly sparked at the end of 2005, when the CEO of AT&T, Ed Whitacre, complained that distant content providers (CPs) were paying another access provider to access the Internet network, but were using the AT&T network for free in order to reach end users, since traffic had to go through their own network to go to destination. Ed Whitacre concluded that CPs should pay AT&T as a contribution to the network infrastructure investments. In case of refusal, the threat was to lower the quality, or even block the traffic, of services from CPs not contributing. This initiated a lot of protests.
- Still in 2005, Madison River Communications, a DSL service provider for the southeast and midwest, blocked ports (a port is a process-specific or an application-specific software construct serving as a communication endpoint) used by the Voice-Over-IP (VoIP) service of Vonage. VoIP services are "for free" as included in the Internet plan but actually compete with regular telephony which are charged differently, in a more lucrative way depending on the connection duration. Madison River was convicted with violating a nondiscrimination principle by the Federal Communications Commission (FCC), the US telecommunications regulator. That was the first case a provider was proven to violate a principle of neutrality. This VoIP situation also illustrates the complexity of neutrality principles: at one point, some European regulators were not officially considering VoIP as Internet traffic due to its naturally competing with regular call services and were tolerating blocking; it did not last though.

- That same year, 2005, it was observed that a Canadian ISP, Telus, blocked its Internet subscribers from accessing a Web page called Voices for Change maintained by the Telecommunications Workers Union (TWU) and supporting union members in strike against the ISP. The official justification given was that striking workers were jamming Telus phone lines and posting pictures of employees crossing the union picket lines. Telus eventually unblocked the Web site after a court granted an interim injunction against posting Telus employee photographs online, but the question of neutrality in Canada became prominent with that incident.
- In 2007, the US Internet provider Comcast blocked several peer-to-peer (P2P) applications such as BitTorrent, arguing that content exchanged through P2P is mostly illegal. P2P applications are resource consuming, and blocking them was also argued to reduce the load on the network and allow a better quality for all other "legal" applications. The decision has provoked strong reactions: Comcast was sued in California, the complaint claiming that BitTorrent blocking was an unfair business practice. In 2008, the FCC concluded that Comcast had "unduly interfered with internet users' right to access the lawful internet content and to use the applications of their choice."
- From 2007 up to 2009, AT&T also asked Apple to block Skype as well as later the Google Voice app and other VoIP services on iPhones (AT&T had exclusive rights to sell the early iPhone models).
- VoIP applications have been regularly throttled worldwide: In Chile, a local ISP Voissnet sued with success (in 2007) the major ISP Telefonica for slowing down its services.
- In April 2009, the German ISP T-Mobile also blocked Skype's VoIP traffic, evoking technical and non-economical reasons, because of a reduced overall performance of its network due to Skype traffic creating congestion about which users of other services would complain about.
- VoIP was not the only type of service targeted by ISPs: the main UK provider, British Telecommunications (BT), was accused in July 2009 of limiting the maximum rate for video streaming from the BBC TV channel; here too, the reason invoked by the ISP was the optimization of network performance.
- In 2010, the DSL provider Windstream Communications based in Little Rock, Arkansas, hijacked the search tool in the tool bar of Firefox, replacing the search engine chosen by the user by its own search portal.
- In 2011, the resource-consuming YouTube traffic was perceivably slowed down by the French ISP Free, the provider claiming that was due to technical (peering) reasons, and not on purpose.
- In 2011, the Web site thepiratebay.org, a torrent Web site mainly used for downloading movies or music, was blocked by Belgian ISPs for copyright reasons following a court decision. This came after thepiratebay.org complained in 2009 about ISPs blocking it, Belgacom and Telenet, a maneuver initially said to be disproportionate in 2010, but overruled by the court of appeal in 2011, even imposing blocking.

- In 2011, several ISPs, including Cogent, Fuse, DirecPC, RCN, etc., were found to redirect search requests for Bing or Yahoo search engines to another page (a practice called a DNS violation) and sharing the resulting gains.
- In 2011–2013, the major ISPs AT&T, Sprint, and Verizon all blocked the mobile-payment Google Wallet, developed by Google, because they were jointly developing their own equivalent service. Blocking was made by removing it from their devices. An interrogation was raised regarding whether or not that was a real neutrality infringement since no traffic was blocked, but here blocking takes place upstream.
- During the same years, the mobile operator MetroPCS proposed a discount phone plan including unlimited talking, texting, and Web browsing, but with YouTube as the *only* possible video streaming service; for any competitor, an extra fee was required. The argument was that users were in general more interested in YouTube. This also raised questions about being a non-neutral behavior.
- In 2012, Verizon was accused of blocking tethering applications (applications for sharing of a mobile device's Internet connection with other connected computers) on their phones by asking Google to remove the apps from Android Market, the former name of Google Play, the android app store. With this move, Verizon was preventing connection sharing and collecting the US$20 fee that Verizon was imposing for this type of service included in its offers.
- In 2012, AT&T blocked FaceTime, the video chat app from Apple, except if customers paid an extra fee. Again, the impact on the overall performance was put forward by AT&T.
- In June 2013 in Zambia, the Web page of the main newspaper watchdog.com was blocked in the country, illustrating a potential hindrance to freedom of speech.
- In 2015, the Dutch telecom companies KPN and Vodafone were fined for blocking VoIP services from their Wi-Fi hotspots, similarly to what Madison River Communications did in 2005.

This list is not exhaustive but illustrates the types of limitations ISPs tried to impose over time, with their motivations.

1.3 New Services: New Difficulties and Potential Hindrance to Society

We have highlighted above some limiting actions that ISPs can implement on . Internet traffic. But it seems important to us to note that Internet telecommunications are not anymore as simple as the supply chain of the Internet first years, with just ISPs standing as intermediaries between users and content. The Internet ecosystem has changed a lot and keeps evolving, with many new actors popping up over time. As some representative illustrations, we can name:

- *Service providers.* They are providing facilitated services to access content and can be classified in several sub-categories. YouTube is a typical example of a service provider, allowing anybody to post video content by offering all the necessary resources for that purpose: one just needs to create an account to have their video content stored and made accessible online. Social networks provide similar facilities, permitting to post photos, personal news, opinions, and links to other Web pages or online resources. Application stores are "sites" where you can access games or applications for mobile devices; there is basically one store per operating system: App Store for Apple, Android Play Store for Android OS, OVI Store by Nokia for Symbian, BlackBerry App World, Windows Store by Microsoft for Windows Mobile, and HUAWEI AppGallery for HUAWEI devices. Ranges of applications may be different and also charged differently, but application stores are compulsory intermediaries for developers. Another major subgroup of service providers is search engines, which offer tools on which Internet users compose keywords to reach the most relevant related content; their role is critical in terms of visibility of content over the Internet.

- *Content delivery networks (CDN)*. CDNs constitute a specific class of service providers: they are systems of servers deployed at the edges of the Internet, which play a key role by storing some content closer to users, thereby reducing transit costs and improving performance for that content. CDNs can also help relieve the pressure on ISPs' infrastructures and improve users' experience and content providers' quality of service. They simplify service and content providers' work by providing and managing the infrastructure. Major CDN companies include Akamai Technologies, Amazon Web Services Inc., CenturyLink, Google Inc., IBM, and Verizon Communications Inc.; they have become key components in the delivery chain. CDN market size value in 2020 is reported to be US\$ 13.3 billion and expected to be US\$ 23.1 billion in 2025.[6]

- *Clouds*. Cloud computing is defined by NIST (National Institute of Standards and Technology) as "a model for enabling ubiquitous, convenient, on-demand network access to a shared pool of configurable computing resources (e.g., networks, servers, storage, applications, and services) that can be rapidly provisioned and released with minimal management effort or service provider interaction." That model includes the collection of hardware and software elements needed to operate an activity without buying and managing your own infrastructure. The main cloud provider is Amazon Web Services, holding around 32% of the cloud infrastructure services market in 2021. Other major cloud providers are Microsoft Azure, Google Cloud Platform, Alibaba Cloud, or IBM. The global cloud computing market is expected to be worth US\$832 billion by 2025. The COVID-19 pandemic and the development of remote work and videoconferencing are accelerating the transition to the cloud: companies are increasingly seeing the cloud as a digital transformation engine as well as a technology that improves business continuity.

Some other actors of telecommunications that also influence the interactions between users and content are *infrastructure equipment providers and device*

---

[6] See   https://www.grandviewresearch.com/industry-analysis/content-delivery-networks-cnd-market.

manufacturers and *regulators*. Infrastructure equipment providers and device manufacturers (e.g., Apple, Nokia, Samsung, Hewlett Packard for devices, Cisco or Alcatel-Lucent for network infrastructures) provide the *physical* tools enabling communications. Regulatory bodies are agencies generally created by governments to establish rules in order to prevent harmful actions and improve the development and use of ICT to benefit the society.

The increasingly complex ecosystem we have just described opens new ways to bypass neutrality laws and differentiate service, even financially. As a first illustration, let us mention *zero rating* in wireless data plans. Wireless providers' offers usually come with a fixed monthly volume of data that customers are allowed to use, after which any extra amount is additionally charged; the principle is to avoid excessive congestion. Zero rating consists in excluding some services/content from counting in the data plan: those services can be consumed without limitation, with the purpose to attract more customers. That data volume can be offered by the access provider or paid by the content provider itself, who could get a return on investment through advertising revenues, for example. Under that framework, packets are treated the same within the network, therefore not infringing a network neutrality rule, but all content providers are actually not treated the same way from an economic point of view. For that reason, zero rating is a behavior under scrutiny, currently considered a gray zone in the network neutrality debate with some countries forbidding it and others accepting it. As of 2022, many zero-rating implementations are experienced worldwide; a updated list can be found on the Wikipedia Web page on the topic;[7] the debate about whether the practice should be included in net neutrality regulation is still vivid; we will develop that issue in Chaps. 2 and 5.

There are many other ways to differentiate the economic performance of some ICT actors through intermediate services in the network, being either ISP-managed services or independent ones. CDNs, with their capacity of reducing the load on the networks and improving the user experience, can also differentiate unfairly the chosen data to be cached, if basing the caching decisions on commercial criteria. For now, they are absent from the neutrality debate, the only official report mentioning CDNs being from the Norwegian regulator [163]. Device builders may also differentiate services, by imposing an operating system, and an operating system may differentiate by imposing a search engine, or application stores may forbid some applications: all this may affect access to content or services and impact social welfare. An often highlighted other intermediate is search engines: when searching for some content, users generally follow advices from search engines, which are supposed to base their proposed list of links on the *relevance* with the user's request. But search engines are also accused of voluntarily biasing their results to favor some content related to them and/or to penalize some other content. This may have an impact on the accessibility of some actors and affect them economically, hence the *search neutrality debate* that we will discuss in Chap. 7.

---

[7] https://en.wikipedia.org/wiki/Zero-rating

Historically, there have been several court actions led by ICT regulatory bodies targeting players other than ISPs. Mostly, the principle was to prevent a dominant position using antitrust rules. As notable examples:

- IBM went to trial in 1975, after being accused of "monopolizing or attempting to monopolize the general purpose electronic digital computer system market, specifically computers designed primarily for business." The case was eventually withdrawn in 1982.
- In 1984, the Bell System was dismantled. The Bell System had been regrouping the dominating actors for all telephone services in North America for more than 100 years. Actions from antitrust regulators started in the 1970s against the Bell System, accused of an abuse of monopoly position. In the early 1980s, the group was estimated at around US$150 billion and separated into seven independent companies, among which AT&T, Verizon, etc.
- In 1998, a suit started against Microsoft, accused since 1994 of preventing competition to protect and extend its software monopoly by imposing its own Internet browser as a part of the installation of the Windows operating system. On June 7, 2000, the court ordered a breakup of Microsoft, but the decision was overturned in appeal, and in 2001 a "trade-off" was obtained, with Microsoft allowing PC manufacturers to adopt non-Microsoft software.
- A similar case occurred in 2012 with the action of the FTC (Federal Trade Commission) against Google[8] about Google favoring its own content over competitors on its search engine, about the use of data obtained from scraping on third-party Web sites without compensation, and about imposing its own advertising tool. Those actions were considered as against competition and the interests of users. The case was eventually settled by exonerating Google from infringing antitrust laws, stating that the purpose of Google was to improve the quality of its services, not to exclude competition.
- In 2018, a scandal popped up worldwide, with millions of Facebook users' personal data collected without consent by the consulting firm Cambridge Analytica and used for political advertising by Ted Cruz and Donald Trump during their presidential campaigns. The data was used to display customized messages on various digital platforms. This was claimed to have influenced the 2016 election and provoked strong reactions, up to requests Facebook be dismantled. Governmental actions have been taken worldwide against the illegal data breach. In the USA, the Federal Trade Commission finally fined Facebook US$ 5 billion to settle the issue.
- An argument popped up in Korea in 2018 when Facebook rerouted connections for its users to a slower network to limit interconnection fees allowed there. That induced protests from users and a penalty from the Korea Communications Commission on March 21, 2018. But the decision was overturned in appeal in court in August 2019.

---

[8] http://competitionlawblog.kluwercompetitionlaw.com/2021/03/28/revisiting-ftcs-2013-google-decision/.

- In July 2020, Epic, a computer game society, filed a civil antitrust lawsuit against Apple, complaining about the monopoly position of Apple on the application store for the iOS operating system. The complaint was initiated by the removal of its major game Fortnite from the App Store due to the implementation of its own payment system that was not in line with the rules imposed by Apple in the guidelines of its store.
- A recent development of behaviors monitored by regulators is the propagation of "fake news" through Web sites or social networks, usually for profit or social influence. That issue is sensitive since related to the notion of freedom of speech, which could then be seen as limited if counter-actions were taken. On the other hand, social networks want to limit fake news to protect the trust in their systems: Facebook, for example, signals potential fake news, and/or limits their display, when a post is being shared by a page known to have spread false news before. Suits related to that matter are generally filed by private individuals or businesses asking for repair when they consider they have been harmed by fake news, and regulators are currently actively thinking of ways to handle the issue. Note that this notion of fake/false news is not limited to ICT, and TV channels are also concerned. For example, Fox News was sued in 2020 for disseminating disinformation on the coronavirus.
- As another application of the antitrust rule, the US Justice Department is expected to prepare by the end of 2021 while we were writing this book a suit against Google, the purpose being its monopoly in the advertising technology market. A trial was set for September 2023.
- Hotel booking sites like Expedia, Booking.com, ebookers, Hotels.com, Agoda, and Trivago are under investigation (and even under legal action in 2019 in the UK) because of their selling rules. The raised issues involve pressure selling (claiming only one room is left when there are several), misleading discount claims, and ranking favorably the hotels paying additional commissions, potentially misleading customers in their choices.
- In Korea in 2021, the ISP SK Broadband required Netflix to pay usage fees for the traffic flowing through its network because of the increase of viewers to Netflix content, an issue exacerbated by the success of the *Squid Game* series.[9] Netflix sued SK Broadband, claiming that their request was against neutrality principles, but the Seoul Central District Court ruled against Netflix in June 2021. Netflix has appealed the decision.

The above list highlights the range of non-neutral issues that can be raised in ICT. In Europe, there is currently a general trend to monitor the activity of some key actors called *structuring platforms*, roughly defined as the largest digital platforms detaining a very significant and lasting market power. Those in the above list are typical examples. The goal of the monitoring is to guarantee market openness and transparency on the used algorithms.

---

[9] https://www.reuters.com/business/media-telecom/skorea-broadband-firm-sues-netflix-after-traffic-surge-squid-game-2021-10-01/

1.4   Toward ICT Neutrality?

The previous section illustrates that there are many different ways for ISPs to differentiate service without infringing the packet-based neutrality principle, and many other intermediaries could have similar non-neutral behaviors, disregarding the principle of an open and "fair" Internet and harming the society. The current focus of the neutrality debate on ISPs behavior may then seem too restrictive. Therefore, a question that could be developed is: should we try to define a more general notion of ICT neutrality to avoid and prevent new types of infringements? The need would then be for a definition of neutrality that could be applied to all actors, the current ones but also if possible the future ones. This would call for an extension of the net neutrality debate but could clearly be related to the discussion about structuring platforms raised in Europe. Of course, this means going beyond the packet level and defining a notion of fairness for each type of activity. Fairness is also related to the issue of transparency of the used algorithms, for example, for platforms operating a ranking, to let the users know why they are advised some content instead of another one.

1.5   Goal and Organization of This Book

The goal of this book is to discuss the pros and cons of net neutrality, trying to be as "objective" (i.e., distant) as possible from arguments of proponents and opponents and giving room to readers to make their own opinion. We present the history of the debate and the various concepts it encompasses but also some mathematical developments illustrating optimal strategies and potential counterintuitive results. One issue barely addressed and that we aim at tackling is the practical monitoring of actors' behavior. Indeed, setting up rules will not be effective if it does not come with measurement tools to monitor whether those rules are followed by all actors; we will discuss that important issue too. We also intend to present the debate in a more general context, as suggested above. According to us, this would help to better grasp all aspects of neutrality and the various bypasses which could be observed in practice.

Analyzing all aspects of the network neutrality debate is a complicated problem because it is highly multidisciplinary. Indeed, the questions we will be considering involve some tools and methods from:

- *Economics.* The interest of net neutrality is often, and probably has to be, studied from the point of view of economics. The questions to be answered, with sometimes opposite responses by proponents and opponents of neutrality, are, among others: should differentiation be allowed to permit return on investment for involved companies? Would differentiation be harmful to innovation and/or user welfare? Who would be the winners and the losers?

- *Law.* Imposing neutrality or some regulations in countries means passing *laws* in a way that is sufficiently clear to avoid problems when prosecutions are brought to court. It imposes to understand and analyze a "specific" language, which needs to be specific enough to avoid misunderstanding but generic enough to apply broadly and remain relevant as technology evolves.
- *Networking.* Of course, knowing how the network is working technically is required to better discuss neutrality issues and challenges. A full understanding of all technologies and protocols is out of the scope of our book, but the interested reader can look at [84, 174] for a description of the technical basics. Packet-based transmissions, TCP and UDP (for User Datagram Protocol) and their performance, routing protocols, and how decisions are made are interesting issues to understand what levels of neutrality are technically implementable. For example, packet-based neutrality, meaning that packets are treated without discrimination at each node of the network, does not necessarily imply that all flows and all users will experience the same performance: when using the TCP protocol for transmission, the throughput of your traffic flow is inversely proportional to the round-trip time between the source and destination. Hence, two end users will experience different performance levels if the round-trip time with their respective used servers differ, which could also be considered unfair.
- *History.* As highlighted in previous subsections, the neutrality debate has historical reasons: the Internet was given birth from cooperative (mostly academic even if initiated by military goals) entities, and since the network inception, users have been used to a free and totally open service they are not ready to give up. There are many other areas in telecommunications (such as telephony) or even public services (the road system, the postal service) where openness and neutrality are not strongly imposed; see [139] for a nice historic view. Keeping in mind the historical developments of the Internet is necessary if one wants to make changes. The historic developments of the Internet can also be related to other disciplines including ethics and freedom of speech, as well as (access to) education.
- *Mathematics.* Modeling and performance analysis, mainly using game theory in this context [65, 141], is useful to represent, analyze, and even predict the outcome of decisions from actors and anticipate the impact of regulation procedures. We will describe a few examples to illustrate the significance of such an analysis, with sometimes counterintuitive results.

Mixing a minimal knowledge in all these domains seems important to us to get a high-level view of the debate and be as objective as possible.

The remaining chapters of this book are organized as follows. Following the violations to an open Internet, regulators felt the need to control and supervise the behavior of ICT actors. Chapter 2 surveys the various laws passed worldwide and compares them; it also discusses some implications of heterogeneous rules over several regions. We discuss in the same chapter the specific cases of so-called specialized services and of the zero-rating practice. Chapter 3 details the pros and cons of neutrality and non-neutrality. We detail there the arguments of proponents and opponents, trying not to take any position to let the reader make her own opinion. Chapter 4 presents how the impact of neutral or non-neutral behaviors can be analyzed mathematically, with sometimes counterintuitive results, emphasizing the interest of modeling to avoid bad decisions. Chapter 5 illustrates that the network neutrality debate is not always as simple as ISPs opposing neutrality and content providers promoting it: there are situations where content providers may have an economic advantage with a non-neutral situation, when they are leaders on a market to create barriers to entry for competitors. In that case, zero rating or side payments to ISPs may actually be beneficial. But given the increasing complexity of the ICT ecosystem, there exist ways for ISPs to circumvent the packet-based rules and being non-neutral without breaking the written law. This is described in more details in Chap. 6, with a discussion about potential extensions of the debate to prevent the issue. Chapter 7 gives more insight on the role and possible non-neutral behavior of a particular and important intermediate actor between content and user, namely, search engines, leading to another debate called the *search neutrality debate*. Chapter 8 focuses on another set of actors, e-commerce platforms and social networks, and investigates how they can influence users' actions and opinions. The question we would like to raise then regards the need or relevance of including them in a more general debate on neutrality. We link that issue to the debate on the transparency of algorithms, which is very active in Europe. Setting rules cannot be effective without monitoring the activity of ICT actors: how to sanction non-appropriate behaviors and be proactive against new conducts without measurements? Chapter 9 explains why this is challenging and what tools are currently available. Finally, Chap. 10 briefly concludes and opens the debate, hoping that readers will have more insight and will be able to make their own opinion about what should be done or expected.

Chapter 2
Definitions

Due to the many complaints from users and content providers, and to the threats on some types of traffic highlighted in Chap. 1, many actors have asked for governmental action, for regulation to be put in place. But ahead of proceeding, states need to formally define what a neutral and acceptable behavior of an ISP should be. Several definitions exist, with different levels of limitations for the ISPs' actions. We first review them in Sect. 2.1, mostly from an historic point of view. A comparison of the different interpretations will be provided in Sect. 2.2. In many implementations, there are special services that are excluded from the regulation, based on security, public health, quality-of-service requirements, or even (hidden or not) revenue concerns; they will be described in Sect. 2.3. Another particular recent issue and potential violation of the neutrality principle, and recently vividly discussed, is the so-called zero-rating and any innovative managing procedure. Those practices are often debated separately; for that reason, we will introduce them in a specific section, in Sect. 2.4, explaining that they are sometimes authorized, sometimes forbidden, or still in a gray zone in the different countries. But in all cases, before enacting (or not) a law, states often launch public consultations; the stakes and induced biases are presented in Sect. 2.5. Several possible definitions also means several worldwide implementations; we review them in Sect. 2.6. Despite the long-lasted debate, the situation is still not fixed, and rules keep evolving, not only due to new services requiring monitoring but more strikingly to changes of codes of conduct in some countries; this is described in Sect. 2.7. A proposed trade-off between allowing differentiation and protecting the right for users to access a service "at will" is to let users decide which service they want to prioritize; this is hinted at in Sect. 2.8. Conclusions on net neutrality definitions and implementations are given in Sect. 2.9.

© The Author(s), under exclusive license to Springer Nature Switzerland AG 2022   15
P. Maillé, B. Tuffin, *From Net Neutrality to ICT Neutrality*,
https://doi.org/10.1007/978-3-031-06271-1_2

2.1   Several Definitions of Neutrality

It may seem surprising after more than 20 years of discussion, but there is still no clear and generally admitted definition of what network neutrality is or should be.

Historically, to our knowledge, the first neutrality principle clearly stated was in 2000 from Lessig and Lemley [95], worried about the convergence of cable and Internet networks and the potential restrictions it may imply on the end-to-end principle. Indeed, the structure of the Internet since its inception has been based on the principle of *end-to-end design*, such that the network relies on a layered system and managed by communications protocols, all applications having to follow the protocols of the different layers, and all applications applying the layered concepts and protocols being considered acceptable. Thanks to the standardized and accepted protocols, "intelligence" (i.e., innovation, creativity) is placed at the ends of the network. An ISP not adhering to the layered rule and imposing its own end-to-end concepts with proprietary architectural standards may be considered according to Lessig and Lemley as a restraint to innovation and be an infringement to the antitrust rule. The end-to-end principle also meant an engineering concept of proper behavior, and it required a valid and "understandable" definition.

The issue strengthened in 2002 when the US regulator, the Federal Communications Commission (FCC), decided to stop considering the Internet service as a regular telecommunication service, but instead as an information service, removing it from the laws regulating telecommunications and potentially allowing ISPs to control and block certain traffic. That change of mind happened after the 1996 Telecommunications Act, in which the FCC was initially declaring ISPs to be "common carriers" providing a public service.

The term *network neutrality* was first coined by Tim Wu in 2003 [178], in line with Lessig and Lemley's concerns. The introduced principle is that broadband operators should be allowed to manage "what they own" (the local network), but not to apply any restriction on inter-network indicia. In his 2003 publication, Tim Wu included a survey of the discriminatory practices and contracts by a number of fixed-line ISPs to emphasize the need for a definition and for regulation and proposed what a neutrality law could be (copying the statement in [178]):

1. Broadband users have the right reasonably to use their Internet connection in ways which are privately beneficial without being publicly detrimental. Accordingly, broadband operators shall impose no restrictions on the use of an Internet connection except as necessary to:

   a. Comply with any legal duty created by federal, state, or local laws, or as necessary to comply with any executive order, warrant, legal injunction, subpoena, or other duly authorized governmental directive

   b. Prevent physical harm to the local broadband network caused by any network attachment or network usage

   c. Prevent broadband users from interfering with other broadband or Internet users' use of their Internet connections, including but not limited to neutral limits on bandwidth usage, limits on mass transmission of unsolicited email, and limits on the distribution of computer viruses, worms, and limits on denial-of service-or other attacks on others

    d. Ensure the quality of the broadband service, by eliminating delay, jitter, or other technical aberrations

    e. Prevent violations of the security of the broadband network, including all efforts to gain unauthorized access to computers on the broadband network or Internet

    f. Serve any other purpose specifically authorized by the Federal Communications Commission, based on a weighing of the specific costs and benefit of the restriction

2. As used in this section:

    a. "Broadband operator" means a service provider that provides high-speed connections to the Internet using whatever technology, including but not limited to cable networks, telephone networks, fiber optic connections, and wireless transmission

    b. "Broadband users" means residential and business customers of a broadband operator

    c. "Broadband network" means the physical network owned and operated by the broadband operator

    d. "Restrictions on the use of an Internet connection" means any contractual, technical, or other limits placed with or without notice on the broadband user's Internet connection

Following this proposed law, Lessig and Wu sent in 2003 a letter to the FCC with a proposed trade-off between full freedom for end users and management policies for ISPs [179].

According to our knowledge, the FCC then provided in 2005 its very first official definition of neutrality, summarized by four items as principles included in a call for an *Open Internet*, in favor again of some neutrality rules [59]:

1. No content access can be denied to users.
2. Users are free to use the applications of their choice.
3. They can also use any type of terminal, provided that it does not harm the network.
4. They can competitively select the access and content providers of their choice.

This corresponds exactly to the proposition/definition described by Professors Timothy Wu and Lawrence Lessig. Even now, that set of principles still constitutes the most commonly given definition. The Oxford Dictionary, as a summary of what is a generally accepted notion, defines network neutrality as:

The principle that internet service providers should enable access to all content and applications equally, regardless of the source, without favoring or blocking particular online services or websites.

Similarly, the Merriam-Webster Dictionary defines it as:

The idea, principle, or requirement that internet service providers should or must treat all internet data as the same regardless of its kind, source, or destination.

The definition is accompanied with a quote from Sarah Rabil (Wall Street Journal):

. . . a philosophical contest that's being fought under the banner of "net neutrality" a slogan that inspires rhetorical devotion but eludes precise definition. Broadly, it means everything on the internet should be equally accessible, that the internet should be a place where great ideas compete on equal terms with big money.

On the third of April 2014, the European parliament voted in favor of network neutrality protection.[1] The definition and associated restrictions are set as:

> The principle of "net neutrality" means that traffic should be treated equally, without discrimination, restriction or interference, independent of the sender, receiver, type, content, device, service or application.

The ISPs have to conform to this principle, but in "exceptional" cases:

1. A legal action
2. To ensure the security and integrity of the network if confronted to attacks
3. In case of *temporary* congestion of the network

All the above definitions forbid any type of differentiation, a definition sometimes labelled as *strong neutrality*. With this definition, ISPs may not intentionally block, slow down, or charge money for specific traffic. There is a less restrictive definition, which we will call *weak neutrality definition* [117, 178], prohibiting user discrimination in the sense that users cannot be charged differently for the same service, *but* under which ISPs can differentiate between applications. For example, videos can be prioritized with respect to email because of more stringent QoS requirements. Strong neutrality prevents that type of differentiation. BEREC, the European regulator [19], actually exempts some so-called *specialized services* from neutrality rules:

> BEREC also finds that it is particularly important to develop common frames of references about internet access service, and find agreement on which traffic management measures are reasonable. Common terminology in these areas can help make information more comparable and easier to understand by end users. It is also vital to adapt the information on net neutrality and traffic management so as to take into account different types of usages, networks and technologies, and different types of offers (access to internet, specialized services, bundles), but also to distinguish between reasonable traffic management measures, and measures that go beyond reasonable traffic management, depending on the effects the measure has on the end user.

BEREC therefore leaves room for possible differentiation, illustrating all the possible exceptions and the new gray zones on neutrality principles. Specialized services are often referred to as "services other than Internet access services" or "non-broadband Internet services" [161]. In 2009 already, specialized services were implicitly discussed in the Norwegian guidelines on neutrality, stating that "if the physical connection is shared with other services, it must be clear how the capacity is allocated between the internet traffic and the other services." The issue of specialized services will be further discussed in Sect. 2.3.

There also exist some notions of *hard* and *soft* neutrality: soft neutrality means that principles are coming from a dialogue between stakeholders or internal codes of conduct (self-regulation, potentially initiated by a regulator), while hard neutrality comes from imposed rules from regulators and laws.

---

[1] See   https://www.europarl.europa.eu/sides/getDoc.do?pubRef=-//EP//NONSGML+AMD+A7-2014-0190+237-244+DOC+PDF+V0//EN

Net neutrality is included in the more general framework and concept of an *Open Internet* requiring not only net neutrality but additionally open standards (that everybody can use, in opposition to proprietary standards), transparency of algorithms (anyone can be aware of what is going on), and low barriers to entry to avoid restricted access for users (financially) and service/content providers (technically).

2.2 Analysis and Comparison

In all the above definitions of neutrality, there is an agreement about the general principle of needing to be "treated the same." The spirit of all definitions is similar: by neutrality, one means in general avoiding unfair discrimination. How to define unfair discrimination on the other hand depends on the granularity and the extent to which it is applied.

There are noticeable differences in the wording about whether the considered scale concerns packets, data, traffic, or even flows. This may seem insignificant, but the meaning of the type of "target" is different, and the notions of neutrality can therefore be discussed appropriately to justify discrimination. When talking about packets, the question of neutrality regards packets inside the network, which should be treated the same regardless of their content, source or destination, and the protocol or service to which they relate to. The notion of data may be considered a bit differently, sometimes more related to content and not the way it is transported or the IP protocol. When talking about flows, the notion of fairness can be discussed since flows being treated by the "best effort" service provided by Internet protocols does not mean any equal treatment in terms of throughput or delay: indeed, such metrics depend on the path from source to destination, and it may require packet differentiation to obtain an equivalent quality-of-service level whatever the source and destination.

In the end-to-end design of Lessig and Lemley, it is stated that the core network should stay neutral and that intelligence can be placed at the edge. This does not explicitly prevent pricing differentiation or zero rating, something neutrality proponents strongly perceive as the most serious infringements to neutrality, which should be included in the definition of an open Internet for which no content access can be denied to users. Moreover, the spatial limitation of neutrality to the core and not the edge does not prevent a "smart" differentiation at the edge, such as through the use of content delivery networks storing selected files at the edge for a better quality of service. This may be seen as files/flows being treated differently, something we will discuss further in Chap. 6.

Another limitation not clearly included in most definitions regards the extent to which the neutrality obligations, whatever they are, have to be applied to wireless services, satellite communications, etc. The Internet is now heterogeneous in terms of used technology to connect users and content, and users are increasingly using their mobile phone to reach the Internet. This again asks the question of the "spatial" limits of the Internet network: to which extent should wireless communications be included? The definitions are heterogeneously clear with that respect, but none is explicit since technologies are not discussed. In practice, wireless providers are offering a limited volume of data in their contracts, with traffic above the limit either being blocked or seeing its speed drastically reduced, which can in some sense be considered an infringement of neutrality rules.

In the European definition, exceptions to the rule are mentioned based on legal action, security, or temporary congestion. But no clear "thresholds" from which such exceptions can be granted are given. For example, how to define a valid reason for a legal action to block some content? Actions in several countries allow to block peer-to-peer Web sites for copyright reasons (we already noted, e.g., what happened in Belgium in 2001 for thepiratebay.org). Legal actions are also launched against sites promoting hatred and pedopornography. Western European countries, despite being often praised for online openness, are far less tolerant than the USA with hateful speech and images. Even Web sites, content providers, or social networks such as Facebook often mark and block pictures of well-known paintings or sculptures, labelling them as pornography,[2] or since recently remove messages tagged as "fake news," the US president himself being the object of such actions, on his comments on the coronavirus in 2020, for example.[3] How to define the frontier between legal and fair protection of social and human rights and infringement to freedom of speech, one of the most emphasized aspects of the Internet philosophy? As an illustration, but many others can be mentioned, services such as those provided by Google or Facebook are forbidden in China, and legal reasons can always be put forward by states to justify restrictions to services. The companies sometimes offer versions of their services conforming to the government's censorship policies and ensure revenue. Some may believe that democracies are safe with this respect of freedom, but at the time we were writing the first version of this chapter in the second half of 2020, the US president was asking for TikTok and WeChat (both Chinese companies) to be banned from the US market due to national security concerns, more precisely concerns about data security and data privacy (and probably for reciprocity reasons as a response to Google, Facebook, and Twitter not being allowed to operate in China). Traffic may also be blocked when it is identified as hacking or voluntarily harming society. Again, this may be subject to interpretation, and the TikTok ban also fits this category. We can also mention the blocking of the Web site and Facebook account of TV channel Russia Today, as a consequence of Russia's military invasion of Ukraine in March 2022, to prevent the spreading of disinformation. Finally, the last possibility evoked for allowing differentiation is in case of "temporary congestion." Here too, two questions arise: how long is "temporary," and when can we say that we are experiencing "congestion"? This is again subjective, and ISPs may jump

---

[2] See, for example, https://www.archaeology.wiki/blog/2018/02/06/facebook-perhaps-confusing-art-pornography/.

[3] https://www.bbc.com/news/technology-54440662.

into this vague definition to justify differentiation; arguments with regulators can be envisioned.

We can additionally emphasize the difference of vision between strong and weak neutrality. Many (strong neutrality proponents) consider any type of differentiation as unfair, except maybe if differentiation is decided by the end users. For the weak neutrality proponents, rules can be less restrictive, and service differentiation may be applied as long as users who pay equally receive the same service and get the same resources. Computer scientists and academics are often viewed as supporters of neutrality as opposed to economists, but most of them are probably supporting weak neutrality. Indeed, historically, to cope with congestion, protocols have been imagined in the late 1990s and early 2000s to differentiate service and prioritize traffic with strong quality of service requirements for, in the end, a better user experience. These methods were called the differential services enhancements (DiffServ) and were defined in the RFCs (Request for Comments, the standardization procedures) 2474 [14] and 2475 [23]. With strong neutrality, this would not be permitted. An even more topical context where weak neutrality is to be required is that of 5G wireless networks. One of the main characteristics of 5G is a possibility to create so-called network slices, obtained by virtually dividing the network for different services according to their needs. This could be in line with weak neutrality, but not with a strong version. This issue of relating 5G and net neutrality is discussed in [158, 181]. Finally, ISPs and infrastructure equipment providers claim that net neutrality regulation risks hindering innovation in networks and threatening the viability of the Internet of Things (IoT); flexibility is claimed to be needed. There are arguments asserting that 5G slices can fit the notion of *specialized services* for which differentiation is allowed, but how to limit such services has to be defined. According to the European Union [158]:

> The requirement for traffic management measures to be non-discriminatory does not preclude providers of internet access services from implementing, in order to optimise the overall transmission quality, traffic management measures which differentiate between objectively different categories of traffic. Any such differentiation should, in order to optimise overall quality and user experience, be permitted only on the basis of objectively different technical quality of service requirements (for example, in terms of latency, jitter, packet loss, and bandwidth) of the specific categories of traffic, and not on the basis of commercial considerations

This is in line with weak neutrality but requires permanent monitoring and supervision from regulators.

For a comparison between European and (initial) US perspectives, see also [160].

2.3   Specialized Services

As we have highlighted, restrictions to network neutrality are framed in the notion of *specialized services* and require further attention. Specialized services, also called sometimes *managed services*, are services or applications which are considered as exceptions and therefore excluded from neutrality rules. For this reason, they are also coined as "non-broadband Internet access services" or "services other than Internet access services" [161]. The questions are: *(i)* What exactly are specialized services? *(ii)* Why are they excluded from the neutrality framework? *(iii)* What are the implications for the society and the potential loopholes associated to specialized services that actors can try to use to escape neutrality?

2.3.1   Perimeter of Specialized Services

In Article 3(5) Regulation (EU) 2015/2120 of the European neutrality rules, specialized services are introduced in the following way:

> Providers of electronic communications to the public, including providers of internet access services, and providers of content, applications and services shall be free to offer services other than internet access services which are optimised for specific content, applications or services, or a combination thereof, where the optimisation is necessary in order to meet requirements of the content, applications or services for a specific level of quality.
>
> Providers of electronic communications to the public, including providers of internet access services, may offer or facilitate such services only if the network capacity is sufficient to provide them in addition to any internet access services provided. Such services shall not be usable or offered as a replacement for internet access services, and shall not be to the detriment of the availability or general quality of internet access services for end-users.

This gives freedom to ISPs to offer "premium" services if not within "Internet access services," which can be differentiated from "regular" Internet services. There is therefore room for interpretation, and regulators have to intervene to ensure that any proposition of specialized services is actually not included in the imagined perimeter. Different countries can also interpret it differently according to their culture and history.

Basically, what regulators (probably) have in mind when thinking of specialized services corresponds to:

- Specific services for which a minimal quality of service is required, in terms of bandwidth, packet loss, jitter, latency, or increased network security. Television over the Internet is a typical example. There exist also services for which a quality degradation, even temporary, may have dramatic consequences: e-health and online surgery are first examples, but assisted driving also falls in this category.
- Not necessarily dissociated from the first item, specialized services are also services not primarily associated to the Internet. Historically, this includes services offered in bundles with Internet access, of which most have migrated over IP: voice over broadband services, television over ADSL/FTTH, and video on-demand. Many of these services (television, etc.) generally used dedicated channels independent of Internet access. It is expected that emerging services such as telepresence or online gaming will enter the category. In this sense, like with telemedicine, we talk about services that have in essence nothing to do with the Internet and are not part of the global Internet but are served on the same technology for economic reasons.

2.3.2   Need for Specialized Services

It seems reasonable, if not clear, that some services (now) carried on the Internet need security and guaranteed quality of service to avoid dramatic consequences. No one would accept the information for assisted driving to be slowed down, augmenting the risk of an accident, because of network congestion! There is a large support for treating in priority some flows like those for telemedicine or assisted driving, due to security and quality of service concerns. Other services are often more subject to debate. Video streaming platforms like YouTube or Netflix could complain about an IPTV receiving a preferential treatment for competition reason, which could indeed be debated. In order to be classified as specialized services, candidates have "objectively" to meet requirements for a specific level of quality of service. This again leaves room for interpretation on the definition of a "threshold" that is by nature subjective, but transparent and predefined rules would simplify a classification.

Another request by regulators is usually that this class of service may be introduced only if capacity is sufficiently provisioned and that it is not at the expense of traditional Internet access and services. If too many specialized services are defined, the standard Internet traffic will lose quality. A threshold is to be defined not only on the requirements from specialized services but on a guarantee on the average quality of the "normal" best-effort service provided to the regular Internet traffic.

Last but not the least, even if it is not often admitted, specialized services can be monetized and permit providers to meet revenue expectations and potentially get return on investment for network capacity. They constitute a way for ISPs to generate revenue and may be seen as a trade-off between a fully neutral (flat rate) network and full (non-neutral) revenue management.

2.3.3   Implications of Introducing a Special Class of Service

If specialized services are permitted to some service providers, then it seems fair to claim that they should also be offered to all entities providing similar services, for equality reasons. Non-exclusivity has to become a rule, and it has to be ensured that a provider is not assigning a higher priority to its own services. Indeed, what could prevent a broadband provider to claim that its own online video service is a specialized service which can be delivered faster than a competitor's? Regulators have to be involved in the process of validating the category. *Transparency* of providers, requiring them to disclose how their specialized services are being offered and what their relationship is to ordinary broadband Internet access service, seems like an acceptable way to proceed.

The separation of specialized services from Internet services has to be as clear and effective as possible; otherwise, neutrality rules can be undermined.

Isolated and reserved capacity is the natural solution, through virtual networks, for example. Network slicing in 5G wireless networks and multiplexing of virtualized and independent logical networks on the same physical network infrastructure provide capabilities to efficiently and cheaply implement that. Note that giving a priority in the Internet does not provide strict guarantees, but only statistical ones. Increasing capacity (also called overprovisioning) is sometimes claimed has a "simple" solution to avoid or at least reduce problems and reserved fast lanes, but still no strict guarantee can be provided.

A requirement is probably to define a valid minimal level of quality required by a specialized service, which needs to be defined by ISPs but then validated by regulators. BEREC Guidelines make the link between specialized services and network slicing by noting that "Network-slicing in 5G networks may be used to deliver specialized services." But all this raises numerous questions yet to be answered:

- What are the objective criteria (QoS, QoE) for being entitled to become a specialized service? Those may be required if one wants to act proactively.
- Who will ask for a service to be of this particular class? The CP? The ISP? If it is the ISP, isn't there a risk to favor commercial partners? What if an ISP does not warrant a request from a CP?
- What are the available monitoring procedures to ensure that rules, and equity within a class of service, are followed?

An additional complication also comes from the difficulty to isolate a class a specialized service: it is hard to differentiate videoconference from video streaming; plus for convenience of tools, distance learning sometimes uses video-gaming platforms.

2.4 Zero-Rating and Sponsored Data

Wireless communications are becoming ubiquitous, and data are increasingly being consumed through mobile phones; it is, for example, admitted that mobile data consumption will be sevenfold larger by 2021 than by 2017.[4] Internet access is increasingly through wireless networks, but data plans proposed by access providers are made of offers with data caps [104], with an upper limit included in the subscription and any additional volume charged or with degraded quality, potentially limiting end users consumption.

ISPs now sometimes propose *zero-rating*, that is, the possibility that an ISP does not account the data volume associated with a particular application in the data cap.

---

[4] See http://www.businessinsider.fr/us/mobile-data-will-skyrocket-700-by-2021-2017-2/ among others.

In this sense, data is "for free," at a price of zero. Wikipedia is more generally defining it as:[5]

> the practice of providing internet access without financial cost under certain conditions, such as by permitting access to only certain websites or by subsidizing the service with advertising or by exempting certain websites from the data allowance.

This definition does not only consider exemptions from data caps (advertising is mentioned).

Implementing zero rating may be interesting for ISPs to attract more customers and therefore generate more revenue through special offers. It was typically the case some time ago in France with wireless provider SFR proposing a data plan called Red by SFR with zero rating for YouTube traffic and targeting young(er) people, the most-demanding customer category in terms of video streaming.

Similarly, content and service providers such as Facebook, Google, and Wikipedia have created programs for the development of ICT in developing countries, with the claimed goal of increasing connectivity and offering universal Internet access, but on which their own services are "for free." This illustrates that content providers may also be interested in zero rating. Indeed, they are economically dependent on the amount of data consumed by users, typically via displayed advertisements: the more volume consumed, the more advertisement and as a consequence the more revenue. For this reason, there might be an incentive for content providers to *sponsor data*, that is, to at least partially pay the ISP for the user's consumption of its own services. There are many such situations worldwide. Representative examples in the USA are Netflix or Binge-On (video streaming) with T-Mobile, DIRECTV and U-verse Data Free TV with AT&T, etc. Verizon (in 2016) zero-rated TV programs for subscribers using Verizon's Fios Mobile App. All these most known examples are for video streaming and TV programs.

Given the commercial advantages they can get from zero rating, ISPs are even developing platforms on which CPs can, if they wish, apply for sponsored data and zero rating. Relevant and major examples are Verizon Wireless with FreeBee Data in 2017,[6] AT&T Mobility with AT&T Sponsored Data,[7] or Orange with DataMI[8] in France, among others. T-Mobile USA was probably the first to zero-rate, for participating music streaming services in a plan called "music freedom."[9] Zero rating has become a lucrative business.

Thanks to sponsored data and zero rating, users may expand their usage, CPs may get more revenue due to advertisement, and ISPs may get paid for the traffic increase. That could be a win-win-win situation, but which actually brings concerns

---

[5] https://en.wikipedia.org/wiki/Zero-rating

[6] https://www.prncwswire.com/news-releases/introducing-freebee-data-the-new-sponsored-data-service-from-verizon-300205928.html

[7] https://developer.att.com/sponsored-data

[8] https://www.datami.com/

[9] https://www.t-mobile.com/support/plans-features/unlimited-music-streaming-with-music-freedom

from user associations and small content providers. Such practices could indeed give an unfair advantage to some content/service providers, eventually preventing some actors from entering the market, due to lower visibility and high entrance costs to the sponsored data system if they want to get the same service as incumbent and big providers already present. Those situations therefore distort user consumption and affect the market access for content providers. For this reason, can it be considered an infringement of neutrality principles even if, within the network, packets are treated equally? Actually, given that zero rating has appeared quite recently, it has not been clearly addressed by neutrality principles. This is a borderline issue where discrimination is commercial, *not* based on access but on how specific content is paid. It also illustrates that any legislation can be circumvented and that regulators have to be proactive about implementing the "spirit" of neutrality principles.

Zero rating is considered a "gray zone" since evaluated differently in different countries. Norway is one of the few in the OECD area where operators don't currently zero rate anything. The others include Finland, Estonia, Latvia, Lithuania, Malta, Chile, and Japan. In the European Union proposition of network neutrality, there is no explicit mention of zero rating, as a trade-off between the Commission being in favor of it and the Parliament against it. Given the situation, Europe leaves the decision to be taken by national regulatory bodies. OECD in 2015 also sees the question as an open or rather ecosystem-dependent case. It states:

> Previous experience in OECD countries has shown that zero-rating becomes less of an issue with increased competition and higher or unlimited data allowances. Indeed, it can be a tool to increase competition. Prohibiting zero-rating may have implications for a market where there is lower competition for transit and may reduce the effectiveness of peering. Nevertheless, in any market with limited competition for access, zero-rating could be an issue of concern.

2.5 Public Consultations

Before enacting a law, authorities often launch public consultations to collect arguments from any entity wishing to respond on questions about the concerned topic. As it has been highlighted in [8], there is a typical bias in responses: respondents are self-selected, and it is primarily strong opponents or proponents who respond, which may lead to a distorted view of the overall public perception of the subject. Public consultations have therefore to be used by regulators and legislators only to grasp and weigh arguments but not as a public poll. From the respondent perspective, it may be frustrating and non-motivating to receive no feedback about the impact of the written response; what is the point of answering then if not actively implicated in the debate? Citizens and media do not always show a lot of interest either. For example, in 2010, when consultations were carried out in Europe, France, and the USA, about 89,000 responses were received in the US consultation, which may seem reasonable, versus only 121 in the French one, with just 7 by individual citizens, all the others coming from ISPs, companies, user consultations, or groups of experts. Again, consultations are tools for legislators to get all arguments and make their own decisions, not to be considered as statistically representative votes.

2.6   Worldwide Implementations

As highlighted in the first sections of this chapter, there are multiple definitions of neutrality, giving room for interpretations and "loopholes" with respect to new behaviors that regulators need to tackle and may manage differently. We review in this section the various laws and rules that have been passed worldwide (see also [137]). We are not exhaustive, given the number of countries in the world, but list the main Internet players and some other active and representative states.

2.6.1   North America

2.6.1.1   USA

The USA is the most regarded country in terms of Internet policy, the most prominent actors of the network being located there, including the famous GAFAM (an acronym standing for Google, Apple, Facebook, Amazon, and Microsoft). The USA is also where the debate on network neutrality started. One of the questions is whether ISPs should be considered as providing a *common carrier* service, a communication service, or an information service. In the former case, ISPs would be under the Communications Act of 1934 and would be regulated by the Federal Communications Commission (FCC); in the latter case, the FCC would not be entitled for regulation. The Communications Act was created to ensure access and openness, stating it was created "for the purpose of regulating interstate and foreign commerce in communication by wire and radio so as to make available, so far as possible to all the people of the United States a rapid, efficient, nation-wide, and world-wide wire and radio communication service with adequate facilities at reasonable charges, for the purpose of the national defense, for the purpose of promoting safety of life and property through the use of wire and radio communication [· · ·]." In 2002, the FCC considered ISPs as an information service, dissociating broadband services from the laws regulating telecommunications [58], actually one of the reasons raising concerns and protests. The classification was officially done to promote broadband deployment and expected to result in better quality, lower prices, and more choices for consumers.

In 2005, the FCC established a set of four rules for an open Internet:

- Consumers deserve access to the lawful Internet content of their choice.
- Consumers should be allowed to run applications and use services of their choice, subject to the needs of law enforcement.

- Consumers should be able to connect their choice of legal devices that do not harm the network.
- Consumers deserve to choose their network providers, application and service providers, and content providers.

The inclusion of no (unreasonable) discrimination was included in 2010 in the revamped version of the Open Internet Order [60]. Given the numerous attempts by ISPs to pass bills against neutrality, the principles were instated by the FCC on February 26, 2015 [61], considering that broadband providers have economic incentives that "represent a threat to internet openness and could act in ways that would ultimately inhibit the speed and extent of future broadband deployment" and that the FCC's 2010 Open Internet rules had limited applicability to mobile broadband. It reinstated ISPs as common carriers and imposed rules banning practices that are known to harm the Open Internet: *(i)* no blocking, *(ii)* no throttling, and *(iii)* no paid prioritization. A reasonable network management provided that it is justified was allowed. But issues such as zero rating were not discussed. Those rules were applied up to 2017 and the election of Donald Trump as a president. The change of policy in 2017 will be discussed in Sect. 2.7.

2.6.1.2 Canada

In Canada, ISPs are also subject to a Federal Telecommunications Act enacted there in 1993, considering their services as utilities and stating that no unreasonable preference can be given to any service or content. But no specific law was passed, despite tentatives, including a proposition issued by the Canadian regulator, the Canadian Radio-television and Telecommunications Commission (CRTC), in 2009 after a public consultation. In 2011, the CRTC allowed usage-based billing, raising many worries about its impact on neutrality, since it may affect the use of resource-demanding applications and entrance of newcomers to the market. In April 2017, Canada enacted rules in favor of network neutrality, *but* allowing to differentiate services in terms of price if the differentiation is based on rates or data caps (as, e.g., not forbidden from the principles of an Open Internet in 2005 by the FCC) [28]. Zero rating is explicitly authorized. The rules are therefore very different from what is implemented in many other countries.

2.6.1.3 Mexico

In early 2020 only, Mexico issued a public consultation on network neutrality after the Mexican telecom regulator released a draft on "Traffic Management and Internet Administration (binding) Guidelines" on December 19, 2019. Up to now, the rules are following the 2014 Federal Telecommunications and Broadcasting Law, where network neutrality is explicitly but briefly addressed in 20 lines in Article 145 *as guidelines* [62]. The guidelines can be summarized as follows: *(i)* free choice in terms of content, application, or service is protected; *(ii)* no differentiation or filtering is allowed; *(iii)* privacy and security have to be preserved; *(iv)* information about the offered service has to be provided; and *(v)* traffic management is authorized only to guarantee quality of service. The regulator is therefore currently working on more precisely addressing the issue after a lawsuit from a user association and a court decision requiring to carry out the public consultation.

2.6.2 Europe

2.6.2.1 European Union

The European Union is among the places where network neutrality is the most actively discussed, probably because of disagreements between members. In 2007, the Commission was considering prioritization as beneficial, provided that users had freedom of choice as regards device, service, and content. The Body of European Regulators for Electronic Communications (BEREC), the association of members telecommunication regulators, was created in 2009. During the 2010s, the European Parliament issued resolution proposals, ignored by the European Commission, which eventually included rules into the more general "Telecommunications Single Market" Regulation, but considered flawed [125]. These neutrality rules are explicated in Article 3 of EU Regulation 2015/2120 [56] (also as stated in the previous section):

1. End-users shall have the right to access and distribute information and content, use and provide applications and services, and use terminal equipment of their choice, irrespective of the end-user's or provider's location or the location, origin or destination of the information, content, application or service, via their internet access service. This paragraph is without prejudice to Union law, or national law that complies with Union law, related to the lawfulness of the content, applications or services.
2. Agreements between providers of internet access services and end-users on commercial and technical conditions and the characteristics of internet access services such as price, data volumes or speed, and any commercial practices conducted by providers of internet access services, shall not limit the exercise of the rights of end-users laid down in paragraph 1.
3. Providers of internet access services shall treat all traffic equally, when providing internet access services, without discrimination, restriction or interference, and irrespective of the sender and receiver, the content accessed or distributed, the applications or services used or provided, or the terminal equipment used.
   The first subparagraph shall not prevent providers of internet access services from implementing reasonable traffic management measures. In order to be deemed to be reasonable, such measures shall be transparent, non-discriminatory and proportionate, and shall not be based on commercial considerations but on objectively different technical quality of service requirements of specific categories of traffic. Such measures shall not monitor the specific content and shall not be maintained for longer than necessary.

This was criticized because of loopholes regarding specialized services, zero rating, and a too vague definition of "reasonable traffic management measures."

2.6.2.2 France

In 2010, ARCEP, the French telecommunications regulator, launched a public consultation about ten non-binding recommendations on traffic management, transparency towards end users, and quality of service. A report was issued on April 12, 2011, by the Commission for economic affairs of the French parliament, proposing net neutrality lines of conduct [9]. The focus was on Internet access, with discussed principles about freedom of use, satisfactory quality of service, and no discrimination between traffic streams, with exceptions to ensure access to the Internet under criteria of relevance, proportionality, efficiency, non-discrimination between parties, and transparency [6]. Specialized services are allowed, provided that they do not degrade the quality of Internet access below a certain satisfactory level and that vendors act in accordance with existing competition laws and sector-specific regulation. Since then, France, as other EU members, has to enforce the EU recommendations of 2015.

Every year, ARCEP releases a report called "state of the Internet in France" about quality of service, interconnection, IPv6, net neutrality, and the openness of devices, for both fixed and mobile Internet networks.[10] The goal of that yearly updated report is to ensure that the network of networks, that is, the Internet, remains an inclusive public resource. It also aims at reacting to evolutions in the networks and at providing explanations about the neutrality application in this evolutive context. French regulation is complicated by the intervention of several regulators: ARCEP for electronic communications markets; CSA (Conseil supérieur de l'audiovisuel) for regulating audiovisual content, regardless of the distribution network; Competition Authority (Autorité de la concurrence) for compliance with competition law; the general directorate for fair trade, DGCCRF, for everything regarding consumers; and the French national commission on computing and freedom, CNIL, for the protection of privacy and freedom in the digital world.

2.6.2.3 Germany

In Germany, a regular report is released by the Bundesnetzagentur, responsible for enforcing the rules on net neutrality under Regulation (EU) 2015/2120 and summarizing all issues related to neutrality (see [68] for the period between 2017 and 2018). The Bundesnetzagentur has prohibited the use of video throttling but authorizes zero rating.

2.6.2.4 United Kingdom

Net neutrality has not been an intense issue in the UK. But before the Brexit, as a member of EU, Ofcom, the UK telecommunications regulator, was asked to

---

[10] See https://archives.arcep.fr/uploads/tx_gspublication/Carto_NN_ENG.pdf.

follow the guidelines published by the Body of European Regulators for Electronic Communications (BEREC).[11] Ofcom is proposing a framework for assessing zero-rating offers and traffic management measures for compliance with the Open Internet Regulation.[12] What is going to happen after Brexit remains to be seen. Ofcom started a review of their existing net neutrality rules in late 2021,[13] being open to an adjustment of the rules due to the changes in the telecommunications environment.

2.6.2.5 The Netherlands

Before the EU legislation 2015/2120, The Netherlands was one of the countries that had been active on neutrality. Net neutrality laws (ratified in 2012) were voted in 2011, forbidding the blocking of Internet services, deep packet inspection, and traffic manipulation. Even after the European regulation was issued, the Netherlands wondered about strengthening the net neutrality law in their country and whether it was relevant to eliminate exceptions for zero rating [92], the Dutch legislation being stricter than what is advocated by the guidelines of joint European telecoms regulators on this matter.

2.6.2.6 Norway

Norway is another country where the debate has been active very early, with strong positions on the matter. The Norwegian Post and Telecommunications Authority (NPT) enacted in 2009 a set of guidelines that ISPs were asked to follow. Even if adherence was voluntary, ISPs had followed them. Three main principles were highlighted: *(i)* transparency, in the sense that users must be given accurate information about the service they are buying, including capacity and quality; *(ii)* users were entitled to send and receive content of their choice, to use services and applications of their choice; and *(iii)* no discrimination was allowed, based on service, content, sender, or receiver. To ensure a sufficient quality of service, demanding traffic like VoIP and streaming video can be prioritized.

When Europe released its guidelines in 2014, Norway as a member of the Union followed the general rule. While zero rating was allowed by EU, Norway quite quickly reacted the same year by stating via its NPT senior advisor that "Internet users are entitled to an internet connection that is free of discrimination with regard to type of application, service or content or based on sender or receiver address." In other words, zero rating would constitute a violation of the guidelines.

---

[11] https://www.ofcom.org.uk/research-and-data/internet-and-on-demand-research/net-neutrality

[12] See https://www.ofcom.org.uk/__data/assets/pdf_file/0014/148100/ofcom-approach-net-neutrality.pdf.

[13] https://www.ispreview.co.uk/index.php/2021/09/ofcom-begin-new-review-of-uk-net-neutrality-rules-post-brexit.html

2.6.2.7 Slovenia

Slovenia also deserves to be pointed out as the second European country releasing a law enforcing strong neutrality in 2012. Three years later, in 2015, the Slovenian regulator, AKOS, banned zero rating, except for three companies owned by the state incumbent. It (of course) led to complaints by other operators arguing that this was against the promulgated rules. The decision was unsurprisingly overturned by court in 2016,[14] then allowing sponsored data.

2.6.2.8 Russia

Russia is not a EU member, but a major country in terms of geopolitics. In 2016, throttling was banned by the Federal Antimonopoly Service, introducing net neutrality in the country. Blocking is banned, *except* for traffic or sites requested by the Federal Service for Supervision of Communications, Information Technology and Mass Media. Russia is accused of making use of this rule to censor content against its leaders under the label of extremism. It has been claimed that nearly 200,000 domains have been blocked under Russian censorship.[15] In November 2019, Vladimir Putin's regime introduced new regulations in the "Sovereign Internet Law," claimed to protect the Internet within Russia from external threats but creating a legal framework for a centralized state management of the Russian Internet.

2.6.3 Asia

2.6.3.1 China

Network neutrality is not enforced in China. Actually, content is regulated in the country by ISPs controlled by the government. As of 2021, sites such as Google, Wikipedia, or Facebook services, for example, cannot be reached from there. This filtering is called the Great Firewall (GFW) [75]. A counter-effect of that censorship is the development of China's internal Internet economy since foreign companies could not be reached.

2.6.3.2 Japan

In Japan, network neutrality principles became official in 2017 as part of the "New Competition Policy Program 2010" enacted by the Ministry of Internal Affairs and

---

[14] For a historical perspective, see [92], starting Page 245.

[15] https://www.inverse.com/article/60771-russia-internet-censorship-trump-net-neutrality

Communications (MIC) [77]. Before that, no rule was imposed, since the (fixed) ISP market was highly competitive and believed to foster innovation. With the advent of bandwidth-demanding applications, zero rating, and Internet accessed through wireless providers with aggressive commercial strategies in a less competitive market than with fixed networks, requests for regulation had soared. Zero rating was not considered an issue as long as the market is competitive. But in November 2019, Japan's communications ministry proposed regulating zero-rating mobile phone services,[16] imposing mobile phone carriers to implement access control to prevent the services from causing Internet congestion and slowing the communication speed for non-subscribers.

2.6.3.3   South Korea

South Korea is one of the world's most highly penetrated broadband markets. It has defined suggestive guidelines for a regulatory framework under which net neutrality is addressed in a case-by-case fashion, meaning that decisions are made *ex post*, while most countries rather try to set up *ex ante* rules [87, 156, 157]. Network neutrality is heavily discussed in the country. Historically, there have been in South Korea a series of enacted Acts, starting with the so-called Electronic Communications Business Act in 1999, whose purpose was to promote e-commerce and under which broadband service can be shared for a reasonable fee. To promote another service, IPTV, another regulation, was passed in 2008 requiring non-discrimination from operators. But since 2016, South Korea has imposed the "Sending Party Network Pays (SPNP)" which, despite being only between ISPs, allows an ISP to charge another one for sending data. In 2021, an amendment to the law allows ISPs to impose fees on CPs for a network access (motivated by the large resource consumption from CPs such as Netflix), limiting even more the neutrality application. In line with this, it is also worthwhile to mention the recent case for the Netflix vs SK Broadband argument and lawsuit we previously evoked,[17] about the ISP SK Broadband requiring Netflix to pay usage fees for the traffic flowing through its network, an issue exacerbated by the traffic increase following the *Squid Game* show success.

2.6.3.4   India

A real debate started in India in 2014 when mobile provider Airtel imposed additional charges for VoIP services, raising protests over the country. Neutrality was not considered a real issue before. The Telecom Regulatory Authority of India

---

[16] See   https://www.nippon.com/en/news/yjj2019111201268/japan-mulls-regulating-zero-rating-mobile-services.html.

[17] https://www.theregreview.org/2021/11/10/kim-can-netflix-win-neutrality/

(TRAI) then launched a public consultation on the matter. Strong net neutrality laws were passed in 2018 in India, guaranteeing a free and open Internet and banning *any* type of discrimination. Exceptions to the rules are for specialized services such as autonomous driving and telemedicine for which guaranteed quality is required.

2.6.4   Oceania

2.6.4.1   Australia

For now, net neutrality has not been considered an issue in Australia, where the market is considered competitive and laws are imposing transparency on the implemented schemes. Zero rating is also implemented (Netflix on with ISP iiNet since 2015) without complaint from the authorities.

2.6.4.2   New Zealand

Like Australia, New Zealand does not have net neutrality regulations in place. According to MediaWorks (New Zealand-based television, radio, and interactive media company): "Until recently there haven't been close links between big ISPs and big media or content companies," meaning that no law was needed up to now since things were running smoothly.

2.6.5   South America

For more analysis on South America, see [169]. We just focus here on Chile as the most active on the subject, and on Brazil, as the most populated country.

2.6.5.1   Chile

The case of Chile can be emphasized, since it was the first country in the world to pass a net neutrality law, in 2010 (the law being initiated in 2007). The law established the four following important characteristics:

1. ISPs cannot arbitrarily block, interfere, or discriminate the right of any Internet user to use, send, receive, or offer any legal content, application, or service through the Internet. But traffic is tolerated provided that it does not affect free competition.
2. ISPs are authorized to block access to certain contents, applications, or services *only* upon users' request.

3. Users can connect through the devices of their choice.
4. ISPs must be transparent about their services in terms of speed, quality of national and international connections, and the nature and guarantees of the service. The establishment of the minimal conditions to be met by the ISPs in regard to their information and publicity obligations is left for a special regulation to be issued by the Telecommunications Under Secretariat. This regulation will set forth the activities that may be considered restrictive to the freedom to use online available content, applications, or services.

Here already, there have been critics about the vague notions of tolerance and about the term "legal," subject to interpretation.

While zero rating was not a topic in 2010, it has been explicitly discussed later, and the practice has been banned starting June 1, 2014.

2.6.5.2 Brazil

Brazil passed a law called "Marco Civil Da Internet" in 2014, on a topic broader than but including neutrality, "guaranteeing equal access to the internet and protecting the privacy of its users in the wake of U.S. spying revelations." The mention to the USA in the law came from Edward Snowden's revelations on surveillance activities by the US government at the time it was on the agenda. From the text of the law, here too there are some exceptions to the rules, with an unclear perimeter.

2.6.6 Africa

Africa has the particularity that 98% of African broadband connections are through mobile networks. Any rule against network neutrality has a stronger impact in this context, particularly with the larger proportion of people with a low income on this continent. To our knowledge, no law has been passed yet, even if active discussions exist in South Africa: high-speed Internet is not prevalent, and Internet access with a sufficient quality is still the priority. Zero rating is also positively perceived, as a means to develop the Internet, as illustrated by Facebook, Google, and Wikipedia programs. It is believed that imposing net neutrality could have negative effects, hindering competition [149].

2.7 A Situation Still Evolving

As highlighted above, the debate is still active in many countries with rules not defined yet in some places, but new issues arising in others, about specialized services or zero rating, for example. As a consequence, there is currently no steady-state worldwide accepted vision about network neutrality.

This evolving situation has been exacerbated with the recent decision of the authorities in the USA to repeal neutrality protections in 2017. The USA being the origin or intermediate of an important part of worldwide traffic, this decision may impact users' perception all over the world and the subsequent decision within all other countries. To recall how it happened, US president Donald Trump appointed Ajit Pai, an opponent of net neutrality, as chairman of the FCC in 2017. The FCC then decided to reclassify the Internet as an information service, thereby re-dissociating broadband services from the laws regulating telecommunications. From that decision, service differentiation has been made possible by ISPs.

Recall that it is not the first time rules have changed in the USA, after the 1996 Telecommunications Act where the FCC declared ISPs to be "common carriers" (with neutrality implications), then the opposed decision in 2002 to consider the Internet as an information service, before again neutrality laws through the 2015 Open Internet Order as described in Sect. 2.6.1.1.

The neutrality repeal ignited many reactions within the country, and even worldwide. On July 12, 2017, more than 200 content providers, including Amazon, Google, Netflix, Pornhub, and Vimeo (video sharing), inserted statements, banners, and illustrative slowed down traffic on their Web sites to warn users about the "dangers" of neutrality repealing. The event was called the Day of Action. According to a poll organized by Mozilla, 76% of Americans were in favor of neutrality. Despite that and the numerous filed comments about the proposal, the Senate endorsed the decision to deregulate the Internet in early 2018, as proposed by the FCC.

Many states, unhappy with this new rule and in favor of neutrality, have tried to impose their own laws. California, for example, has passed its own net neutrality act, which the US Department of Justice was challenging on a legal basis.[18] California is as of October 2020 the only state law that comprehensively restores all the net neutrality protections from the FCC's 2015 Open Internet Order.

As a consequence, major US ISPs have been shown to differentiate service for some resource-demanding providers or applications.[19] Using a measurement application called Wehe (detailed in Chap. 9) and extensive tests carried out at the end of 2018, a significant slowdown was identified for YouTube, for example, (sometimes with speed divided by 10), while Spotify was not throttled. Many ISPs denied it (explaining it by other reasons) or refused to comment. AT&T and Verizon were the providers shown to throttle the most at that time.

The COVID-19 crisis also exacerbated neutrality issues. Due to the traffic increase, with significantly increased consumption from home to watch on-demand videos and participate in online meetings, worries were raised about congestion, and many actors pointed out the potential necessity of service differentiation.

---

[18] http://cyberlaw.stanford.edu/blog/2020/09/california-defends-its-net-neutrality-law

[19] https://www.bloomberg.com/news/articles/2018-09-04/youtube-and-netflix-throttled-by-carriers-research-finds   or   https://www.cnet.com/how-to/your-carrier-could-throttle-your-streaming-netflix-and-youtube-videos-heres-how-you-test/

Major service providers such as Netflix and Google were asked to downgrade the quality of their videos to reduce the load on the network and give more capacity to those working from home [76]. The request is to apply measures at the application layer (of the OSI, for Open Systems Interconnection, model) rather than within the network, hence not directly in opposition to neutrality rules, even if "reasonable traffic management" measures are allowed. No real *major* congestion issues were reported even if a traffic increase was observed [162], especially during lockdown periods, with variations among countries [29, 165] and more seen on lower income and/or countries with slow networks, with a few exceptions including France [63]. The pandemic induced some relaxation of neutrality requirements in many countries. It was, for example, the case in India, which waived zero-rating prohibition for applications such as the World Health Organization and India's Ministry of Health and Family Welfare, pointing out that they contribute to social welfare [41]. South Africa also zero-rated its COVID alert mobile application to incentivize the citizens to use it in order to reduce the virus propagation.

But with heterogeneous definitions and implementations of network neutrality worldwide and end-to-end traffic potentially flowing through several countries, it is not possible to guarantee that a traffic be neutral in the sense of the regulator, given that some criteria may not have been fulfilled on a leg of the journey from source to destination. In a string of papers [2, 110], game-theoretic models are built representing the interactions between users, network providers, and content providers to investigate the impact of two neutrality relaxation policies in a part of the world on all actors, compared with a fully neutral network. Results show that neutrality repeal may only favor the ISP in the differentiation-authorized zone, but no other actor, and that it can be worse off for everybody if the regulation procedures are very strict in the neutral area.

2.8   A Trade-Off with Users Deciding Differentiation?

The network neutrality debate can be very roughly summarized as the opposition between, on one side, end users and content providers wishing no limit or constraint on their possible use of the Internet and on the other side ISPs claiming that there is a stress on the network architecture due to resource-demanding applications and that service differentiation should be applied to ensure quality of service and get a return on investment.

One option gaining interest, and not addressed by regulators yet, is to allow differentiation but *only* if initiated by users. Quoting H. Schulzrinne in [154]:

> Rather than focusing on network behavior only, it may be more helpful to consider end-user choice as the principle for deciding whether a particular traffic management or other policy is reasonable if it cannot be readily justified as protecting the network against attack or abuse.

In other words:

1. Service differentiation is often seen as a restraint to innovation, but users should be able to choose to favor new services if they find them relevant, and innovative CPs could also gain from this.
2. With user-driven differentiation, the ISP stays "neutral" in the sense that it does not choose to differentiate.
3. Such an approach would allow ISPs to operate some differentiation, release the necessity to invest on capacity, and get a reasonable share of revenue.

All these seem a decent trade-off respecting arguments of both sides of the debate.

This type of problem has been mathematically analyzed in [85] to investigate whether the option of allowing differentiation, operated by users, is worthwhile with respect to neutrality or differentiation operated by the ISP. The scenarios are compared: a unique class of service (neutral scenario); a situation with two priority classes but for which the ISP decides which class should get priority; and the same two-priority classes but for which each user decides its service class. According to the model, letting users decide the differentiation is a viable and balanced solution.

This suggestion leads to technical questions about *(i)* the implementation of user-driven differentiation and *(ii)* the implementation of an associated charging scheme. Historically, in the 1990s and early 2000s, there has been a large amount of works on techniques for service differentiation (DiffServ being one of them); see [86] among the many references on service management and related existing standardization. Less has been done up to now about charging and accounting.

2.9 Conclusions

As conclusions, network neutrality, treating all traffic flows and/packets without differentiation, has been extensively debated. Legislation has been discussed in many countries worldwide, and laws still have to be enacted (or not) in many places. But as we highlighted, there is no absolute consensus about the definition of neutrality, strong or weak, nor about the appropriate level of implementation, if any. The subject is far from closed, with changing rules, such as with the repeal in the USA in 2017.

Our goal in this book is to be as neutral as possible with respect to the debate. The notions of "neutrality" and "openness" are sensitive issues. As David Clark, a Vice Chair to the FCC's Open Internet Advisory Committee, declared:

> Now openness has taken on a sort of religious tone. Openness is a slippery word. It doesn't mean much. I have cynically observed that it's a word you put in front of another to create a positive value (open borders, open conversation, open continents, open relationship). It's obvious that it's opposite of closed, which is a bad word. Openness is not a goal, nor is network neutrality a goal.

Trying to avoid (or to clearly identify) any religious tone, the next chapter will list and discuss arguments from both sides of the debate.

Chapter 3
Pros and Cons: The Arguments in the Debate

In this chapter, we list and organize the arguments that have been developed on both sides of the net neutrality debate since its beginning. Our goal is to provide the logics behind each argument, together with concrete examples, while avoiding taking any passionate stance. The next chapters will develop mathematical models illustrating the relevance of some arguments but also, interestingly, potential counter-intuitive and opposite results.

As we intend to show here, it is often difficult to claim that one recommendation naturally follows from higher principles; indeed, it is frequently the case that different interpretations of the same principle lead to recommending net neutrality be protected or not.

We propose in this chapter an organization based on those higher principles, namely, freedom, competition and innovation, security and privacy, and user welfare. When several arguments—possibly on different sides of the debate—can be derived from a principle, we give them with no specific order (still trying to remain neutral and just state the arguments).

Also, note that the arguments are sometimes difficult to compare and oppose, since they tend to consider slightly different definitions of net neutrality: generally net neutrality proponents tend to exaggerate what operators would be allowed to do without specific regulation, while net neutrality opponents tend to exaggerate the constraints that neutrality regulation would impose. But those biased interpretations are certainly helpful to highlight what extremes should be avoided and to fine-tune the definitions of net neutrality.

P. Maillé, B. Tuffin, *From Net Neutrality to ICT Neutrality*,
https://doi.org/10.1007/978-3-031-06271-1_3

3.1   The "Freedom" Arguments: Whose Freedom?

The freedom principle (which is rarely disputed in itself) is used as the basis for arguments by both sides of the neutrality debate. Which side the freedom principle leads you to defend mainly comes down to whose freedom you consider needs more protection, among Internet users and operators. Indeed, net neutrality regulations (are expected to) set a balance between freedom of speech and freedom of enterprise.

3.1.1   [Pro-NN] Net Neutrality Is Needed to Guarantee Free Speech

The Internet has become an extraordinary medium for sharing thoughts and ideas without any form of censorship, some of the most notable illustrations being the catalyst role that social platforms played in the "Arab Spring" in the early 2010s [164], seen as a very positive means of liberation of the peoples, or the influence they may have had on the 2016 US presidential election [3, 71], then seen by some, depending on their political stance, as a manipulation of opinion or a means to receive alternative news with respect to "biased" regular media.

Despite all the inevitable problems that come with that freedom of speech (like misinformation, incitement to violence, or privacy issues), most people are extremely attached to it and advocate for its protection in all expression domains, in particular on the Internet. And net neutrality principles naturally contribute to that protection, since some actors being allowed to select which Web pages are available is equivalent to censorship.

A standard example is China implementing the so-called Great Firewall of China, blocking Web sites such as Wikipedia, YouTube, and Google. Russia also passed laws to authorize censorship, the latest one in 2019, fining people and sites spreading government-considered fake news or "disrespectful" content toward authorities. But this may also happen in established democracies: Another example of such a censorship was implemented by the Canadian operator Telus in 2005: in the midst of a fight with its unionized employees, Telus simply barred all its subscribers from accessing the "Voice for Change" Web site managed by union members to support the strike. Also note that as a side effect, all Telus subscribers had lost the access to more than 700 other Web sites, hosted on the same server as "Voice for Change." Despite Telus explaining their action was to protect the company and its workers, they finally had to unblock the Web site as per a court injunction. Democracies support freedom of speech but limit or block content linked to pedopornography, terrorism, security, etc. This is the typical kind of arguments used for censorship when willing to limit freedom too, illustrating how thin the frontier can be with this respect. The question was exacerbated during the COVID-19 pandemic, such as with South Africa blocking sites and imposing criminal penalties for misleading coronavirus-related speech.[1] On a related note, some Web sites give a score to countries according to Internet freedom criteria.[2]

The argument for neutrality regulation is therefore straightforward: **We do not want an Internet where operators decide what we can and cannot see or what we can and cannot write.**

3.1.2   *[Anti-NN] Net Neutrality Hinders Operators' Freedom of Enterprise*

Now let us take the point of view of an **ISP!** (**ISP!**), which has invested enormous amounts to be able to provide high-quality connections to its subscribers by building large-capacity "pipes": shouldn't that **ISP!** be allowed to manage its pipes how it sees fit? For such an actor, any regulation is synonymous to extra constraints that limit its range of actions. It is therefore natural that ISPs ask for as little regulation as possible, with the simple argument that **ISPs are for-profit companies, how they manage their activity is part of their freedom of enterprise, and no specific law for them is needed**.

To elaborate on that stance, recall the ever-growing needs in terms of communication bandwidth, mainly driven by high-definition video streaming services (like YouTube and Netflix). ISPs just provide the support for those bandwidth-demanding services, i.e., they bear the burden of the increased communication load, without getting any direct benefit since service/content providers directly perceive subscription revenues from users and/or advertisement revenues from advertisers. When that extra load incurs difficulties in terms of network management, it seems that the margin of maneuver of ISPs is very limited if they are not allowed to shape the traffic (i.e., slow down some services) or even to ask the most bandwidth-consuming service providers to participate financially for capacity expansions. Is that fair to ISPs? What if some flows are sent to the ISP's network with the sole purpose of saturating it, shouldn't the ISP be allowed to cut or throttle that malicious flow?

3.2   The "Investment" Arguments

3.2.1   *[Anti-NN] Returns on Investments Are Needed*

This is probably the main argument developed by ISPs: they are in charge of ensuring a good quality of service to users by providing a sufficient capacity, but

---

[1] https://freedomhouse.org/country/south-africa/freedom-net/2020

[2] https://freedomhouse.org/countries/freedom-net/scores

on the other hand, CPs are more and more demanding in terms of resources with an increasing traffic. Moreover, ISPs claim that the share of revenue of CPs in the delivery chain to users keeps increasing, something easily observable with Google or Facebook, while all CP activity is based on high-performance infrastructures, hence CPs should naturally be involved in the infrastructure investment. In short, the argument is that **CPs are the ones benefiting the most from network infrastructures and needing upgrades, so the most resource-consuming ones should contribute to the upgrade investments**. In 2017, to motivate its decision to overturn neutrality, the FCC followed a close reasoning, claiming that neutrality was reducing investment and jobs and was inducing billions of dollars of losses. See Chap. 4 or, for example, [26] for mathematical models analyzing this claim about potential negative impacts.

3.2.2 [Pro-NN] More Customers, More Investments

On the other hand, neutrality proponents usually claim that the more users are satisfied with the diversity of services provided by CPs and the quality of service of service provided by ISPs, the larger the number of end-user subscriptions (hence revenue for ISPs) in a kind of virtuous circle and that **ISPs wanting CPs to pay for the network is just them wanting to make money from both ends of the chain**.

3.3 The "Competition and Innovation" Arguments

Favoring competition is widely seen as a good thing, since the emulation it creates among competitors elicits innovation and drives prices down, hence benefiting customers. But here again, both sides of the debate have arguments to support their view (see also [88]).

3.3.1 [Pro-NN] Non-neutrality Biases the Competition Among Services

The question of unfair competition is among the first triggers of the whole net neutrality debate. Indeed, as early as in 1994, then US vice-president Al Gore [69] raised concerns regarding the promising Internet ecosystem:

> How can government ensure that the information marketplace [...] will permit everyone to be able to compete with everyone else for the opportunity to provide any service to all willing customers?

Even if Gore may not have specifically thought about neutrality-related problems, it is quite clear that **to compete on a level playing field, services need to be treated the same by ISPs**. Otherwise, how could an innovative **VoIP! (VoIP!)** company thrive if blocked by some ISPs offering comparable services, as was Vonage by Madison River in 2005, or more recently Skype and Google Voice on iPhones by AT&T between 2007 and 2009? In the same vein, differentiated treatment like *zero rating* of some services (not counting them in the data amount the user has paid for) gives those services a huge advantage.

A possible response to that argument may rely on the already existing legal arsenals to ensure fair competition, but the question remains whether such measures (not specific to the Internet) are really applicable in networking ecosystems that evolve very fast relative to the timescale of judicial procedures. Another question is: Would existing laws against anti-competitive actions be sufficient to protect a brand new type of service needing a fair access?

3.3.2   *[Anti-NN] ISPs Favoring Some Content Providers Stimulates ISP Competition (Through Content)*

Imagine a non-neutral Internet, where ISPs favor some content providers over others (e.g., through contracts or by even owning those content providers in a "vertical integration" construction); to simplify the picture, one can think that some contents are only available through a specific ISP, although in practice the distinction can be more subtle (with, e.g., in video streaming, the high-quality version being only available on the associated ISP). To attract subscribers, ISPs therefore need to be able to offer content that at least matches the content controlled by their competitors, hence an incentive to innovate on the content side. And to provide that content with high quality, ISPs will also be incentivized to increase their capacities or invent new technologies.

As an illustration of this phenomenon, we can cite, from the television domain, the case of the competition between cable and satellite TV in the USA, where cable networks had to intensively invest in content creation to compete with the satellite TV provider DirecTV's obtaining the exclusive rights of the "NFL Sunday Ticket" [96].

To summarize, the argument in this case could be rephrased as follows: **let ISPs associate with content providers and then compete, they will innovate both on content and on quality-of-service**.

3.3.3 [Pro-NN] Neutrality Is Needed to Allow Innovating Newcomers

But the "innovation" argument is mostly used by neutrality proponents, with a more straightforward scenario: just think about all services that have appeared on the Internet and succeeded because of its low barrier-to-entry, and imagine whether they could have survived had they faced a non-neutral network. In a non-neutral world, ISPs would be expected to favor their partnered services and relegate all other flows to a slow lane, so that the next Google, the next Facebook, or the next TikTok would have a much harder time building an audience and succeeding: what to do if the only options are either to pay an enormous premium to ISPs or to stay in slow lanes? Note that each of those three examples needed the best connection quality available at the time of their appearance, with low latency, high reliability, and sufficient transmission rates being key reasons for their success.

To sum up, the point is simply that **non-neutrality would create high entry barriers for innovating services**, hence the need for a level playing field.

3.4 The "Security and Privacy" Arguments

3.4.1 [Anti-NN] Encryption Already Prevents Discrimination

To perform some differentiation with respect to any aspect other than the source or recipient IP address (e.g., application, type of device used), a non-neutral ISP would need to perform a so-called Deep Packet Inspection of the packets it treats, which is already a costly operation in terms of time and computational power [91]. But in addition, now most applications use encryption to guarantee the integrity and confidentiality of their exchanges, so that the ISP cannot even identify the application that is used. In summary, **net neutrality is just unnecessary because ISPs cannot technically differentiate among encrypted flows**.

3.4.2 [Pro-NN] Neutrality Helps Protect Privacy

The principle of privacy protection is mainly used by net neutrality proponents, to argue that Internet carriers should just act as "dumb pipes" and simply send the packets they receive toward their destination, without further inspection that would be needed to perform differentiation. Indeed, the fear associated with ISPs being allowed to decapsulate packets to determine their treatment (depending on the user, the protocol used, the service, etc.) is that **governments or companies could implement a society of surveillance and act according to their agenda, without the users' consent**.

At a time when people get scared about what companies like Facebook know about them and do with that data, it should be even scarier to imagine that ISPs, being allowed to inspect our traffic, would know everything about our online activity, not only related to one Web site as Facebook. Therefore, explicitly forcing ISPs to remain "dumb pipes," forbidding them to look into the traffic they carry, would seem a necessary guarantee against such data collection.

3.5 The "Welfare" Arguments

The arguments in this section rely on economic theory, and even when taking the specific point of view of users, both sides of the debate can find ground to defend their position.

3.5.1 [Pro-NN] Non-neutrality Would Lead to a Fragmented Internet, Which Is Bad For Users

A fear of net neutrality proponents is that without any regulations, in order to maximize profit and attract subscribers, each ISP will be associated with some "package" of content providers, through vertical integration (the ISP controlling those content providers) or some commercial agreement. As a result, users will not be able to access all content providers—or with comparable qualities—but only those included in their ISP's package. This means that depending on the ISPs available in their region **some content may be unreachable, or users would have to subscribe to several ISPs to get access to all content**: such a fragmentation of content into "several Internets" is clearly to the detriment of users. This fragmentation is experienced with TV content: one soccer fan wanting to watch all games often needs to subscribe to several providers (Canal+, BeIn Sport, Eurosport, Amazon Prime, RMC Sport, e.g., in France as of 2022), leading to expensive fees; the same happens for TV series fans.

3.5.2 [Anti-NN] Content Providers Should Contribute to the Infrastructure Costs to Reduce Users' Share

That argument is advanced by ISPs, complaining that a few content providers with bandwidth-consuming services (such as YouTube or Netflix) saturate the networks and therefore incur enormous infrastructure and maintenance costs bore by ISPs only. On the other hand, those content providers extract continuously increasing revenues, either directly (through subscriptions) or indirectly (through advertisements). The solution put forward to avoid passing all the extra costs to end users is then that **ISPs should be allowed to charge content providers for part of their infrastructure costs, to keep low Internet prices for users**. And net neutrality prevents the appearance of such business models.

3.5.3   [Anti-NN] A Free Market Finds the Most Efficient Outcome

Somewhat linked to the previous argument is the more general belief that markets naturally reach efficient situations, due to competition and utility optimization from self-interested actors:

> Agriculture, manufactures, commerce, and navigation, the four pillars of our prosperity, are the most thriving when left most free to individual enterprise.[3]

In the context of net neutrality, this can be formulated as follows: **let the invisible hand of the digital market find the optimal models without constraining it**. Note however that markets being "welfare maximizers" only holds under some specific conditions (in particular, sufficient competition is needed) which are far from verified in reality.

3.6   Conclusions

Opponents and proponents have developed arguments, respectively, against and in favor of neutrality. Many arguments, pro or con, seem reasonable, and the list above may lead to mixed feelings about the degree of neutrality to be implemented. In what follows, we are going to describe simple yet representative mathematical models illustrative of the impact of neutrality or non-neutrality on the various Internet actors and sometimes remark that some outcomes are counterintuitive with respect to raised arguments.

---

[3] Thomas Jefferson, First Annual Message to Congress. December 8, 1801.

Chapter 4
Mathematical Analysis

The purpose of this chapter is to point out that the so-called common sense may be dangerous concerning neutrality (or non-neutrality) ideas or decisions. This is done through the design and analysis of mathematical models by non-cooperative game theory, which studies the interactions between selfish actors. It is well known in this field that such interactions may lead to counterintuitive outputs. Hence, a particular care should be taken before claiming assertions.

Any reader not interested in or not comfortable with mathematical developments can directly jump to the interpretations and conclusions that we will specifically highlight in the text in subsections.

Of course, the conclusions of models, in particular from our examples in this chapter, are not necessarily to be taken for granted either: they in most cases depend on the mathematical assumptions we made. But working with models can help emphasize issues not generally thought of and open discussions and arguments toward a need or not for regulation.

In this chapter, Sect. 4.1 reminds or introduces the main notions of mathematical modeling and game theory that we will use in this chapter and in the remainder of this book. We focus on the minimal material that is needed to understand the derivations in the present and next chapters. Section 4.2 introduces a basic model analyzing the relations between one ISP and one content provider (CP) that, even if looking simple, illustrates issues and counterintuitive outcomes, sometimes in contradiction with assertions from participants to the debate. Again, even if not to be taken for granted, such results show how intricate the debate is. Section 4.3 extends the previous model to the situation with two CPs, to compare the outcomes with strong and weak neutrality. Since many issues related to neutrality have been analyzed in the literature, we summarize the results in Sect. 4.4. Given that the models are very diverse, we cannot dig into all of them but present the main conclusions. Section 4.5 presents final notes.

P. Maillé, B. Tuffin, *From Net Neutrality to ICT Neutrality*,
https://doi.org/10.1007/978-3-031-06271-1_4

4.1   Introduction to Mathematical Modeling and Game Theory

When trying to understand the impact of decisions, or to anticipate that impact for decision-making, there are several options. The first and simplest one is to base choices on intuition and experience. But this is often considered dangerous since experience may be limited and even misleading and outcomes may be counterintuitive. At the other extreme, we can implement in real life or at least in a controlled environment the system or choices we want to investigate and see what results occur from it. But this can be very costly and long, and a test or implementation could be perceived as a politically incorrect way to introduce a rule. An intermediate procedure is to build a mathematical model as representative as possible of real life and analyze it. It is a "cheap" way to explain and make predictions about the behavior of a system of components. In the situation of understanding interacting components behaving selfishly, the relevant framework is that of *non-cooperative game theory*.

4.1.1   Elements of Non-cooperative Game Theory

The Internet is made of numerous actors, the main ones in the network neutrality debate being the end users, the ISPs, and the CPs, even if much more could be involved as we will hint in next chapters. It is interesting to represent the impact of *my* decisions as an actor on the others, and how they can even influence the decisions of others which have to anticipate my choices, but knowing that also influences my decision, and so on. This is the purpose of non-cooperative game theory: to represent and analyze the output of interactions between non-cooperative and strategic entities. For textbooks on game theory, the reader can look at [65, 141] or the many courses available on the Web. More on game theory in the context of network economics can be found in [104].

A stakeholder of the Internet with decision power is called a *player* in the game theory vocabulary. Assume we have a set of n players among whom we want to analyze interactions. We index them such that the set is $I = \{1, \ldots, n\}$.

Each player i has a set of actions that we will denote by $\mathcal{A}_i$, and an *action* will be denoted by $a_i \in \mathcal{A}_i$. Actions can be of different nature: a price setting for an ISP and a CP or ISP subscription for end users are the simplest examples. The outcome will be defined in terms of the *action profile*:

$$a := (a_1, \ldots, a_n).$$

The set of action profiles is then:

$$\mathcal{A} := \prod_{i=1}^{n} \mathcal{A}_i = \{(a_1, \ldots, a_n) | a_i \in \mathcal{A}_i, \forall i \in \mathcal{I}\}.$$

The preferences of players among the possible action profiles (and the resulting outcome on the system) are generally represented through *utility functions*. Denote by U_i the utility function for Player $i \in \mathcal{I}$. The principle is to map the set of action profiles to $\mathbb{R}$ (i.e., $U_i : \mathcal{A} \to \mathbb{R}$) such that Player i will strictly prefer action profile $a = (a_1, \ldots, a_n) \in \mathcal{A}$ over $a' = (a'_1, \ldots, a'_n) \in \mathcal{A}$ if and only if $U_i(a) > U_i(a')$. Player i will be said to be indifferent between a and a' if $U_i(a) = U_i(a')$. Typical examples of utility include the revenue (expressed in monetary units) for service providers, or a quantified level of quality of service (such as throughput) for end users.

An underlying assumption in game theory is that players are *rational*, meaning that they choose actions maximizing their utility functions.

Two other important notions used throughout the next sections are *social welfare* and *user welfare*. Social welfare, denoted by SW, is often defined as the sum of utilities over all players (assuming that all utilities are expressed in similar units, typically monetary units):

$$\forall a \in \mathcal{A}, \quad \text{SW} := \sum_{i \in \mathcal{I}} U_i(a). \tag{4.1}$$

In other words, social welfare measures the aggregated level of satisfaction over all stakeholders and is a kind of measure of satisfaction for society. It can sometimes constitute the utility function of a regulator, wanting to maximize the total value extracted by some market.

The other notion, user welfare, denoted by UW, is more specific to a game with players made of several types, where one subset $\mathcal{I}_u \subset \mathcal{I}$ represents end users. Mathematically:

$$\forall a \in \mathcal{A}, \quad \text{UW} := \sum_{i \in \mathcal{I}_u} U_i(a). \tag{4.2}$$

Isolating end users, when relevant in terms of model, makes sense when a government or a regulator is trying to investigate the impact of an action profile on people.

We will redefine SW and UW in the next sections to fit a different modeling of end users, not expressed individually, but keeping the same spirit of aggregating actors' utilities.

4.1.2   Output Analysis

The process leading a player i to select their action a_i, based on their preferences, their knowledge, or beliefs, is called their *strategy*. In most cases in this book, we will only consider so-called *pure* strategies, i.e., strategies leading to play one deterministic action (in contrast, *mixed* strategies only give distributions over the set of actions, and the action that is played is selected randomly according to that distribution). For that reason, unless specified otherwise, we will, by a slight abuse, use the terms *action* and *strategy* interchangeably.

Each rational player $i \in I$ wishes to maximize their utility $U_i(a)$, a function depending on the strategies of all players, including Player i's decisions as represented by the fact that the vector $a = (a_1, \ldots, a_n)$ contains a_i. To better separate the decision of the considered Player i from that of other players, we often use the notation:

$$a = (a_1, \ldots, a_n) = (a_i; a_{-i}) \text{ where } a_{-i} := (a_j, j \neq i),$$

meaning that a_{-i} is the vector including the strategies of all players *except i*.

In a non-cooperative context, Player i can only play with their strategy a_i, not with any part of a_{-i}. The most important notion of equilibrium in game theory is the notion of *Nash equilibrium* [133]. Basically, the principle is that a profile a is a Nash equilibrium if no player can improve their utility through a unilateral deviation. More formally:

Definition 4.1 A Nash equilibrium is a profile $a^* \in \mathcal{A}$ such that for every player $i \in I$:

$$U_i(a_i^*; a_{-i}^*) \geq U_i(a_i; a_{-i}^*) \quad \forall a_i \in \mathcal{A}_i. \tag{4.3}$$

Equation (4.3) expresses that the action profile a_{-i}^* being fixed, Player i cannot improve their utility U_i by moving from the strategy a_i^* to any other strategy a_i. Again, the *unilateral* (non-cooperative assumption) comes from playing with only the strategy of Player i, no common move from a group of players is here "allowed" (this would fit the framework of cooperative game theory).

To compute a Nash equilibrium, one can look at the *best response* correspondence of each player $i \in I$, denoted by BR_i, which gives the set of actions maximizing Player i's utility when faced with an action profile a_{-i} from the opponents. Formally:

$$\mathrm{BR}_i : \prod_{j \in I \setminus \{i\}} \mathcal{A}_j \mapsto \mathcal{P}(\mathcal{A}_i)$$

$$a_{-i} \mapsto \arg \max_{x \in \mathcal{A}_i} U_i(x, a_{-i}), \tag{4.4}$$

where $\mathcal{P}(\mathcal{A}_i)$ is the set of subsets of $\mathcal{A}_i$. Then a Nash equilibrium is an action profile a^* such that for all player $i \in I$, $a_i^* \in \mathrm{BR}_i(a_{-i}^*)$, since in this case, every player is maximizing their utility given the others' strategies; hence, no player has an interest to make a unilateral move.

A Nash equilibrium therefore constitutes an expected or at least a stable outcome since no player will change their action. For a game, there may be one, none, or even several Nash equilibria. If there is a unique Nash equilibrium, the rationality of players should lead all players to deduce that they should play their equilibrium strategy and to anticipate that all other players will do the same reasoning.

Example 4.1 To illustrate the notion, consider the simple game presented in Table 4.1 with two players, Player 1 being the ISP with two strategies, *differentiate* (Diff) or *not differentiate* (Ndiff) represented over lines, and Player 2 being the CP with two strategies represented over columns, *invest a lot* (Hinv) or *invest not much* (Linv). A couple in the table corresponds to the value $(U_1(a_1, a_2), U_2(a_1, a_2))$ with $a_1 \in \{\text{Diff, Ndiff}\}$ and $a_2 \in \{\text{Hinv, Linv}\}$, where U_i is the utility (revenue) of Player i. The content of Table 4.1 then contains all the information of the game.

It can be readily checked that (Diff, Hinv) is the only Nash equilibrium for this game. Indeed, the ISP has then no interest to move to Ndiff, since that would reduce its utility U_1 from 8 to 5; similarly, the CP moving to strategy Linv would reduce its utility from 4 to 2. For all other strategy profiles on the other hand, there is an interest to move for at least one player.

Note that this simple example abusively excludes end users from the equation; it is introduced here to illustrate basic notions.

It may also be interesting to see what would happen if all actors were collaborating, which can be interpreted as finding the optimal action profile maximizing social welfare. Formally:

Definition 4.2 The socially optimal strategy profile, or *social optimum* is

$$\tilde{a} := \arg\max_{a \in \mathcal{A}} \sum_{i \in I} U_i(a)$$

and the social optimum outcome is $\sum_{i \in I} U_i(\tilde{a})$.

In the case of Example 4.1, it can be checked in Table 4.1 that the action profile maximizing the sum of utilities is $\tilde{a} = $ (Ndiff, Hinv), different from the Nash equilibrium strategy, and leading to $U_1(\tilde{a}) + U_2(\tilde{a}) = 14$. For this example, the CP (Player 2) has the same best strategy in the Nash and Social optimum situation,

Table 4.1 A network differentiation and investment game: the ISP (Player 1) selects the line and the CP (Player 2 the column. Terms in the cell are of the form (U_1, U_2))

	Hinv	Linv
Diff	(8, 4)	(7, 2)
Ndiff	(5, 9)	(3, 5)

but it may happen that it is the case for no player, and even that no player would prefer the Nash equilibrium to the social optimum; such a situation is called the prisoner's dilemma [104], something *a priori* counterintuitive.

A metric comparing the social welfare at the *worst* Nash equilibrium to the social optimal outcome is the *price of anarchy* (PoA), defined below.

Definition 4.3 Let $\mathcal{A}^*$ be the set of Nash equilibrium action profiles. The PoA is the ratio between the social optimum outcome and the worst social value at a Nash equilibrium:

$$\text{PoA} := \frac{\max_{a \in \mathcal{A}} \sum_{i \in I} U_i(a)}{\min_{a^* \in \mathcal{A}^*} \sum_{i \in I} U_i(a^*)}. \tag{4.5}$$

The PoA is always larger than 1. In the case of Example 4.1, the sum of utilities at the Nash equilibrium being 12, the PoA is $14/12 = 7/6$.

There are much more notions of strategy and associated equilibrium in the vast domain of game theory. Again, an interested reader can go to [65, 141]. We just briefly mention here a concept named the *Nash bargaining solution* [134], which is relevant when the players need to find some agreement through a negotiation, and each one has a "threat" action they would play in case the negotiation fails. The concept is further explained in Sect. 5.1.4; it basically consists in managing the trade-off between the utilities of all players by maximizing the product of their gains with respect to the "no agreement" outcome.

4.1.3 Principle of Mechanism Design

The idea of *mechanism design* consists in defining the rules of the game, either by limiting or modifying the set of actions of players or by introducing components modifying the utilities of players, such that the outcome of the game (a Nash equilibrium) is a situation beneficial to all or at least to "society." Such an approach is typically applicable to regulators, who can set rules to define the range of allowed actions or introduce monetary incentives. A situation that can be seen as optimal from the regulator side is when the (introduced) rules are such that the resulting Nash equilibrium coincides with the social optimum outcome, yielding a price of anarchy of 1, and if possible with an outcome at least as good as what the social optimal outcome without the rules was.

Coming back to Example 4.1, imagine that a regulator imposes a tax t to the ISP implementing differentiation and giving back the corresponding amount to the CP. The resulting game utilities are displayed in Table 4.2, where we recall a couple in the table corresponds to the value pair $(U_1(a_1, a_2), U_2(a_1, a_2))$ with $a_1 \in \{\text{Diff}, \text{Ndiff}\}$ and $a_2 \in \{\text{Hinv}, \text{Linv}\}$, with U_i the utility (revenue) of Player i. With a level of tax $t = 4$, we end up with a (still unique) Nash equilibrium (Ndiff, Hinv), the social optimum situation. Given that the whole tax level t is re-injected

Table 4.2 A network differentiation and investment game with a level of tax t transferred to the CP if the ISP applies differentiation

	Hinv	Linv
Diff	$(8-t, 4+t)$	$(7-t, 2+t)$
Ndiff	$(5, 9)$	$(3, 5)$

into the system and given to the CP, the sum of utilities is not changed whatever t, and the new Nash equilibrium corresponds to the social optimum situation of the game without tax.

4.2 A Basic Model

To illustrate more precisely the interest of modeling in the network neutrality debate, we present in this section a basic model that will be used to compare various scenarios. More refined, but more complicated models and analyses used in the literature will be summarized in Sect. 4.4, along with the associated results.

The model we will present in the next section consists of one ISP and two content providers (CPs), but we start for now with the simpler situation with a single CP, whose parameters will be indexed by 1, while parameters for the (single) ISP will be indexed by A.

There is a *flat rate* subscription price, denoted by p_A, charged to users to access ISP A. To access any content, the ISP subscription is compulsory. Subscription to the CP is also assumed to be through a flat rate,[1] denoted by p_1. We additionally introduce the notion of side payment, that ISP A may want to impose to CP 1 for the traffic going through its network. This payment is often considered as a value $q_1' > 0$ *per unit of volume* that CP 1 has to pay to ISP A, but we will assume here for simplicity that the price is $q_1 > 0$ *per unit of user*, which is equivalent if we assume that each user "consumes" the same volume w, so that $q_1 = wq_1'$. In the literature, that type of model with side payments is also referred to as inducing *two-sided pricing*, since ISPs can charge both sides of the market: end users and CPs. The charges/costs imposed by actors to other players are summarized in Fig. 4.1. In the neutral case, we will consider that side payments are prohibited, i.e., $q_1 = 0$.

Now let us model the user side. We assume a continuum of end users, of mass one without loss of generality. That assumption yields a type of model different from what we presented in the general introduction to game theory in Sect. 4.1, where a discrete number of users was considered and included in the discrete set

---

[1] Remark that we could similarly consider that the CP gives a free access but earns money, thanks to advertisement. In that case, the more advertisement is placed on content, the more money the CP gets, but the more disturbance, or cost, for the users. Then p_1 could be the perceived cost by users due to advertisement, with a revenue proportional to p_1 for the CP, thanks to a mapping between money earned by the CP and the perceived cost by users.

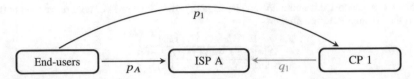

Fig. 4.1 Charging interactions between stakeholders with one CP and one ISP

$\mathcal{I}$ of players, or even when no user was explicitly considered in Example 4.1 (but users could be considered as hidden in the model, since leading to the providers' revenues). Here, infinitesimal users have three action choices: either they subscribe to the ISP and the CP or only to the ISP (taking benefit from other available services only) or they do not subscribe at all to anything. We assume that users' subscription to CP+ISP depends on the full price $p = p_1 + p_A$ they will have to pay. If subscribing to the ISP only, the perceived price is $p = kp_A$ with $k > 1$ representing the increased perception of price for not benefiting from the CP's service. Finally, there is also a "cost" $p = p_0$ for not subscribing to anything, i.e., not having Internet access.

To represent user choices, we consider a discrete choice/stickiness model (see [104] for more details). In such a model, the valuation V of a user is the sum of two components:

$$V = v + \kappa.$$

The value v corresponds to the average valuation for a service that has a price (cost) p, which we represent by the standard logarithm relation:

$$v = \alpha \log \left(\frac{1}{p} \right) \tag{4.6}$$

where $\alpha > 0$ is a sensitivity parameter. Using such a function comes from psychophysics, stating that in many situations, the perception of a physical stimulus is logarithmic in its magnitude [148]. We consider $1/p$ as the argument of the log, since the larger the price, the smaller the valuation/interest for the service. The second term, denoted by κ, is user specific and treated as a random part representing user differences in perception. As in standard discrete-choice modeling, κ is assumed to follow a Gumbel distribution with mean 0.

As a result of our assumptions, there is a random valuation $V_i = v_i + \kappa_i$ corresponding to each option (with $i \in \{1, A, 0\}$), with respective prices $p_1 + p_A$, kp_A and p_0 in (4.6), and the κ_i are independent and identically distributed Gumbel random variables for each option and user. A rational user typically selects the option with the largest valuation. Over the full mass 1 of users, this leads to a simple expression for the mass (or proportion) σ_1 of users subscribing to the ISP+CP service (see again [104] for more details):

$$\sigma_1 = \begin{cases} \dfrac{(p_A + p_1)^{-\alpha}}{(p_A + p_1)^{-\alpha} + (kp_A)^{-\alpha} + p_0^{-\alpha}} & \text{if } (p_A + p_1) > 0 \\ 1 & \text{if } p_A + p_1 = 0. \end{cases} \tag{4.7}$$

The mass σ_A of users subscribing to the ISP *only* is similarly:

$$\sigma_A = \frac{(kp_A)^{-\alpha}}{(p_A + p_1)^{-\alpha} + (kp_A)^{-\alpha} + p_0^{-\alpha}}$$

and the mass σ_0 of users not subscribing to anything is:

$$\sigma_0 = 1 - \sigma_1 - \sigma_0 = \frac{p_0^{-\alpha}}{(p_A + p_1)^{-\alpha} + (kp_A)^{-\alpha} + p_0^{-\alpha}}.$$

With those proportions, the revenue of ISP A can be expressed as:

$$U_A = (p_A + q_1)\sigma_1 + p_A\sigma_A. \tag{4.8}$$

Similarly, the revenue of CP 1 depends on revenues generated by subscriptions and on the side payment q_1:

$$U_1 = (p_1 - q_1)\sigma_1.$$

We can also define *User welfare* UW' as the aggregated utility from users, with respect to the "no service" situation:

$$\text{UW'} = \mathbb{E}[\max(0, V_1 - V_0, V_A - V_0)],$$

where the expectation is over the population, and the max comes from each user selecting their preferred option. To simplify notations, define $Z := \max(0, V_1 - V_0, V_A - V_0)$ so that UW' $= \mathbb{E}[Z]$. Now, for any $z \geq 0$:

$$\mathbb{P}[Z \leq z] = \mathbb{P}[(V_A - V_0 \leq z) \cap (V_1 - V_0 \leq z)]$$
$$= \mathbb{P}[(V_0 \geq V_A - z) \cap (V_0 \geq V_1 - z)]$$
$$= \frac{\exp(v_0)}{\exp(v_0) + \exp(-z)(\exp(v_A) + \exp(v_1))},$$

where the last line stems from Gumbel distributions, similarly to how (4.7) is obtained. Then:

$$
\begin{aligned}
\text{UW'} = \mathbb{E}[Z] &= \int_{z=0}^{+\infty} \mathbb{P}[Z > z]\, dz \\
&= \int_{z=0}^{+\infty} \frac{\exp(-z)(\exp(v_A) + \exp(v_1))}{\exp(v_0) + \exp(-z)(\exp(v_A) + \exp(v_1))}\, dz \\
&= \left[-\log\left(\exp(v_0) + \exp(-z)(\exp(v_A) + \exp(v_1))\right) \right]_{z=0}^{+\infty} \\
&= \log\left(1 + \exp(v_A - v_0) + \exp(v_1 - v_0)\right) \qquad\qquad (4.9) \\
&= \log\left(1 + \left(\frac{p_0}{kp_A}\right)^{\alpha} + \left(\frac{p_0}{p_A + p_1}\right)^{\alpha}\right).
\end{aligned}
$$

We take the option to express user welfare in monetary units instead of the above unit-less notion of perceived value. This will be relevant later, to express social welfare as the sum of users' and providers' benefits in monetary units. We therefore convert UW' by applying the transformation $p_0 \times (\exp(\cdot) - 1)$, somehow inverting the logarithmic perception of costs, which yields:

$$
\text{UW} = p_0 \left(\frac{p_0}{kp_A}\right)^{\alpha} + p_0 \left(\frac{p_0}{p_A + p_1}\right)^{\alpha}. \qquad\qquad (4.10)
$$

Note also that this transformation is consistent, in the sense that if no service from the ISP or the CP is available, then the corresponding prices can be thought of as infinite, leading to UW=0.

To compute the social welfare SW, we can simply add to the user welfare UW the revenues of the ISP and the CP:

$$
\begin{aligned}
\text{SW} = \text{UW} + U_A + U_1 &= \text{UW} + (p_A + p_1)\theta_1 + p_A\theta_A \\
&= p_0 \left(\frac{p_0}{kp_A}\right)^{\alpha} + p_0 \left(\frac{p_0}{p_A + p_1}\right)^{\alpha} + \frac{p_A + p_1}{1 + \left(\frac{p_A+p_1}{kp_A}\right)^{\alpha} + \left(\frac{p_A+p_1}{p_0}\right)^{\alpha}} \\
&\quad + \frac{p_A}{1 + \left(\frac{kp_A}{p_A+p_1}\right)^{\alpha} + \left(\frac{kp_A}{p_0}\right)^{\alpha}}. \qquad\qquad (4.11)
\end{aligned}
$$

Decision variables are p_1 for the CP and p_A and q_1 for the ISP. But they are chosen at different time scales. At the largest time scale, ISP A chooses q_1, then p_A (equivalent to doing it at the same time since it is the same actor), and at a finer time scale, CP 1 chooses p_1. Even if ISP A decides first, we consider here that it can anticipate the decision of CP 1. The ISP is therefore the *leader* in a so-called *Stackelberg game*. The analysis of decisions among providers is therefore realized by *backward induction*: since CP 1 will maximize its utility U_1 for any values of p_A

and q_1 set by ISP A, ISP A makes use of the optimal choice of p_1 to select p_A and q_1 maximizing its utility U_A.

To simplify notations, let $Q := (kp_A)^{-\alpha} + p_0^{-\alpha}$. The first-order condition in the optimization of CP 1 revenue U_1 in terms of p_1 then gives (with p_A and q_1 fixed):

$$\frac{\partial U_1}{\partial p_1} = \frac{-Q\alpha p_1 + Q\alpha q_1 + (p_A + p_1)^{1-\alpha} + Q(p_A + p_1)}{(p_A + p_1)^{1+\alpha}((p_A + p_1)^{-\alpha} + Q)^2} = 0. \tag{4.12}$$

Solving this equation to get an exact expression for p_1 is intractable in general, but it can be solved numerically. In the remainder of the section, we will focus on the case where $\alpha = 2$, since it simplifies the computations (but again, all the analysis can be carried out numerically for a general α). Note also that it is reasonable to assume that $\alpha > 1$, since otherwise $U_1 = \dfrac{p_1 - q_1}{1 + \left(\frac{p_A + p_1}{p_0}\right)^\alpha + \left(\frac{p_A + p_1}{kp_A}\right)^\alpha}$ increases with p_1, in which case setting an infinite price would be optimal.

Specific $\alpha = 2$ Case For $\alpha = 2$ though, we can obtain explicit results for p_1. In that case:

$$\frac{\partial U_1}{\partial p_1} = -\frac{Qp_1^2 - 2Qp_1q_1 - Qp_A^2 - 2Qp_Aq_1 - 1}{(Qp_1^2 + 2Qp_1p_A + Qp_A^2 + 1)^2},$$

so solving (4.12) amounts to solving a second-degree equation in p_1 in the numerator, $p_1^2 - 2p_1q_1 - p_A^2 - 2p_Aq_1 - 1/Q = 0$, with only one non-negative solution:

$$p_1 = q_1 + \sqrt{(p_A + q_1)^2 + \frac{1}{Q}}. \tag{4.13}$$

For the upper level of optimization, when ISP A chooses p_A and q_1 to maximize its utility U_A, we solve the problem numerically, taking the above expression of p_1 as a function of p_A and q_1 in utility U_A.

Neutral Case The neutral situation corresponds to the situation where $q_1 = 0$. Equation (4.13) is then reduced to $p_1 = \sqrt{p_A^2 + \frac{1}{Q}}$, and the optimization for ISP A is reduced to finding the single parameter p_A (instead of two parameters p_A and q_1) maximizing the utility U_A.

Non-neutral Case The non-neutral case means optimizing U_A in terms of the two values p_A and q_1.

As an example, with $\alpha = 2$, $p_0 = 0.4$ and $k = 2$, we get the results displayed in Table 4.3 for the neutral and non-neutral cases. In Table 4.3, the optimal non-neutral option sets a strictly positive side payment q_1 and allows ISP A to increase its revenue, even if here not to a huge extent (only an improvement of 2.3%). That

Table 4.3 Comparison of neutral and non-neutral outputs when $\alpha = 2$, $p_0 = 0.4$, and $k = 2$

	q_1	p_A	p_1	U_A	U_1	UW	SW
Neutral	0	0.281	0.4303	0.1268	0.07465	0.3291	0.5306
Non-neutral	0.127	0.245	0.6111	0.1297	0.07078	0.3539	0.5544

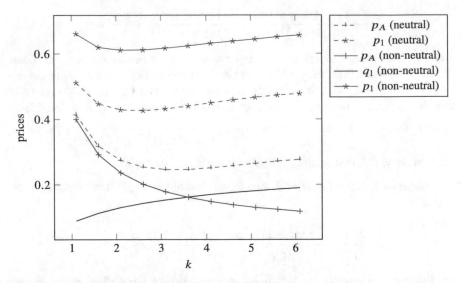

Fig. 4.2 Prices in terms of k when $\alpha = 2$, $p_0 = 0.4$

non-neutral setting allows the subscription price of ISP A to be reduced, but it increases the price p_1 set by CP 1. CP 1 revenue is decreased if non-neutrality is allowed, but quite surprisingly, it is *not* the case of user welfare, nor social welfare, for which a non-neutral scenario is preferred, contrary to what user associations would expect. That simple example illustrates that a proper model investigation of policies is worthwhile and that counterintuitive results are sometimes obtained.

To push the analysis further, we illustrate and compare in Figs. 4.2, 4.3, and 4.4 the variations of, respectively, prices, provider utilities, and welfares, for both the neutral and non-neutral scenarios, in terms of the parameter $k > 1$ representing the cost of subscribing to the ISP without the CP (k can be interpreted as the ratio between the amount of content available with the CP and the amount available without it). That will show how the actors' decisions, and the impact of neutrality, vary depending on the power of the CP (the larger k, the more powerful the CP).

As the curves show, prices are not in general monotone in terms of the power k of the CP, but the more powerful the CP, the higher the side payment, and the lower the ISP subscription price in the non-neutral case. From the providers' utilities, as expected, the more powerful the CP, the larger its revenue, and the smaller the ISP revenue. As expected too, the CP prefers neutrality, while it is the opposite for the ISP. The gain of being non-neutral (the difference between the non-neutral and the neutral curves) increases for the ISP as k increases. But the loss for the CP does not

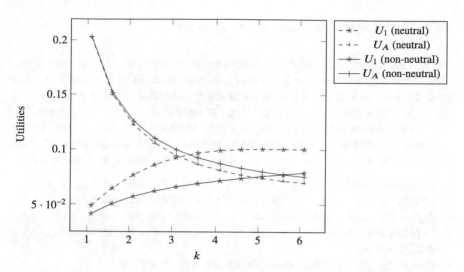

Fig. 4.3 Utilities in terms of k when $\alpha = 2$, $p_0 = 0.4$

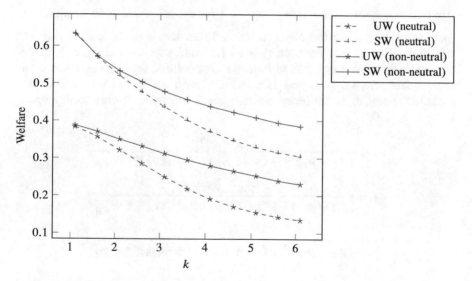

Fig. 4.4 Welfares in terms of k when $\alpha = 2$, $p_0 = 0.4$

increase nor decreases with k. In Fig. 4.4, user welfare and social welfare decrease as the CP becomes more powerful, which somewhat justifies the scrutiny over major CPs. But non-neutrality is better for both metrics than neutrality, which is (again) counterintuitive and contradicts some arguments of user associations against non-neutrality. Notably, the more powerful the CP, the better it is to allow differentiation.

4.3   Model with Two Content Providers

We now extend the model of the previous section, by assuming the presence of two CPs, denoted by CP 1 and CP 2. All parameters are indexed by 2 instead of 1 when related to CP 2 instead of CP 1, with, for example, subscription prices p_1 and p_2. We also introduce a parameter β representing the reputation of CP 2 relative to CP 1, leading to a *perceived* subscription price βp_2 when choosing CP 2. The CPs are assumed to be *substitutes*, meaning that an end user will either choose to subscribe to CP 1 or to CP 2 or to none, but never to both of them. The options are therefore:

- Option denoted by 1: Subscription to ISP A and CP 1, with price $p_A + p_1$;
- Option denoted by 2: Subscription to ISP A and CP 2, with price $p_A + \beta p_2$;
- Option denoted by A: Subscription to ISP A only, with perceived price $p = k p_A$, as before $k > 1$ represents the increased perception of price for not having access to CPs' services;
- Option denoted by 0: No subscription at all, with "cost" p_0.

As in (4.6), the average valuation v for a service for a price p is represented by the standard logarithm relation $v = \alpha \log \left(\dfrac{1}{p} \right)$ for the price/cost p, to which a user-specific part κ_i representing user perception differences is added to form a random valuation $V_i = v_i + \kappa_i$ for each option i and each user. As before, κ_i is treated as a random variable assumed to follow a Gumbel distribution with mean 0 and independent across options and users, which leads, when each user selects their preferred option, to the following masses (proportions) θ_i of users selecting option $i, i = 1, 2, A, 0$:

$$\sigma_1 = \frac{(p_A + p_1)^{-\alpha}}{(p_A + p_1)^{-\alpha} + (p_A + \beta p_2)^{-\alpha} + (k p_A)^{-\alpha} + p_0^{-\alpha}}$$

$$\sigma_2 = \frac{(p_A + \beta p_2)^{-\alpha}}{(p_A + p_1)^{-\alpha} + (p_A + \beta p_2)^{-\alpha} + (k p_A)^{-\alpha} + p_0^{-\alpha}}$$

$$\sigma_A = \frac{(k p_A)^{-\alpha}}{(p_A + p_1)^{-\alpha} + (p_A + \beta p_2)^{-\alpha} + (k p_A)^{-\alpha} + p_0^{-\alpha}}$$

$$\sigma_0 = \frac{p_0^{-\alpha}}{(p_A + p_1)^{-\alpha} + (p_A + \beta p_2)^{-\alpha} + (k p_A)^{-\alpha} + p_0^{-\alpha}}.$$

Here too, we will incorporate side payments to represent non-neutral situations, but we will compare three scenarios instead of two in the previous section, thanks to the competition between CPs:

1. In the non-neutral case, ISP A charges CP 1 (respectively, CP 2) a price q_1 (respectively, q_2) per unit of user to that CP.
2. In the *weak* neutrality case (see Sect. 2.1), a side payment is possible, but no differentiation between CPs is possible. In other words, $q_1 = q_2 = q$.

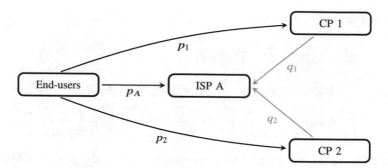

Fig. 4.5 Charging interactions between stakeholders with two CPs and one ISP; arrows are labeled with prices per unit of user. The side payments q_1 and q_2 are unconstrained in the non-neutral setting, and they should satisfy $q_1 = q_2$ in the weakly neutral setting, while strong neutrality corresponds to imposing $q_1 = q_2 = 0$

3. In the *strong* neutrality case, no side payment is permitted, meaning that $q_1 = q_2 = 0$.

The different players and corresponding charges are represented in Fig. 4.5.

In this context, the revenue of IP A is:

$$U_A = (p_A + q_1)\sigma_1 + (p_A + q_2)\sigma_2 + p_A\sigma_A, \qquad (4.14)$$

and the revenues of CPs are:

$$U_1 = (p_1 - q_1)\sigma_1$$
$$U_2 = (p_2 - q_2)\sigma_2.$$

Similarly to the case with a single CP, user welfare UW' is the aggregated utility from users, with respect to there being no service:

$$\text{UW'} = \mathbb{E}[\max(0, V_1 - V_0, V_2 - V_0, V_A - V_0)].$$

Repeating the computations steps of the previous section with the additional option, and redefining $Z := \max(0, V_1 - V_0, V_2 - V_0, V_A - V_0)$ to simplify notations, we get for $z \geq 0$:

$$\mathbb{P}[Z \leq z] = \mathbb{P}[(V_A - V_0 \leq z) \cap (V_1 - V_0 \leq z) \cap (V_2 - V_0 \leq z)]$$
$$= \mathbb{P}[(V_0 \geq V_A - z) \cap (V_0 \geq V_1 - z) \cap (V_0 \geq V_2 - z)]$$
$$= \frac{\exp(v_0)}{\exp(v_0) + \exp(-z)(\exp(v_A) + \exp(v_1) + \exp(v_2))}.$$

Following the developments for (4.9):

$$\text{UW'} = \mathbb{E}[Z] = \int_{z=0}^{+\infty} \mathbb{P}[Z > z]\, dz$$

$$= \log\left(1 + \exp(v_A - v_0) + \exp(v_1 - v_0) + \exp(v_2 - v_0)\right) \quad (4.15)$$

$$= \log\left(1 + \left(\frac{p_0}{kp_A}\right)^\alpha + \left(\frac{p_0}{p_A + p_1}\right)^\alpha + \left(\frac{p_0}{p_A + \beta p_2}\right)^\alpha\right).$$

To express it in monetary units, as before we apply the transformation $p_0 \times (\exp(\cdot) - 1)$, yielding:

$$\text{UW} = p_0 \left(\frac{p_0}{kp_A}\right)^\alpha + p_0 \left(\frac{p_0}{p_A + p_1}\right)^\alpha + p_0 \left(\frac{p_0}{p_A + \beta p_2}\right)^\alpha. \quad (4.16)$$

Social welfare SW is then:

$$\text{SW} = \text{UW} + U_A + U_1 + U_2$$

$$= p_0 \left(\frac{p_0}{kp_A}\right)^\alpha + p_0 \left(\frac{p_0}{p_A + p_1}\right)^\alpha + p_0 \left(\frac{p_0}{p_A + \beta p_2}\right)^\alpha$$

$$+ \frac{p_A}{1 + \left(\frac{kp_A}{p_A + p_1}\right)^\alpha + \left(\frac{kp_A}{p_A + \beta p_2}\right)^\alpha + \left(\frac{kp_A}{p_0}\right)^\alpha}$$

$$+ \frac{p_A + p_1}{1 + \left(\frac{p_A + p_1}{kp_A}\right)^\alpha + \left(\frac{p_A + p_1}{p_0}\right)^\alpha + \left(\frac{p_A + p_1}{p_A + \beta p_2}\right)^\alpha}$$

$$+ \frac{p_A + p_2}{1 + \left(\frac{p_A + \beta p_2}{kp_A}\right)^\alpha + \left(\frac{p_A + \beta p_2}{p_0}\right)^\alpha + \left(\frac{p_A + \beta p_2}{p_A + p_1}\right)^\alpha}. \quad (4.17)$$

Following the principles described in the previous section, decisions are taken at different time scales. First, ISP A chooses q_1, q_2 (if relevant) and then p_A (equivalent to doing it at the same time). Then, charges imposed by the ISP being fixed, there is a game between CPs on subscription prices p_1 and p_2, to attract users and maximize their revenues. Even if ISP A decides first, we assume it can anticipate the decision of CPs. The ISP is therefore the *leader* in a so-called *Stackelberg game*. The analysis of decisions among providers is therefore realized by *backward induction*.

To simplify the analysis, we will limit ourselves to the specific case when $\alpha = 2$.

4.3.1 Pricing Game Between CPs ($\alpha = 2$)

Proceeding by backward induction, let q_1, q_2, and p_A be fixed, and analyze what prices should be set by CPs, when CP i ($i \in \{1, 2\}$) chooses p_i maximizing U_i. Since U_i depends not only on p_i but also on the price of the opponent, we end up with a non-cooperative game, with the Nash equilibrium as the solution concept (see Definition 4.1).

We therefore look for CP best responses. Differentiating U_1 as in (4.12) with respect to p_1 and looking at the value p_1 such that $\dfrac{\partial U_1}{\partial p_1} = 0$, we get similarly to (4.13), with $\alpha = 2$, the best response $\mathrm{BR}_1(p_2)$ of Player 1 to Player 2 setting p_2:

$$p_1 = \mathrm{BR}_1(p_2) = q_1 + \sqrt{(p_A + q_1)^2 + \frac{1}{Q_1}} \qquad (4.18)$$

with $Q_1 = (p_A + \beta p_2)^{-2} + (kp_A)^{-2} + p_0^{-2}$. Doing the same by differentiating U_2 with respect to p_2, the best response $\mathrm{BR}_2(p_1)$ of Player 2 to p_1 is (from $\dfrac{\partial U_2}{\partial p_2} = 0$):

$$p_2 = \mathrm{BR}_2(p_1) = q_2 + \frac{1}{\beta}\sqrt{(p_A + \beta q_2)^2 + \frac{1}{Q_2}}$$

with $Q_2 = (p_A + p_1)^{-2} + (kp_A)^{-2} + p_0^{-2}$. A Nash equilibrium is derived from the system of the two above equations with two unknowns p_1 and p_2 (the other parameters being considered fixed). Solving the system analytically is intractable, but it can easily be done numerically. Figure 4.6 draws the best-response curves $\mathrm{BR}_1(p_2)$ and $\mathrm{BR}_2(p_1)$ of, respectively, CP 1 and CP 2 in terms of the price of the opponent when $p_A = 1$, $p_0 = 0.1$, $q_1 = 0.3$, $q_2 = 0.2$, and $\beta = 1.5$, $k = 2$. We observe a unique Nash equilibrium as the intersection of the two best-response curves. Here it looks like we have constant best-response curves, but they are actually not, even if variating in a very limited way. To see why it is the case, look at the expression of p_1 in terms of p_2 in (4.18): p_1 is a decreasing function of Q_1, itself decreasing in p_2, meaning that p_1 is increasing in p_2. So the value varies between $q_1 + \sqrt{(p_A + q_1)^2 + \dfrac{1}{p_A^{-2} + (kp_A)^{-2} + p_0^{-2}}}$ (for $p_2 = 0$) and

$q_1 + \sqrt{(p_A + q_1)^2 + \dfrac{1}{(kp_A)^{-2} + p_0^{-2}}}$ for $p_2 = \infty$, leading to minor variations. With our above parameter values, the range goes from 1.603793137 to 1.603830918; hence, it is almost invisible in the figure, but the price selection has a minor (even if existing) impact on the opponent, which may be larger with other parameter values. The same analysis can be done for p_2 in terms of p_1.

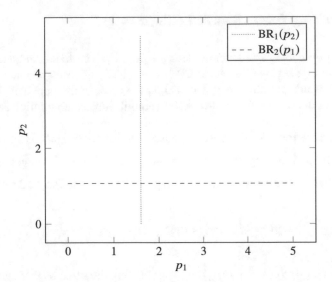

Fig. 4.6 Best responses with $p_A = 1$, $p_0 = 0.1$, $q_1 = 0.3$, $q_2 = 0.2$, $\beta = 1.5$, and $k = 2$

4.3.2 Fully Neutral Case ($\alpha = 2$)

The fully neutral case assumes $q_1 = q_2 = 0$. The ISP then has to maximize its revenue in (4.14), which is just $U_A = p_A(\sigma_1 + \sigma_2 + \sigma_A)$, in terms of p_A, making use of the prices p_1 and p_2 at the Nash equilibrium of the above game.

For example, with our (above) parameter values $p_0 = 0.1$, $\beta = 1.5$, and $k = 2$, we obtain an optimal price $p_A = 0.088$, for a maximal ISP A utility $U_A = 0.03882$.

4.3.3 Weakly Neutral Case ($\alpha = 2$)

In the weakly neutral case, $q_1 = q_2 = q$, that is, the ISP is not allowed to differentiate between CPs. The ISP can select p_A and q to maximize its revenue in (4.14), which becomes $U_A = (p_A + q)(\sigma_1 + \sigma_2) + p_A\sigma_A$.

Still for the example with parameter values $p_0 = 0.1$, $\beta = 1.5$, and $k = 2$, we obtain optimal prices $p_A = 0.088$ and $q = 0$, for a utility $U_A = 0.03882$, which corresponds to the fully neutral case. In other words, for the parameter values we considered, if weak neutrality is authorized or imposed, then there is no interest for the ISP to charge side payments to CPs.

4.3.4   Non-neutral Case ($\alpha = 2$)

In the non-neutral case, the ISP selects p_A, q_1, and q_2 to maximize (4.14).

We again compute the optimal prices for our parameter values $p_0 = 0.1$, $\beta = 1.5$, and $k = 2$ and obtain $p_A = 0.083$, $q_1 = 0.0178$, and $q_2 = 0$, resulting in $U_A = 0.03898$. Note that in this case, non-neutrality is preferred but that side payments are "imposed" only to CP 2, the CP with the worst reputation. It somewhat means that well-established content providers, usually having a good reputation, may be favored in this context, a point that can be raised by neutrality proponents.

4.3.5   Comparison

Let us now compare in Table 4.4 the outputs for the three scenarios, not just comparing the optimal prices and ISP revenue.

Again, with the presented set of parameters, in a weakly neutral rule, the ISP does not have interest to impose side payments. Comparing with the non-neutral case, side payments to CP 2 "allow" the ISP to decrease its price p_A, and CP 1 then also increases its price p_1, while CP 2's price decreases. As a consequence the share of users subscribing to the ISP only increases, as well as that subscribing to CP 2, probably due to the decrease of p_A, part of the cost when interested in CP 2. On the other hand, it is not the case for CP 1. The revenue experiences surprisingly the same trend, when one would expect CP 1 to benefit from the situation. User and social welfare also increase with non-neutrality, something not initially expected. So, even if imposing a side payment to the non-established CP seems unfair, as said previously, it actually increases user welfare, something user associations should be keen on. Again here, some counterintuitive results are observed.

Table 4.4 Comparison of outputs with two CPs when $p_0 = 0.1$, $\beta = 1.5$, and $k = 2$

Scenario	Fully-neutral	Weakly-neutral	Non-neutral
q_1	0	0	0.0178
q_2	0	0	0
p_A	0.088	0.088	0.083
p_1	0.1190	0.1190	0.1456
p_2	0.07936	0.07936	0.07695
σ_A	0.1804	0.1804	0.2007
σ_1	0.1304	0.1304	0.1058
σ_2	0.1304	0.1304	0.1405
U_A	0.03882	0.03882	0.03898
U_1	0.01552	0.01552	0.01352
U_2	0.01035	0.01035	0.01081
UW	0.07894	0.07894	0.08082
SW	0.1436	0.1436	0.1441

4.4   Other Conclusions from the Literature

The two previous sections detail a model and give conclusions, or rather hints, about potential outputs regarding neutrality or non-neutrality decisions that can be derived from it. There has been a recent but non-negligible amount of research activity around modeling and analysis of decisions in the neutrality debate context. Let us briefly describe here several important existing works in that direction, along with indications about the modeling assumptions, the properties that are investigated, and the conclusions.

The papers [4, 5] study the implications of non-neutral behaviors using a model of consumer demand diminishing linearly in usage-based price, with a monopolistic ISP and a CP. Several scenarios are studied: taking into account an advertising revenue for the CP, considering both cooperative and non-cooperative scenarios, and with several orders of decision. Without side payments, it is shown that all actors are better off cooperating. When the value of the side payment is decided by the regulator, two cases happen according to a threshold on the price: under the threshold, providers set their price so that consumer demand equals the demand values in the competitive case without side payments, while above the threshold, usage-based prices are set to zero. Advertising is shown to increase providers' revenues. In [30], the previous model is extended to non-monopolistic cases, with a model for demand that combines linear demand in usage-based prices with some "stickiness" demand equivalent to the one presented in the previous sections, accounting for customer loyalty. A game-theoretic analysis shows for that model the unexpected result (a paradox) that at the Nash equilibrium, side payments reduce the revenue of ISPs applying them. With CPs "selling" different types of content, say Web services and file sharing (P2P), with different price sensitivity and willingness to pay, it is nevertheless shown that ISPs and Web CPs benefit from non-neutral practices, which is not the case for file-sharing CPs.

In a simple two-sided market with an ISP charging both CPs and end users, assuming that the type parameters of the consumers and the CPs are power-law distributed (a distribution often observed in "nature", e.g., for content popularity), [45] shows that net neutrality is not socially optimal unless CPs' operating costs are very small.

In [101–103], the authors propose to share the revenue among providers using the Shapley value, the only mechanism that satisfies a set of axioms representing a sense of fairness. In that case, CPs participate to the network access cost. Two categories of ISPs are even considered to better take into account the topology of real-life Internet: transit and eyeball (access) ISPs. Thanks to revenue sharing according to the Shapley value, it is shown that selfish ISPs would yield globally optimal routing and interconnecting decisions.

In the previous section, like in many works, there is in general a single ISP and one or several CPs. Though, in practice, in countries such as France (even if not everywhere), we often have ISPs in competition for customers, while for many services, the CPs are in a quasi-monopolistic position, a characteristic ISPs complain about. Typical examples of quasi-monopolies are YouTube for non-copyrighted videos and Netflix for movies and TV shows. ISPs complain that this aspect is often forgotten in the debate. For that reason, the issue has been specifically addressed in [38] with a model close to the one presented above with end users, one CP but two ISPs in competition. Similarly to what we have presented here, the model is analyzed as a three-level game corresponding to three different time scales where at the largest time scale, side payments (if any) are determined; at a smaller time scale, ISPs decide their (flat-rate) subscription fee; and then the CP chooses the (flat-rate) price to charge users. Users spread themselves according to the same type of model as developed in this chapter. As a conclusion, non-neutrality is, there again counterintuitively, shown to be potentially beneficial to the CP, and not necessarily to ISPs, unless the side payments values are decided by ISPs. The same problem was previously studied in [25] with a demand model linearly decreasing in price as in [4] and such that users were assumed to always go with the cheapest provider. As a consequence, the game ends up with a price war (a classical Bertrand competition) such that ISPs keep decreasing their subscription price in order to attract all demand. Even with such a demand model, it is observed that the purpose of introducing side payments, that is, to recover costs and reinvest in the architecture, is not fulfilled since ISP revenues are not increased.

A model involving many components has been proposed in [138]. The model proposes to include investment incentives for ISPs and competition between two ISPs on subscription prices and on quality, to which end users are sensitive. A CP chooses its ISP, and as a consequence users, to connect to, at a predefined cost. As we did in this chapter, all the decisions are assumed to be taken at different time scales, and the interaction is analyzed by backward induction. In the non-neutral scenario, ISPs' investments are shown to be larger than in the neutral case because it is easier to extract surplus through appropriate CP pricing. As a consequence, CPs' revenues may also increase, as well as user welfare. Non-neutrality has therefore a rather globally positive impact with that model. The impact of imposing neutrality on CP and ISP investments is also studied in [35].

In [130, 131], parameters characterizing advertising rates and end-user price sensitivity are introduced. It is shown that a two-sided pricing (i.e., introducing side payments) is valuable only if the ratio between parameters is either low or high. The works also analyze how neutrality or non-neutrality affects provider investment incentives, network quality, and user prices. In each case, at the equilibrium of the game, the levels of investment in content and architecture are determined. Using a different model, [152] investigates the case when ISPs negotiate joint investment contracts with a CP in order to enhance the quality of service and increase industry profits. It is found that an unregulated regime leads to higher-quality investments but that ISPs have an incentive to degrade content quality.

Another place where a discrete choice/stickiness model is also used is [39], with two ISPs and, similarly to [138], users having access to the network only through one ISP. In other words, ISPs have different geographical locations and market shares. CPs also have different locations and can access the network (i.e., users) through a designed ISP. Thanks to game-theoretic tools, three different situations of interactions *between* ISPs are analyzed and compared: *(i)* the case of peering between the ISPs, where ISPs interconnect and do not charge for the traffic through their network, *(ii)* the case where ISPs do not share their traffic and therefore not all content is accessible from all users, and *(iii)* the case where they fix a transfer price per unit of volume charged to the other ISP. The paper supports the transit price scenario and suggests a limited regulation (enforcing global connectivity) to prevent incumbent ISPs from having a dominant position in the bargaining.

As highlighted in Chap. 2, the application of neutrality principles is heterogeneous across countries. One can then wonder: how does a local strategy or rule affect a global Internet? In [2, 110], a model is built and analyzed to investigate this issue. The model represents the interactions between users, network providers, and content providers located in different areas, where ISPs are allowed or not to differentiate services. Even users and CPs located in neutral areas would be affected by alien non-neutral countries since accessing users or content there requires passing through the non-neutral ISP. The results show that repealing neutrality, as done by the Trump administration in the USA may *only* favor the ISP in the differentiation-authorized zone, but no other actor, and that it can be worse off for everybody if the regulation procedures are very strict in the neutral area.

4.5   Additional Notes

Even if we do not address it here, many mathematical analyses of zero rating and sponsored data have been carried out in the literature (see [78, 80, 109, 111, 159, 173, 180, 184]), many of them illustrating that ISPs may be the ones benefiting the most from sponsoring, and in particular for [111] that, surprisingly, the possibility of sponsored data may actually reduce the benefits of content providers and on the other hand increase the revenue of ISPs in competition, with a very limited impact on user welfare. Some of those models are developed within the next chapter.

Chapter 5
Non-neutrality Pushed by Content Providers

Content providers (CPs) are generally on the "pro-neutrality" side of the debate, since relaxing neutrality constraints would give more power to ISPs, for example, allowing them to charge CPs more for high-quality traffic management. But for some (big) content providers, allowing differentiation may be beneficial since it may harm smaller competitors. This might explain some apparently contradictory positions, like Netflix that generally claims to be pro-neutrality, even publicly opposing differentiation practices like zero rating in the Netherlands in 2014, but paid the main Australian operator to be zero-rated when the service was launched in that country in 2015 [92]. Although in that example an interpretation is that neutrality can protect incumbents against powerful newcomers (that could otherwise use differentiation to enter the market with an edge, like Netflix did in Australia), it is in general believed to help keep the barrier to entry low for small actors, by preventing wealthy players from purchasing a preferential treatment by ISPs.

In this chapter, we develop the idea that, in a variety of contexts and ways, (some) content providers may not always be so inclined to defend net neutrality. On the contrary, non-neutrality may help incumbents remain in place by raising the barrier to entry, even if this means paying a fee (a side payment) for that purpose. We will, for example, see in Sect. 5.1 that this can occur if the incumbent anticipates a demand decrease upon the arrival of competitors; it is therefore willing to pay side payments up to the corresponding revenue loss, just to avoid that loss.

Other a priori non-neutral –or at least, at odds with neutrality principles– practices include *sponsored data* (the CP paying for the user's data usage to access its services) and *zero rating* (the CP agreeing with the ISP that access to its services will be ignored in the user's data cap). For a CP, having the possibility of using such tools appears to offer extra degrees of freedom to maximize revenue, and can therefore be desirable, as is illustrated through some simple models in Sect. 5.2. However, the order in which decisions are made can have a strong influence: if ISPs can anticipate how CPs will sponsor data, and integrate that into their choices (e.g.,

P. Maillé, B. Tuffin, *From Net Neutrality to ICT Neutrality*,
https://doi.org/10.1007/978-3-031-06271-1_5

of quality/network investments), then they may be able to extract most of the benefits from such practices, possibly leaving CPs worse off than without sponsoring.

Finally, a third direction developed in this chapter deals with reputation effects, which may enable big content providers, even without paying for differentiation, to incentivize ISPs to favor them in order to be seen as performing well. This is illustrated in Sect. 5.3, where we develop a 2-CP model to encompass the fact that users are most sensitive to the quality of their preferred services, creating an incentive for ISPs to favor the most popular CPs.

5.1   Non-neutrality as a Barrier to Entry Protecting Incumbents

The effect analyzed in this section is among the pro-neutrality arguments developed in Chap. 3: a non-neutral network, where CPs can pay ISPs for their traffic to be favorably treated, creates a barrier to entry for newcomers who could not afford that quality premium. Such practices would hinder innovation, hence the point being raised by neutrality defenders.

But in practice, some large CPs are accepting to pay ISPs for preferential treatment even while being publicly pro-neutrality. This is the case for Google, paying the main French ISP Orange[1] or Netflix that pays Comcast and Verizon.[2] Is that only because they have no choice but to comply with the ISPs' requests? Couldn't they hope to have those *side payments* prohibited though fighting them, knowing that user associations and governments tend to favor a neutral vision of the Internet? Or, could it be that those large CPs are actually fine with the current situation, with side payments preventing possible competitors from entering the market, at a cost below the possible loss from competition?

In this section, we develop that idea through a simple model, initially introduced in [108, 167]. Note that the situation with side payments also needs to be profitable to the ISP(s), which would be the case here if the revenues from side payments exceed the extra revenues that could stem from newcomer CPs.

Initially defined as "anything that allows incumbent firms to earn above-normal profits without the threat of entry" [13], the *barrier to entry* concept has been refined over time in the economics community [146]. One can in particular distinguish barriers to entry with regard to their impact, introducing:

- The *economic* barrier to entry, a cost undergone by a newcomer but not by incumbents

---

[1] http://www.theverge.com/2013/1/19/3894182/french-isp-orange-says-google-pays-to-send-traffic.

[2] http://arstechnica.com/information-technology/2014/05/21/see-which-isps-google-microsoft-and-netflix-trade-internet-traffic-with/.

- The *antitrust* barrier to entry, a cost that delays entry, thereby reducing social welfare with respect to an equally costly immediate entry

Regarding how those costs operate, it is also possible to separate:

- The *primary* barrier to entry, a cost that constitutes a barrier to entry on its own
- The *ancillary* barrier to entry, a cost that (indirectly) strengthens the impact of already existing barriers to entry

Some examples of each combination are given in [146].

To address the question, in the rest of this section, we define and analyze a model with two CPs –an incumbent one and a potential new entrant– for a specific type of service. The other CPs (for the other services) are abstracted out to focus only on the competition between the incumbent and new entrant.

5.1.1 Modeling the Impact of a New Entrant CP

Unlike the attraction model defined in Chap. 4, here we assume that both CPs have negligible market power, so that their presence does not affect the subscription decisions of users to the ISP services. CPs are assumed here to make revenue through advertisement, sales, or even subscriptions but without treating subscription prices as decision variables; we model those revenues as being proportional to the amount of traffic of each CP.

Summarizing, and to introduce, the model notations:

- Users are charged the ISP subscription price, denoted by p_A, when subscribing, and can then access the services offered by the CPs in the market.
- When non-neutrality is allowed, CPs have to pay the ISP a side payment proportional to the generated traffic volumes; through a unit change, we write the side payment as q per mass unit of requests from users using that service.
- The incumbent (resp., entrant) CP earns a revenue r_i (resp., r_e) per mass unit of requests to its service.

Note that in this section we will not consider CP-specific side payments, but instead a common value q, corresponding to what we called *weak neutrality*. The situation we consider is represented in Fig. 5.1.

To have simpler analytical expressions, we will not consider the same attraction model as in Chap. 4, but instead a simpler linear model, also often used in economics [104], in particular in the context of entry barriers [48]. In that model, we still assume a continuum of potential users, whose total mass is denoted by D_{max}, but out of which the mass choosing to subscribe to the ISP is a linear decreasing function of the price. This leads to a mass of subscribers D of the form:

$$D = [D_{\mathrm{max}} - sp_A]^+,$$

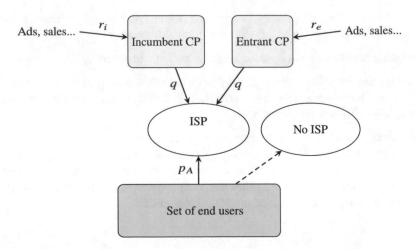

Fig. 5.1 Representation of relations between users, ISP, and CPs [108]; plain arrows indicate monetary transfers and are labelled with amounts per unit (of user mass for p_A, of service requests for the other values)

where s is a sensitivity parameter and $[x]^+ := \max(0, x)$ for any $x \in \mathbb{R}$.

Let us now describe how we model the mass D_i (resp., D_e) of requests for the incumbent (resp., entrant) CP service:

- When only the incumbent CP is in the market, the ISP subscribers (of mass D) generate some requests. Without loss of generality, we define the unit of volume requests so that the total volume D_i equals D. Also, the entrant CP not being present, we have $D_e = 0$.
- When both CPs are reachable by the mass D of users, we assume that the requests spread between them, with volumes $\gamma_i D$ and $\gamma_e D$ for the incumbent and entrant, respectively, for some positive parameters γ_i and γ_e. We make the reasonable assumptions that demand for the incumbent will shrink due to the arrival of a competitor (i.e., $\gamma_i < 1$) but that the overall demand for the service will increase (i.e., $\gamma_i + \gamma_e > 1$) because users have more options and may feel more comfortable with one or the other CP, or some may even use both.

Such a simple model captures the main phenomena that we would expect in this situation, namely, that **entrants are good for users, but hurt the incumbent** who might thus want to prevent them from entering.

In the next subsections, we analyze the actors' (here, mostly, the ISP and incumbent CP) utility functions and actions, to identify some conditions under which side payments can constitute a barrier to entry that is beneficial to the incumbent CP and to the ISP.

5.1.2   *Actors' Revenues and Decision Time Scales*

We first define the revenues for CPs and the ISP and then specify how decisions are taken before computing them.

5.1.2.1   CP Revenues

The incumbent (resp., entrant) CP obtains revenues r_i (resp., r_e) per unit of request and a request volume denoted by D_i (resp., D_e) and has to pay side payments with a unit price q per unit of request,[3] leading to a utility function or revenue R_i (resp., R_e) where:

$$\begin{cases} R_i = (r_i - q)D_i \\ R_e = (r_e - q)D_e. \end{cases}$$

5.1.2.2   ISP Revenue

The ISP receives revenues from subscriptions (p per mass unit of subscribers) and from side payments (q per mass unit of request), leading with our notations to a revenue:

$$R = p_A D + q(D_i + D_e).$$

5.1.2.3   Order of Decisions

As in Chap. 4, decisions are taken at different time scales, leading to a Stackelberg game model. Here decisions occur as follows:

1. First (at the largest time scale), the side payment q is decided—if such side payments are allowed.
2. Second, the entrant CP decides whether to enter the market or not.
3. Third, the ISP sets the subscription price p_A.
4. Finally, users decide to subscribe or not to the ISP and use the available services.

Note that the decision of the entrant CP (to enter the market or not) is not explicitly mentioned here; we could insert it after the subscription price p_A is

---

[3] Note that the model in [108] had two more parameters corresponding to the volume of traffic per unit of request, so that side payments were in terms of traffic volume and not per (mass) unit of request like we do here.

decided by the ISP, but we will rather analyze each of the two situations (with and without the new entrant) separately and compare them afterward.

5.1.3 Analyzing the Game for Fixed Side Payments

As with previous models, we will use the backward induction method to study the outcomes of those interactions. Here we focus on the last stages of the game, assuming the side payment q is given.

5.1.3.1 User Decisions

Users are the last players in our model. Their decisions are completely described by our assumptions, and we just summarize them here before studying how the ISP sets its subscription price:

- The mass of subscribers will be $D = [D_{max} - s p_A]^+$, whether the entrant CP is present or not.
- The mass of requests for the incumbent (resp., entrant) CP will be $\bar{\gamma}_i D$ (resp., $\bar{\gamma}_e D$), where:

$$\bar{\gamma}_i := \begin{cases} 1 & \text{without the entrant CP} \\ \gamma_i & \text{with the entrant CP} \end{cases}$$

$$\bar{\gamma}_e := \begin{cases} 0 & \text{without the entrant CP} \\ \gamma_e & \text{with the entrant CP.} \end{cases}$$

5.1.3.2 ISP Subscription Price p_A

The ISP revenue can be written in terms of p_A as $(p_A + q(\bar{\gamma}_i + \bar{\gamma}_e)) [D_{max} - s p_A]^+$ and is maximized when $p_A = \left[\dfrac{D_{max}}{2s} - \dfrac{q(\bar{\gamma}_i + \bar{\gamma}_e)}{2} \right]^+$.

To avoid null subscription prices, from now on, we will assume that $q(\bar{\gamma}_i + \bar{\gamma}_e) < \dfrac{D_{max}}{s}$. The mass of users subscribing to the ISP is then $D = \dfrac{D_{max}}{2} + \dfrac{sq(\bar{\gamma}_i + \bar{\gamma}_e)}{2}$, and the ISP revenue equals:

$$R^{opt} = (D_{max} + qs(\bar{\gamma}_i + \bar{\gamma}_e))^2 / (4s). \tag{5.1}$$

5.1.3.3 Should the New CP Enter the Market?

Our model does not include fixed costs, so the entrant CP decides to participate as soon as its expected revenue $(r_e - q)D_e$ is positive, i.e., $q < r_e$. As a result, an easy way to prevent that CP from entering the market is to set a sufficiently large side payment, above what the CP can make from requests. But note that if $q \geq r_i$, then the incumbent CP also has a negative revenue, an undesirable situation leading to no CP offering the service of interest; so a candidate side payment acting as a barrier to entry can be found only if $r_i > r_e$, within the interval $[r_e, r_i]$.

5.1.3.4 Illustration Example: Impact of the Side Payment

Figure 5.2 displays the utilities of the three actors (ISP and the two CPs) when the side payment q varies. Note the discontinuities at $q = r_e$, when the entrant CP stops entering the market: the ISP revenue drops (due to less revenues from side-payments), and the incumbent CP's increases (due to $\bar{\gamma}_i$ switching from γ_i to 1, i.e., more traffic). For values above r_i, providing the service is not profitable even to the incumbent CP.

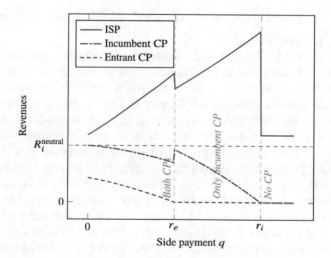

Fig. 5.2 Utilities (net revenues) for the ISP and both CPs, for $D_{\max} = 10, s = 1, r_i = 6, r_e = 3, \gamma_i = 0.7, \gamma_e = 0.6$

5.1.4   Can the ISP and the Incumbent CP Agree on Side Payments?

5.1.4.1   Side Payments Maximizing the ISP Revenue Are Not Sustainable

Let us first take a look at the ISP point of view. From (5.1) and the expressions for (γ_i, γ_e), the ISP revenue R^{opt} is maximized for a side payment q set just below r_e if $r_e(\gamma_i + \gamma_e) > r_i$ and just below r_i otherwise. As illustrated in Fig. 5.2, none of those situations is satisfying to the incumbent ISP, who would prefer a neutral situation (no side payments) to any of those values for q. Faced with such side payments, the incumbent CP would therefore join the "pro-neutrality" movement, which is not what we are looking for here.

5.1.4.2   Can Side Payments Benefit Both the Incumbent CP and the ISP?

Let us formalize the conditions that need to hold for the situation we want to highlight:

- The ISP always prefers the non-neutral situation over the neutral one: indeed we directly see from (5.1) that the ISP revenue is $\left(\dfrac{D_{\max}}{2s}\right)^2$ in the neutral case and can only be larger when $q > 0$.
- The incumbent CP must also prefer the non-neutral situation over having no side payments and facing the new entrant, i.e., there must be some side payment value in the interval $[r_e, r_i]$ yielding the incumbent CP a larger revenue than the neutral situation. We see graphically in Fig. 5.2 that it might not be the case: for our parameter values, if $q \in [r_e, r_i]$, R_i is always below the revenue that the incumbent CP can make in the neutral case. On that interval for q, we have $R_i = (r_i - q)(D_{\max} + sq)/2$, while in the neutral case, it is $\gamma_i r_i D_{\max}/2$; hence, side payments can benefit the incumbent CP for any $q \geq r_e$ such that $(r_i - q)(D_{\max} + sq) \geq \gamma_i r_i D_{\max}$. After some algebra, that is, rewriting the inequality as one for a polynomial of degree 2 in terms of q (more exactly $sq^2 + (D_{\max} - r_i s)q + (\gamma_i - 1)r_i D_{\max} \leq 0$) and investigating whether r_e is smaller than the largest (if any) root of the polynomial since its negative values are only between its two potential roots), we find that such side payments exist if and only if $r_e \leq r^*$, with:

$$r^* := \frac{r_i - D_{\max}/s + \sqrt{(D_{\max}/s - r_i)^2 + 4r_i(1 - \gamma_i)D_{\max}/s}}{2}.$$

If the condition $r_e \leq r^*$ holds, then the side payments satisfying the condition coincide with the interval $[r_e, r^*]$. For the parameter values of Fig. 5.2, we have $r^* \approx 2.69$.

Intuitively, if the entrant CP cannot generate much revenue from requests (r_e small), then a low side payment can be sufficient to deter it from entering the market, with its cost to the incumbent CP remaining below the gain from avoiding competition. On the contrary, if r_e is high, then the incumbent CP prefers a neutral situation –even if that means facing competition– to being charged side payments, since they would need to be high to constitute a barrier to entry.

5.1.4.3 How Can the ISP and Incumbent CP Agree on a Side Payment Level?

Consider a situation like in Fig. 5.3, where it can be in the interest of both the ISP and the incumbent CP to use side payments and keep the newcomer CP out of the market. With respect to Fig. 5.2, we have only changed the value of r_e (taking $r_e = 3$) in order to display an example where barrier-to-entry side payments benefit the incumbent CP: the figure effectively shows a range of side payment values for which the incumbent CP revenue is larger than in a neutral situation. As the figure illustrates, the gains for the ISP and incumbent CP differ when the side payment level varies: the incumbent CP would prefer a side payment just above r_e, while the ISP would like to set it as large as possible.

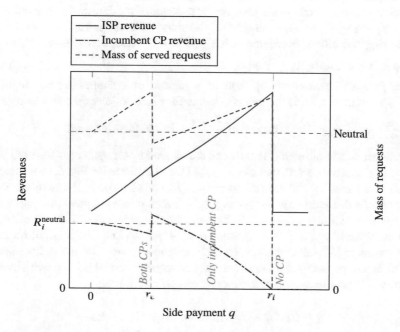

Fig. 5.3 Utilities (net revenues) for the ISP and the incumbent CP, and mass of served requests from both CPs, for the same parameter values as in Fig. 5.2 (except $r_e = 2$)

For such situations where two actors have to agree on a decision through a
negotiation, one can use the concept of *Nash bargaining solution*, which can be
proved to be the most likely to be played under some assumptions [141]. That
concept relies on the existence of a "threat," that is, a situation that is reached in case
the negotiation fails. Here, a reasonable threat situation is that of a neutral network
(no side payments): we can indeed assume that the incumbent CP could reach
that outcome using neutrality-related complaints if the ISP sets unsatisfying side
payment levels, and reciprocally the ISP could just decide to let the newcomer CP
enter without charging side payments. The Nash bargaining solution is then defined
as a maximizer of the *product of the gains from the negotiation for both actors*: here
that would be a side payment value q maximizing $(R(q) - R(0)) \times (R_i(q) - R_i(0))$,
where $R(q)$ (resp., $R_i(q)$) is the revenue of the ISP (resp., the incumbent CP) if the
side payment equals q. We will not perform those computations here since they can
become heavy, but just intended to highlight some situations where side payments
can be an efficient barrier to entry benefiting both the ISP and incumbent CP, and
show how a specific level of side payment can be found through negotiations.

5.1.4.4   What About Users? Should the Regulator Intervene?

The impact on users is not trivial to analyze with this model, since it does not
define satisfaction levels in the presence or absence of the entrant CP. Nevertheless,
one simple metric we may consider is the mass of users subscribing to the ISP
(indicating the ISP subscription price p_A is low enough for those users). As
computed previously, that mass is $D = \dfrac{D_{\max}}{2} + \dfrac{sq(\bar{\gamma}_i + \bar{\gamma}_e)}{2}$ and is always
larger in a non-neutral setting than in a neutral one, suggesting the regulator
would be in favor of side payments because they lead to lower subscription prices
$\left(\left[\dfrac{D_{\max}}{2s} - \dfrac{q(\bar{\gamma}_i + \bar{\gamma}_e)}{2}\right]^+ \text{ instead of } \dfrac{D_{\max}}{2s}\right)$, hence favoring users.

Another metric of interest that can be considered by a regulator is the total mass
of requests that are served, that is, $(\bar{\gamma}_i + \bar{\gamma}_e)D$, and is plotted in Fig. 5.3. In a neutral
situation, the mass of ISP subscribers is $D_{\max}/2$, and since both CPs are present, the
mass of served requests equals $(\gamma_i + \gamma_e)D_{\max}/2$. But if side payments are preventing
the newcomer CP from entering the market, the (larger) mass of ISP subscribers is
only multiplied by $\bar{\gamma}_i + \bar{\gamma}_e = 1$ (instead of $\gamma_i + \gamma_e$) to obtain the mass of requests,
so the mass of ISP subscribers much be large enough, i.e., side payments must be
sufficiently large. As a result, the total mass of requests served is larger with barrier-
to-entry side payments than in a neutral setting if and only if:

$$q \in (r_e, r_i) \text{ and } D_{\max} + sq \geq (\gamma_i + \gamma_e)D_{\max},$$

or equivalently, q should be both in the interval $\in (r_e, r_i)$ and larger than
$(\gamma_i + \gamma_e - 1)D_{\max}/s$.

Summarizing, depending on the metric considered by the regulator, any side payment or only some values would be preferable to a neutral setting. For the set of parameters used in Fig. 5.3, if the regulator focuses on maximizing the mass of served requests, then the side payments benefiting the incumbent CP would be refused (since leading to fewer requests served than in the neutral case), but such side payments would be accepted if the regulator focuses on the mass of ISP subscribers.

5.1.5 Refining the Model

The model we considered in this section remains quite simple; apart from the specific form of the demand functions that can always be criticized and/or refined, we underline here two assumptions that we made and how their relaxation can be treated (at the cost of a more complex model):

- A strong assumption we made regards the knowledge of all the consequences of the newcomer's entrance in the market, before that entrance takes place (if at all). Indeed, how can one –in particular the ISP or the incumbent CP– guess in advance the values of r_e (revenue of the newcomer CP per unit mass of request) and of the parameters γ_e, γ_i (impact of the newcomer entrance on demands)? Assuming they are perfectly known seems unrealistic. A possibility to relax that assumption is to assume that the ISP and incumbent CP treat those parameters $(r_e, \gamma_i, \gamma_e)$ as random variables and consider an *a priori* joint distribution over their values to compute *expected* revenues when opting for a side-payment level [108].
- Another aspect that is ignored in our model is the temporality of user decisions. Indeed, it is not realistic to assume an immediate jump of the mass of requests to the incumbent CP from D to $\gamma_i D$ and an immediate mass of requests $\gamma_e D$ for the newcomer CP the instant it enters the market. In reality, demand should take some time to adjust, and the values we took in the model should only be asymptotically approached. The convergence phase cannot in general be ignored, for example, if it is too long, the newcomer may not be able to recover from possible initial investments it made to enter. That aspect is developed further in [108], where decision makers reason upon a given time horizon, also considering a time discount factor (similar to an interest rate and representing the preference for present incomes over future ones). As could be expected, such considerations in the model render the barrier to entry even more effective (or equivalently, it is easier for the ISP and incumbent CP to create a barrier to entry) than with our simplified model.

5.2   Sponsored Data and Zero Rating

While wireless communications are more and more ubiquitous and mobile data consumption continues to grow,[4] data plans proposed by ISPs (here, wireless operators) are still mostly based on data caps [104], after which service is degraded or charged extra. Hence, there is an incentive for CPs to *sponsor* data, i.e., to bear the communication cost on behalf of users in order to gain in attractiveness (and in the end in revenue, from advertising and/or subscriptions).

Such practices are implemented by operators like T-Mobile with the Binge-On program. Note that AT&T's Data Free TV plan (that excluded DIRECTV and U-verse from data caps) as well as its Sponsored Data program ended in March 2021, due to a legislative change. But some ISPs are still applying the sponsored data business model, commercializing it through tools and programs like FreeBee Data for Verizon or DataMI for Orange. Some new third-party actors like Aquto (acquired by Mavenir in 2018) can also enter the market to facilitate exchanges.

As evoked in Chap. 2, sponsored data (and its close version zero rating, which involves a direct agreement between the CP and the ISP) practices can be questioned in terms of net neutrality. In a September 2021 decision, the Court of Justice of the European Union precisely argued neutrality protection to rule against the practice of zero rating by two German operators, Telekom and Vodafone.[5] That decision contributes to clarifying the "gray area" where zero rating has been with respect to net neutrality, at least in the EU.

It is therefore of interest to study the impact of sponsored data and zero rating on all actors and on society. As regards economic modeling and analysis of such practices, one can mention [78], where for a single ISP, several (complementary) CPs, and a discrete set of users, the authors observe that the benefits from sponsoring are likely to be higher for users than for the CPs implementing it.

The model studied in [80] considers a monopoly ISP with inelastic user participation (the pricing equilibrium in the case of many competing ISPs is said to be reduced to a monopoly network). Assuming there are two types of content (high benefit and low benefit), the authors show how content providers select the sponsored-data option or not depending on their type and on the overall proportion of high-benefit content; conditions are also derived for the practice to increase total welfare. But the impact on ISP competition is not studied closely. That competition aspect was not included in other contributions like [159], which instead focuses on CP competition, or [180, 184] where the focus is on modeling network externalities. Note that other interesting approaches include investigating the combination of sponsored data and data caching strategies, as is done in [142].

---

[4] See http://www.businessinsider.fr/us/mobile-data-will-skyrocket-700-by-2021-2017-2/ among others.

[5] https://fortune.com/2021/09/02/in-boost-for-net-neutrality-top-eu-court-plunges-dagger-into-controversial-zero-rating-practice/.

In this section, we propose to have a look at a different model, initially introduced in [109] and refined in [112], involving users, CPs, and competing ISPs. Also, a key component that we include in the model is the negative impact that advertising has on user quality of experience and therefore on their decisions. To our knowledge, the main other contribution considering ISP competition is [173]: the authors conclude –in the same direction as we do here– that ISPs may be the ones benefiting the most from sponsoring, but advertising is not covered in the model, and user choices are based on a to-be-motivated Hotelling framework.

The main components of the interactions we intend to model are as follows: CPs will have to decide whether to sponsor data or not but also select the amount of advertising to include with their content. Competing ISPs will have to fix subscription prices to attract users, who will make decisions regarding which ISP to use (if any) and their data consumption from each CP.

5.2.1 Modeling Sponsored-Data Practices in a Competitive ISP Context

We present here the model from [112], which considers several CPs and 2 ISPs (indexed by i). Assuming CPs are complements (i.e., there is no CP competition), we will without loss of generality only consider one CP (see [112] for more detail).

5.2.1.1 Users' Decisions and Preferences

Each user will have to select an ISP, and an amount of volume (without advertisements) to consume from the CP over some period of time, say a month. To include user heterogeneity while keeping a relatively simple model, we assume there are only two types of users, differing by their willingness-to-pay θ for connectivity, a parameter that will also affect data consumption. More specifically, a proportion ψ_h of users are type-h (for high valuation) users, with willingness-to-pay θ_h, while a proportion $\psi_\ell = 1 - \psi_h$ have a willingness-to-pay $\theta_\ell < \theta_h$.

Denoting by p_i the subscription price of ISP i, we model the connectivity-related utility of a type-k user ($k \in \{\ell, h\}$) as the term $a_i(\theta_k - p_i)$, with $a_i > 0$ a constant representing the reputation of ISP i.

Now let us model data usage: if a type-k user selects ISP i, we denote by $v_i(\theta_k)$ the data volume consumed, chosen by the user in order to maximize their utility. We assume here a linear marginal valuation for data usage, of the form $[\theta_k - \alpha s^2 x]^+$ per extra unit of content when already consuming x, where $[\cdot]^+ := \max(\cdot, 0)$, α is a fixed parameter (sensitivity to advertisements), and $s \geq 1$ represents the relative increase of volume due to the advertising introduced by the CP. For example, $s = 2$ would mean that for each volume unit of (useful) content, an equivalent volume unit of advertising is added. We take a quadratic form to represent the fact that advertisements get increasingly annoying to the user, so that they stop being profitable if excessively introduced. Summarizing, the willingness-to-pay for a type-k user subscribing to ISP i and consuming a volume x (without advertising) of CP data is modelled with a (while non-decreasing) quadratic concave function, expressed as [34, 106]:

$$r_k(x) := \begin{cases} \theta_k x - \alpha s^2 \frac{x^2}{2} & \text{if } x \leq \frac{\theta_k}{\alpha s^2} \\ \frac{\theta_k^2}{2\alpha s^2} & \text{otherwise.} \end{cases}$$

If we denote by c_i the unit data usage price with ISP i, the user would have to pay an amount $c_i s v_i(\theta_k)$ in addition to the subscription price. Note how, through the multiplicative term s, all data is charged, whether it is the original CP data or added advertising.

The overall utility of a type-k user selecting ISP i is then the sum of the connectivity-related utility and the data usage utility, yielding:

$$U_i(\theta_k) := a_i(\theta - p_i) + r_{\theta_k}(v_i(\theta_k)) - c_i s v_i(\theta_k). \tag{5.2}$$

With our model, the data consumption volume if subscribing to ISP i can easily be computed, and equals:

$$v_i(\theta_k) = \left[\frac{\theta_k - c_i s}{\alpha s^2} \right]^+,$$

which then gives the usage-related utility.

Finally, users can make that reasoning for both ISPs, and select the one giving the largest overall utility $U_i(\theta_k)$: we denote by i_k the ISP chosen by type-k users (we can for simplicity assume that if both ISPs give the same utility, then users select the one with the best reputation).

5.2.1.2 The CP Side: Advertising and Sponsoring

We focus on CPs making revenue only from advertising in this model, i.e., they are not paid by users. Their goal is therefore to display as much advertisement as possible while remaining attractive to users, even possibly by sponsoring data.

CP revenues are supposed to be per advertisement volume unit, with a unit price β. With our model, the advertisement volume for a type-k user subscribing to ISP i is $(s-1)v_i(\theta_k)$; aggregating over all users, the CP revenue per mass of user is then:

$$\psi_h \beta(s-1)v_{i_h}(\theta_h) + \psi_\ell \beta(s-1)v_{i_\ell}(\theta_\ell) = \frac{\beta(s-1)}{\alpha s^2} \left(\psi_h \left[\theta_h - c_{i_h} s \right]^+ + \psi_\ell \left[\theta_\ell - c_{i_\ell} s \right]^+ \right).$$

In the remainder of this section, without loss of generality, we will normalize the mass of users to 1.

A first decision variable for the CP is the amount of advertising added to the "legitimate" content, through the ratio $s \geq 1$ representing the relative volume increase due to introducing ads.

The other CP decisions regard data sponsoring. To model those, we use the binary notation γ_i (for $i = 1, 2$), which equals 0 if the CP fully sponsors its data on ISP i and 0 if it chooses not to sponsor. Note that this allows the CP to decide to sponsor data only with both ISPs, with one, or with none. But unlike [106], we only consider here "all-or-nothing" decisions, i.e., the CP cannot decide to partially sponsor data consumption.

To express the utility (revenue) of the CP when sponsoring, we need to introduce one last notation, namely, the price q_i per volume unit charged by each ISP i, for $i = 1, 2$. This also allows to express the price c_i paid by users per volume unit: in the absence of sponsoring, we have $c_i = q_i$, while $c_i = 0$ if data is sponsored; this can be written mathematically written as:

$$c_i = (1 - \gamma_i)q_i.$$

Subtracting potential sponsoring costs to advertising revenues, the overall CP revenue equals:

$$\psi_h(\beta(s - 1) - \gamma_{i_h}q_{i_h}s)v_{i_h}(\theta_h) + \psi_\ell(\beta(s - 1) - \gamma_{i_\ell}q_{i_\ell}s)v_{i_\ell}(\theta_\ell). \tag{5.3}$$

5.2.1.3 ISP Price Competition

At the largest time scale we consider in the model, the two ISPs play a price competition game, each ISP i deciding what amount q_i to charge the user (a charge bore by the CP if sponsoring is implemented) per volume unit of data. ISPs also make revenue from subscriptions, but we will assume here that subscription prices $(p_i)_{i=1,2}$ are fixed, either from previous decisions or from regulation.

Total revenues for an ISP i can then be expressed as:

$$\psi_h \mathbb{1}_{\{i_h=i\}} (p_i + q_i s v_i(\theta_h)) + \psi_\ell \mathbb{1}_{\{i_\ell=i\}} (p_i + q_i s v_i(\theta_\ell)).$$

To account for traffic management costs, we subtract to those revenues an amount κx^2, with x the total traffic managed by the ISP (the factors of q_i in the expression above) and $\kappa > 0$ a parameter. We take a convex function to represent congestion effects: the more traffic there is, the harder it is to handle.

5.2.1.4 Order of Decisions

As for some of our previous models, we consider that decisions are taken over different time scales and that at each one, the decision-makers are able to anticipate the subsequent decisions that will be made. The classical *backward induction* method can then be used to analyze the game. Here, we will assume that the largest time scale is the one where ISPs decide their prices $(q_i)_{i=1,2}$; then the CP takes its decisions regarding the amount of advertising and the (possibly different over ISPs) levels of sponsoring; finally users select an ISP and consume some data from the CP.

The model we have developed in this section is quite rich and therefore complex to treat analytically. For that reason, in the following subsections, we will use it to illustrate some phenomena that *can* occur, through some numerical computations for some specific parameter values, rather than try to prove general results.

5.2.2   How Does the CP Decide to Sponsor and Add Advertisement?

The CP has to choose the advertisement overhead $s \geq 1$, as well as the data sponsoring levels $(\gamma_1, \gamma_2) \in \{0, 1\}^2$. Note that there might be some regulation decision forbidding sponsored data, in which case $\gamma_1 = \gamma_2 = 0$, and the only strategic decision is s, or allowing sponsored data but only if the practice is the same on all ISPs, i.e., forcing $\gamma_1 = \gamma_2$. Those three possibilities (no sponsored data, sponsored data with constrained equality, unconstrained sponsored data) are considered and compared.

Figure 5.4 *(left)* shows the CP optimal sponsoring decision for the two cases where sponsored data is allowed (equal sponsoring and unconstrained sponsoring), when the advertising level s varies.We notice a threshold policy regarding sponsoring, which could be expected since introducing more advertising increases revenues (per volume of data) which can be used to sponsor data. Also, the threshold for constrained sponsoring ($\gamma_1 = \gamma_2$) lies between the two thresholds (one per ISP) for unconstrained sponsoring.

However, the negative effect of excessive advertising on the overall revenue is visible on Fig. 5.4 *(right)*, where we display the revenue as s varies, when optimal sponsoring decisions are taken for each of the three possible regulation scenarios (no sponsoring allowed, equal sponsoring only, unconstrained). In each case, the curves have a maximum: as advertising decreases the value of the content for users, demand for the CP tends to decrease, as will eventually the volume of advertisement that is seen by users.

Those sponsoring decisions by the CP have consequences on the revenues of ISPs and on user welfare, both plotted in Fig. 5.5 for fixed values of the ISP prices, again in the three possible regulation contexts regarding data sponsoring.

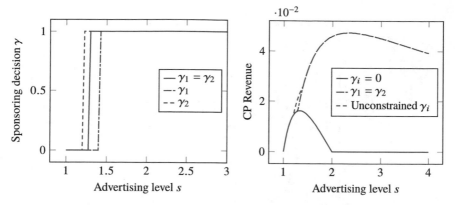

Fig. 5.4 Optimal γ *(left)* and CP revenue *(right)* when $\psi_\ell = 0.7$, $\theta_\ell = 1$, $\theta_h = 3$, $\beta = 1$, $r_1 = 2$, $r_2 = 1$, $p_1 = 0.16$, $p_2 = 0.1$, $q_1 = 0.2$, $q_2 = 0.1$, $\alpha = 1$ [112]

5.2.2.1   The Pricing Game Played by ISPs

We can note that with the parameters we took, allowing sponsoring (with constrained equality over ISPs or not) benefits users and tends to reduce the gap between ISP revenues.

But this is without considering the largest time scale of our model, namely, the price competition among ISPs. Given the complexity of the subsequent stages of the game, with threshold effects for the sponsoring decisions, and possibly several local maxima when varying one's price, the ISP best responses are not always continuous, and the Nash equilibrium of the pricing game is difficult to predict (even existence and uniqueness are not guaranteed). For our set of parameters, an example is displayed in Fig. 5.6, where we can observe very different-looking best-response functions depending on the regulatory scenario. In each case, we (numerically) found one Nash equilibrium (the black dot in the figure), which happens to be the same in both situations allowing sponsoring since at the unconstrained case equilibrium, the CP chooses to sponsor data on both ISPs.

5.2.3   A Practice Finally Mostly Benefiting ISPs?

The main values of interest at the equilibria of the ISP pricing game with our set of parameters ($\psi_\ell = 0.7$, $\theta_\ell = 1$, $\theta_h = 3$, $\kappa = \alpha = r_2 = 1$, and $r_1 = 2$) are given in Table 5.1. As pointed out before, the unconstrained sponsoring equilibrium leads to full sponsoring, hence the same situation as when sponsoring is constrained, so we only compare that common outcome to the one when sponsoring is forbidden. There is much more advertisement in the former case, which was expected, but a counterintuitive observation can be made about CP revenues: the CP actually

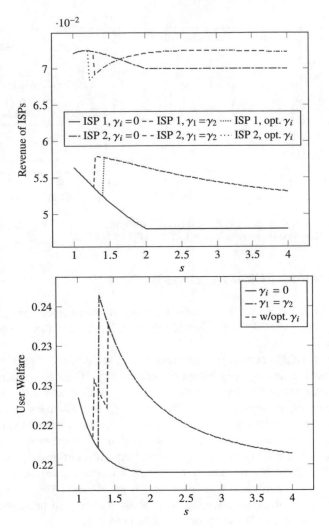

Fig. 5.5 ISP revenues *(top)* and user welfare *(bottom)* when $\psi_\ell = 0.7$, $\theta_\ell = 1$, $\theta_h = 3$, $\kappa = 1$, $\beta = 1$, $r_1 = 2$, $r_2 = 1$, $p_1 = 0.16$, $p_2 = 0.1$, $q_1 = 0.2$, $q_2 = 0.1$, $\alpha = 1$ [112]

makes less with the possibility of sponsoring data than without it! When sponsored data is allowed, we notice higher volume prices charged by ISPs; that increase is not experienced by users since it is covered by the sponsoring. So in essence, most of the extra revenue coming from advertising finally ends up benefitting ISPs, through higher volume prices (despite competition). This is likely to come from the ISPs' position in the game, as leaders that can make their decisions anticipating the (follower) behavior of CPs.

Such observations (data sponsoring benefitting ISPs rather than CPs) may explain the efforts by ISPs to develop sponsored data platforms on their networks.

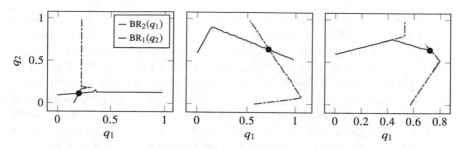

Fig. 5.6 Best responses of ISPs, with $\psi_\ell = 0.7$, $\theta_\ell = 1$, $\theta_h = 3$, $\kappa = 1$, $\beta = 1$, $r_1 = 2$, $r_2 = 1$, $p_1 = 0.16$, $p_2 = 0.10$, $\alpha = 1$, in the no-sponsoring (neutral) case (*left*), constrained (*center*), and unconstrained (*right*) sponsoring cases [112]

Table 5.1 Output at equilibrium points (revenues and UW scaled by 10^4) when $\psi_\ell = 0.7$, $\theta_\ell = 1$, $\theta_h = 3$, $\kappa = \alpha = r_2 = 1$, and $r_1 = 2$ [112]

Strategy	(q_1, q_2)	(γ_1, γ_2)	s	CP	ISP1	ISP2	UW
No sponsoring	$(0.201, 0.112)$	$(0, 0)$	1.304	141	534	724	2163
Constrained sp.	$(0.720, 0.645)$	$(1, 1)$	6.242	67	615	840	2150
Unconstrained sp.	$(0.720, 0.645)$	$(1, 1)$	6.242	67	615	840	2150

To take the regulator point of view, one can focus on the impact on user welfare. For our model and with the parameters we chose, we observe a very limited impact of allowing data sponsoring; hence, a regulator may not want to intervene to forbid the practice. However, some careful monitoring may be needed to ensure user welfare does not deteriorate (since our model is of course a simplification of reality, and/or the outcome can be different with other parameter values).

5.3 When Big CPs Designate the "Good" ISPs: Incentivizing Non-neutrality Without Paying

In this section, we take into account the fact that the biggest CPs are more and more powerful, to the point that the neutrality questions may even be reversed: instead of the ISPs asking for payments from CPs to get preferential treatment, some CPs may just "force" ISPs to favor them, with the threat of otherwise driving users toward competing ISPs. In this section, we propose and analyze a model, based on those in [107, 113], to study that kind of situation.

5.3.1 ISP Competition: The Importance of Looking Good

The idea that it is in ISPs' interest to favor big CPs is actually quite simple: if the quality of experience with a small content provider is bad, users are more likely to blame that newcomer and its server management than if the quality is bad with a huge actor like YouTube or Netflix. In the latter case, users may be more tempted to blame the ISP, especially if the ISP's impact on quality is highlighted by those content providers. That's precisely what some CPs do, by grading ISPs with respect to the performance each ISP gives them, depending on the user location: on its Web page https://www.google.com/get/videoqualityreport/, Google provides ISPs with quality badges labeled "YouTube HD Verified," "standard definition," or "lower definition." Similarly, Netflix uses an "ISP speed index" and ranks ISPs according to the streaming speed of its services (see https://ispspeedindex.netflix.com/). Of course, such actions have much more impact on ISPs' reputation than if a small CP were to implement them. As a result, in order to look good, ISPs may be incentivized to upgrade their networks but can also be tempted to give preferential treatment –for free– to those "influencer CPs" whose opinion matters, at the expense of smaller CPs.

In the following subsection, we build a model to represent that situation, with two competing ISPs (so that each one may lose subscribers churning to the other) and two CPs. Each ISP will have to decide how to share their network resource between the two CPs and may take into account the CPs' popularity to make that decision, in order to attract as many subscribers as possible. The popularity of CPs will be modelled through a distribution of the usage time for each one over the population: each individual user will then consider their average perceived service quality as the metric to select an ISP, i.e., they will care more about the service quality with their mostly-used CP.

Note that in the model considered here, only the ISPs and the users are decision-makers, and the CPs are just passive in the interaction (they may however publish the quality their traffic is experiencing with each ISP to help users make their decision for an ISP). Summarizing, we will define a Stackelberg game [141], where:

1. first, ISPs decide what treatment (share of their capacity) to offer to each CP, in a competitive manner;
2. then, given the ISP decisions, users choose based on their preferences what ISP to subscribe to. Some congestion effects may also take place, hence we will look for equilibria among users.

Our objective is to propose a model and method to quantify and understand the best strategies that competing ISPs may want to implement with regard to differentiated treatment of CPs, without any payment between those actors. We in particular intend to investigate whether it is in the best interest of ISPs to favor the largest CPs to "look good," or they should remain neutral and allocate their capacity proportionally to each CP's traffic.

5.3.2   A Two-ISP, Two-CP model with Heterogeneous Users

We introduce here the mathematical modeling for the interactions we want to study. As argued before, we limit the setting to two competing ISPs and two CPs. The CPs are not in direct competition here, and their relative popularity among the population of users is assumed given and will be represented by a continuous distribution.

To avoid confusions, we will label ISPs with A and B and CPs with 1 and 2. The capacity of ISP i ($i = A, B$) will be denoted by C_i, of which a proportion $\beta_i \in [0, 1]$ will be allocated to CP 1 traffic, hence a capacity $(1 - \beta_i)C_i$ reserved for CP 2 traffic.

5.3.2.1   Modelling Consumer (Heterogeneous) Usage of Different CPs

A simple way to think of users having different preferences or sensitivities to the quality with each of the two CPs is to consider the relative amount of *time* they spend on each one. Let us denote by $\theta \in [0, 1]$ the proportion of online time a given user spends using services offered by CP 1. Since our model only counts two CPs, that user would spend with CP 2 a proportion $(1-\theta)$ of their online time (say, during the peak hour). The value θ characterizes the user; we can call them a type-θ user.

To introduce some heterogeneity in the model, we assume a very large number of users (treated as a continuum) and consider that the parameters θ over the user population are distributed according to a distribution function F, which admits a density and is strictly increasing over its support $[0, 1]$.

We also denote by $\bar{\theta}$ the expected value of θ, i.e.:

$$\bar{\theta} := \mathbb{E}[\theta] = \int_{\theta=0}^{1} \theta \, dF(\theta) = \int_{\theta=0}^{1} (1 - F(\theta)) d\theta.$$

5.3.2.2   ISPs Deciding How to Allocate Their Capacity Affects CP Quality

As previously mentioned, the ISP decision variable considered in this model is the share β_i of ISP i's capacity C_i that is allocated to CP 1 (the rest being allocated to CP 2). Of course, that choice will impact the quality on each CP's service, because of congestion. Let us denote by T_{ij} the total throughput (again, at the peak hour) of CP j for ISP i subscribers ($i = A, B$; $j = 1, 2$); then the quality for that traffic, which we will denote by Q_{ij}, will increase with the allocated capacity and decrease with the traffic load. In this section, to maintain some analytical tractability, we will just take the ratio between those quantities, i.e., consider that:

$$\begin{cases} Q_{i1}:=\dfrac{\beta_i C_i}{T_{i1}}, \\ Q_{i2}:=\dfrac{(1-\beta_i)C_i}{T_{i2}}. \end{cases} \tag{5.4}$$

Users will take those qualities into account to decide which ISP to subscribe to.

5.3.2.3 Introducing Some Asymmetry Among CPs: Required Throughput

To link users' online behavior to the global traffic values (T_{ij}), we need to specify how much traffic is generated by a (mass unit of) user with each CP. This is an opportunity to introduce some asymmetry in the model: without loss of generality, we can set one value (say, for CP 2) to 1 and say that one unit of mass of users spending all their time with CP 1 corresponds to γ traffic units. Several interpretations can be used to understand that parameter:

- A value of γ above 1 could indicate that the type of service provided by CP 1 is more bandwidth-demanding by nature than CP 2's service (e.g., a video-streaming service *versus* an online radio).
- If services are comparable, γ may represent the relative efficiency of CP 1 with respect to CP 2, for example, CP 1 can apply some data compression to reduce the bandwidth usage of its service.

A final simplifying assumption we will make is that there is independence between the type θ of a user and their probability of being online, so that we can use the distribution of types to express the volume T_{ij} of each type of traffic ($i = A, B; j = 1, 2$). Without loss of generality (up to a traffic rate unit change), we set that probability to 1.

With those assumptions, at the peak hour, the traffic rate T_{i1} corresponding to ISP i subscribers using CP 1 services is:

$$T_{i1} = \int_{\Theta_i} \gamma \theta \, dF(\theta),$$

with Θ_i the set of subscribers (their types in $[0, 1]$) who chose ISP i ($i = A, B$). Similarly, for CP 2 services we have:

$$T_{i2} = \int_{\Theta_i} (1-\theta) \, dF(\theta).$$

5.3.2.4 Users Care About the Quality of the Services They Use!

The title of this subsection may seem obvious, but can be seen as in direct contradiction with neutrality principles, according to which all services should be treated the same. Here we take into consideration the fact that users will perceive the quality provided by their ISP only through their use, and, therefore, only for the CPs they spend time on.

To model that fact, we assume that each user is sensitive to the *average* quality they experience over their online time, which is a weighted sum of the qualities for each CP, weighted by the proportion of online time spent with each. A type-θ user spends a proportion θ of their (online) time with CP 1 and $(1 - \theta)$ with CP 2, so their average perceived quality is:

$$\theta Q_{i1} + (1 - \theta) Q_{i2}, \tag{5.5}$$

with the qualities expressed in (5.4).

5.3.2.5 A (Simple) Game on Differentiation

In the remainder of this section, we summarize the results of the analysis for the model just defined; for more details and proofs, the reader is referred to [113].

Note that we only focus here on the decision variables $(\beta_A, \beta_B) \in [0, 1]^2$ of ISPs deciding how to allocate their capacity (and the subsequent subscription decisions by users). In particular, we do not consider pricing decisions: ISPs are not charging CPs for improved services here, and the ISP subscription prices paid by users are assumed to be equal, and sufficiently low (say, below the valuation for basic services such as e-mail) to have all users deciding to subscribe. We also assume the possible quality improvement from subscribing to both ISPs is not worth the extra cost, so each user in the considered population subscribes to one and only one ISP, that is, their preferred one in the sense of the average perceived quality (5.5). For those reasons, ISP subscription prices are not included in the model. Similarly, the ISP capacities C_A and C_B are assumed fixed in this model.

We consider that ISP revenues are proportional to their market share, so that each ISP i ($i = A, B$) will try to maximize the mass of subscribers, which we denote by m_i, that it manages to attract.

5.3.3 User Equilibria: How ISP Decisions Affect User Subscription Choices

Following the classical *backward induction* method, we focus on user subscription decisions for fixed values of the decision variables β_A and β_B. Users interact because of congestion effects through the qualities expressed in (5.4), and the expected outcome can be called a *user equilibrium* [18, 141], which is a partition of the set of users (seen as the interval [0, 1] containing their types) into two subsets Θ_A and Θ_B, such that no user can strictly improve their average experienced quality by switching ISPs.

Mathematically, the following relation should hold:

$$\theta \in \Theta_i \quad \Rightarrow \quad \theta Q_{i1} + (1 - \theta) Q_{i2} \geq Q_{\bar{i}1} + (1 - \theta) Q_{\bar{i}2} \tag{5.6}$$

for $i \in \{A, B\}$ and $\bar{i} = \{A, B\} \setminus \{i\}$.

The rigorous study of all user equilibria is carried out in [113], the main results being listed below:

- There always exists a user equilibrium that is unique in the sense that the traffic volumes $(T_{ij})_{i=A,B; j=1,2}$ are unique and the market shares m_A, m_B are also unique. (As a consequence the qualities $(Q_{ij})_{i=A,B; j=1,2}$ are unique as well.)
- The equilibrium can be of one of two types:

    - Either $Q_{A1} = Q_{B1}$ and $Q_{A2} = Q_{B2}$, i.e., each CP has the same quality on both ISPs.
    - Or CP1 quality is strictly better with an ISP than with the other, while CP2 quality is strictly worse.

- If the ISP decisions β_A and β_B are sufficiently close, then the equilibrium is of the first type ($Q_{A1} = Q_{B1}$ and $Q_{A2} = Q_{B2}$).

The mathematical conditions and characterizations of the equilibria are detailed in [113]; we only give here an illustration for the case when user types follow a power-law distribution over [0, 1], i.e., the cumulative distribution function F is of the form $F(x) = x^\kappa$ for some $\kappa > 0$. Such distributions are widely found in physics, biology, mathematics, or economics [136]. For our case, the value of κ can be used to model popularity imbalance between CPs among users.

For the rest of this section, we fix some default parameter values: unless stated otherwise, we will consider that $\kappa = 2, \gamma = 2, C_A = 10, C_B = 5$, and $\beta_B = 0.7$ (β_A will vary, to illustrate the impact of one ISP changing its capacity allocation).

In Fig. 5.7, we plot the qualities $(Q_{ij})_{i=A,B; j=1,2}$ at the user equilibrium as functions of β_A. As stated below, there is a zone that includes β_B, in which each CP has the same quality on both ISPs (but that quality is not the same for each CP), so that users end up being indifferent among ISPs. But when β_A takes more extreme values and decides to clearly favor one CP, this can result in different qualities among ISPs, the other CP being better treated by ISP B.

The proportions of CP 1 and CP 2 traffic on each ISP at the user equilibrium are plotted in Fig. 5.8. We again observe the three different equilibrium zones. In the middle zone (where each CP has the same quality on both ISPs), as expected, we observe that a higher β_A leads to ISP A treating more traffic from CP 1 and less from CP 2. Note however that this might not be true in the two extreme zones, which can be interpreted as follows: Consider, for example, the "high-β_A" region, and then

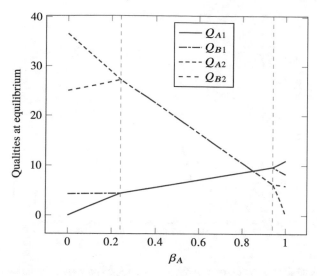

Fig. 5.7 Qualities at equilibrium versus β_A. The vertical dashed lines indicate the frontiers between equilibrium zones [113]

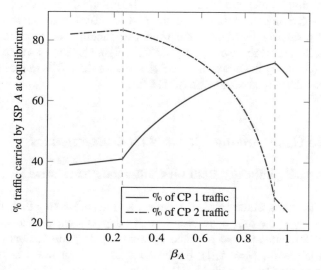

Fig. 5.8 Proportions (percentages) of traffic from each CP carried by ISP A at user equilibrium, versus β_A. The vertical dashed lines indicate the frontiers between equilibrium zones [113]

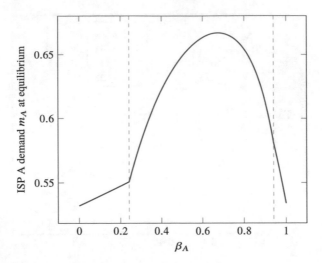

Fig. 5.9 Demand for ISP A at user equilibrium versus β_A. The vertical dashed lines indicate the frontiers between equilibrium zones [113]

further increasing β_A means decreasing β_B and significantly degrading CP 2 quality, possibly incentivizing some users (with their CP 1 traffic) to switch to ISP B.

We finally display in Fig. 5.9 the objective function of the decision-maker (ISP A), i.e., its market share $m_A = \int_{\Theta_A} dF$. The figure here shows that the capacity allocation decision β_A that maximizes ISP A's market share falls in the middle zone, which is often the case as established in [113].

5.3.4   The Game Among ISPs and Its Consequences

5.3.4.1   At the Equilibrium, Both ISPs Differentiate the Same Way

Figure 5.9 illustrates what each ISP i cares about when making their decision: its market share m_i at the user equilibrium, which depends on the allocation choices (β_A, β_B). In the game played between ISPs on capacity allocations (through the decision variables β_i, $i = 1, 2$), the best response of an ISP i is the value of β_i maximizing m_i, and a pair $(\hat{\beta}_A, \hat{\beta}_B)$ is an equilibrium if and only if $\hat{\beta}_A \in \arg\max_{\beta_A} m_A(\beta_A, \hat{\beta}_B)$ and $\hat{\beta}_B \in \arg\max_{\beta_B} m_B(\hat{\beta}_A, \beta_B)$.

The analysis of the game is carried out in [113], involving some algebra. The main conclusion is that when ISP capacities C_A and C_B are of the same order of magnitude and the CP imbalance parameter κ is not too large (below 5 if the ratio C_A/C_B is around 2, which leaves some room for significant differences among CPs), then there is only one stable Nash equilibrium, which is simply both ISPs allocating the same proportion $\bar{\theta}$ of their capacity to CP 1 traffic, where $\bar{\theta}$ is the average proportion of time spent by users with CP 1, i.e.:

$$\beta_A = \beta_B = \bar{\theta} = \int_{[0,1]} \theta \, dF(\theta).$$

5.3.4.2   Equilibrium *vs* Neutral Capacity Allocation: Neutrality Hindering Innovation?

So far, we have not defined what a *neutral* allocation would be in the model of this section. Based on the principle that all traffic should be treated the same, a reasonable definition is that capacity should be shared proportionally to the overall traffic, i.e., each ISP i should set β_i to the share that the total CP 1 traffic represents. Computing that share yields:

$$\beta^{\text{neut}} := \frac{\gamma \bar{\theta}}{\gamma \bar{\theta} + (1 - \bar{\theta})} = \frac{1}{1 + \frac{1}{\gamma}(1/\bar{\theta} - 1)}.$$

Note that when $\gamma = 1$, we have $\beta^{\text{neut}} = \bar{\theta}$, meaning that the equilibrium and neutral decisions coincide.

But if we consider that CPs offer comparable services, with CP 1 investing to be more bandwidth-efficient (i.e., reduce γ), then the neutral and equilibrium situations differ: while the equilibrium values remain unchanged, the neutral capacity share allocated to CP 1 traffic decreases when γ decreases, which can be seen as a disincentive for CP 1 to improve its service efficiency.

5.3.4.3   Equilibrium *vs* Neutral Capacity Allocation: No Impact for ISPs

An interesting observation from the analysis of the two situations (neutral and non-neutral) is that in each one, the ISP market shares are proportional to their capacities: ISP A attracts a proportion $m_A = \dfrac{C_A}{C_A + C_B}$ of subscribers, and ISP B convinces the rest $m_B = \dfrac{C_B}{C_A + C_B}$.

As a consequence, with that model, ISPs are indifferent whether neutrality is enforced or not.

5.3.4.4   Equilibrium *vs* Neutral Capacity Allocation: What About Users?

Finally, let us have a look at the consequences for users of imposing neutrality. With our model, those consequences can be measured in terms of *average user perceived quality*, that is, the average value over the whole population of the individually perceived qualities $\theta Q_{i1} + (1 - \theta) Q_{i2}$ (with i the index of the selected ISP).

Therefore, we need to express the quality that each ISP provides to each CP for both cases, which we get after some algebra (see [113] for details):

- When neutrality is imposed, by design, both CPs are served with the same quality, which we denote by Q^{neut} and equals $Q^{\text{neut}} = \dfrac{C_A + C_B}{1 - \bar{\theta}(1 - \gamma)}$;

- Without neutrality constraints, the Nash equilibrium is $(\beta_A, \beta_B) = (\bar{\theta}, \bar{\theta})$, and each CP j, $j = 1, 2$ is served with the same quality Q_j^{NE} on both ISPs, with

$$Q_1^{\text{NE}} = \frac{C_A + C_B}{\gamma}, \qquad Q_2^{\text{NE}} = C_A + C_B.$$

In other words, at the Nash equilibrium, CP qualities differ by a factor γ, and we find again the incentive to innovate: if a CP optimizes its protocols to reduce the bandwidth use by some factor, then its quality as perceived by users will increase by the same factor, leaving the quality of the other CP unchanged. By contrast, in the neutral case, an improvement by one CP benefits both CPs. Such an interpretation can be seen as net neutrality introducing some unfairness among CPs, since it seems fairer to have one CP's efforts benefit that CP (or reversely, one CP's lack of effort not affecting negatively the others).

Going back to our global metric –the average user perceived quality– we just compute the expected value of $\theta Q_1 + (1 - \theta) Q_2$ for each case (removing the ISP-related index to simplify the writing), which is simply $\bar{\theta} Q_1 + (1 - \bar{\theta}) Q_2$.

- In the neutral situation, all qualities are equal so the average is just that common value $Q^{\text{neut}} = \dfrac{C_A + C_B}{1 - \bar{\theta}(1 - \gamma)}$.

- In the non-neutral case, at the equilibrium, the average user quality is $(C_A + C_B)\left(1 - \bar{\theta}(1 - \dfrac{1}{\gamma})\right)$.

One can check analytically that the latter is always above the former, i.e., from the point of view of user-perceived quality, the non-neutral situation should be preferred. The ratio between those metric values is plotted in Fig. 5.10 for different values of $\bar{\theta}$ and γ, highlighting the extent of the impact of neutrality here.

5.3.5 A Model Yielding Unexpected Conclusions

The model developed in this section seems to favor a non-neutral (laissez-faire) approach, since imposing an equal treatment of CPs by ISPs implies that users would perceive a lower overall quality, and introduces some disincentives for CPs to design bandwidth-frugal services.

While ISPs are indifferent about neutrality being enforced or not, the results suggest that non-neutrality could be pushed by regulators/users and CPs willing to control their performance, somewhat the opposite of the arguments we encounter most of the time.

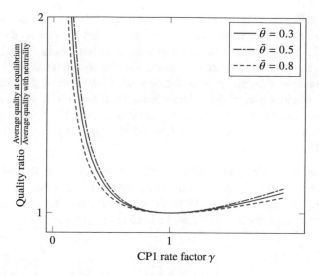

Fig. 5.10   Relative average qualities in the equilibrium and neutral cases [113]

To conclude, let us go back to our initial concern and motivation for this model: that without neutrality, newcomer CPs could not thrive because ISPs will try to "look good" and favor big CPs. The results of this section suggest that this concern may be unfounded: even in the non-neutral case, the quality CPs are served with depends only on their bandwidth consumption (the parameter γ). A small CP would not be disfavored, because if it is small, the capacity gain from disfavoring would be small as well, and below the loss corresponding to the dissatisfaction of that CP's users.

5.4   Conclusions

The three models developed in this section provide some elements of response to the initial questions we had regarding big content providers preferring non-neutral situations over neutrality enforcement. Let us summarize the takeaway message for each question:

- *Can big CPs use non-neutrality (through side payments) as barriers to entry to deter potential competitors?* According to our model of Sect. 5.1, yes they can; more precisely, they can reach an agreement with their ISP that both would prefer to a neutral situation. But that depends of course of several parameters, like the expected impact of the newcomer on the incumbent CP.
- *Is it in the interest of CPs to participate in sponsored data schemes?* The model in Sect. 5.2 suggests that such mechanisms may end up mostly benefitting the ISP, instead of CPs or even users.

- *Can big CPs elicit favorable differentiation by ISPs just because being widely used gives them more weight toward users?* The answer provided by the model in Sect. 5.3 is negative: while a non-neutral situation would likely be preferred by users, the potential service differentiation that would occur with selfish ISPs trying to attract subscribers does not depend on the size of the CPs, but rather on their efficient use of throughput. Here also, the model suggests (contrary to common arguments) that imposing neutrality could hinder innovation, in the sense that it would dis-incentivize CPs from optimizing the resource usage of their services.

Of course, some different models might lead to other conclusions, we mostly highlighted what *might* happen, and the main message is that the interactions make the outcomes difficult to predict. In particular, regulatory decisions must be made with great care, since their impact may be hard to anticipate.

Chapter 6
A More General View of Neutrality

In the previous chapters, the vivid interactions between ISPs and CPs, with fears from end users, have been described. We have highlighted the pros and cons of neutrality and the various definitions, all mainly focusing on ISPs' actions on Internet packets flowing through the network. In the two previous chapters, we have also illustrated using game-theoretical models some counterintuitive results on winners and losers of non-neutral behaviors. But we claim here, as developed in [121], that the restriction of neutrality principles to ISPs' actions on Internet packets may be too restrictive for several reasons:

1. There are many potential ways to circumvent the (packet-based) neutrality laws, which could be seen as infringements of the neutrality spirit; we believe they have to be supervised with care if neutrality is to be really implemented.
2. The content delivery chain is now quite complex, with many (non-ISP) intermediaries which may be non-neutral and impact quality of service.

Our purpose in this chapter is to emphasize these aspects, an examination supported by the literature [52].

6.1 Is It Relevant to Generalize Network Neutrality?

The network neutrality debate has raised many discussions and led to several definitions and laws. The whole debate seems centered on a quite simplistic delivery chain of content to users, of the form:

Content/service providers—ISPs—users,

hence focusing on ISPs as the intermediaries potentially differentiating service, thanks to packet- or flow-specific treatments within routers over the path from sender to receiver. But the Internet network ecosystem has changed and keeps evolving fast, with many "newcomers" playing specific roles, or even "old" actors

© The Author(s), under exclusive license to Springer Nature Switzerland AG 2022
P. Maillé, B. Tuffin, *From Net Neutrality to ICT Neutrality*,
https://doi.org/10.1007/978-3-031-06271-1_6

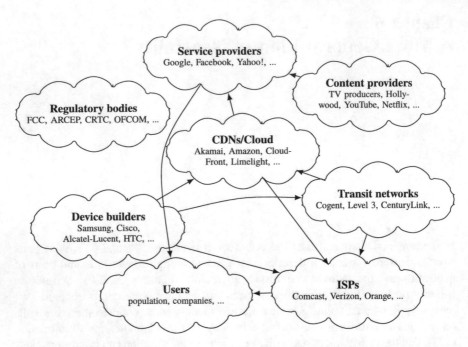

Fig. 6.1 Schematic description of Internet actors, taken from [121]. Arrows represent a provider-customer (seller-buyer) relationship

trying to get a return on investment by potentially proposing differentiated services. A schematic, even if incomplete, description of the ecosystem is provided in Fig. 6.1. It can be readily seen that even if playing an inescapable role in the delivery chain, ISPs are not the only players which can restrain access to content. The success and quality of a connection between a CP and an end user partly depend on their interactions with other actors. Some examples of such actors in Fig. 6.1 are:

- Content delivery networks (CDNs), storing content closer to users with the goal of reducing transit costs and improving users' quality of experience. But since all content can hardly be stored at the edge, the choice of the favored one can be questioned; this will be detailed in Sect. 6.2.
- Transit networks, which run the network core and may not be in direct contact with ISPs, in a multi-tier architecture of the Internet network topology. A transit network bridges a connection between two other networks. The business models of transit networks vary according to location, but there are usually peering agreements between transit networks, or prices can be on a per-megabit-per-second (Mbps) basis. Being part of the network infrastructure, transit networks are naturally submitted to neutrality rules.
- Device builders and operating system developers. When buying a device, a smartphone, laptop, desktop, or tablet, an operating system and applications may be pre-installed, meaning those tools are favored. On desktops, the most well-

known example is Microsoft, pre-installing its Web browser Explorer from 1994 and prosecuted in 1998 because of that (see Chap. 1). Moreover, applications often have to be downloaded through an application store imposing fees and rules; it is generally the case for smartphones. This creates issues as highlighted by the argument in 2020 between the online game Fortnite and Apple, Fortnite trying to install its own payment rule and being removed from the App Store because of that. In addition, some applications may be available on some operating systems only, for any technical or strategic reason. These general risks of limitation of access to applications have ignited the *neutrality of terminal* issue, which several regulators have started to discuss. It will be hinted in Sect. 6.4.

- Another major class of intermediaries which can strongly affect the visibility of content providers is search engines, which are used to reach specific content from keywords, users expecting to see the most relevant content mentioned first. If search engines manipulate the results, accessibility may be controlled. The whole Chap. 7 will be devoted to that sensitive topic.
- Even news aggregators, social networks, and why not regular news Web sites can be questioned about newsfeed algorithms, as well as Web merchant sites about what they place first, potentially favoring some "content." This related issue will be developed in Chap. 8, since it constitutes a very general problem, not specific to an actor.

All the above bullets illustrate that the current focus on ISP behavior may be too restrictive, particularly in the era of cloud-based content delivery. There is indeed a paradigm change on the management of network operations due to the advent of new actors. As another example, thanks to the virtualization of networks and services, there are more possibilities to dynamically sell network resources and operations. It means here too that ISPs, as well as all other actors, can act on network management in different ways, not only at the packet or flow level, hence many ways to circumvent the packet-based neutrality rules. From an economic point of view, vertically integrating other services on which differentiation can be applied or imposed side payments internalized is another option, investigated in Sect. 6.3. So, can restraining neutrality to a packet-level interpretation of neutrality effectively prevent intermediaries from biasing the competition among CPs? It does not seem easy, and the goal of this chapter is to emphasize that threat.

6.2   Content Delivery Networks: Intermediaries Flying Under the Radar?

6.2.1   Introduction to CDN Role and Impact

A first illustration of a quite recent intermediary, different from an ISP but who can play selfishly and create discrimination, is the case of content delivery networks

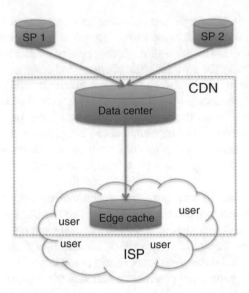

Fig. 6.2 CDN description with here two service providers (SP 1 and SP 2). The CDN stores content in a (remote) data center or at (closer) edge servers

(CDNs). CDNs have appeared in the late 1990s and are "in charge" of taking care of content distribution on behalf of CPs, who can therefore focus on their content generation activity. One of the principles underlying the activity of a CDN is that, instead of sending data from a remote data center each time there is a request, the most frequently asked content can be stored at the edge of the network, as described in Fig. 6.2, or in other possible strategic network positions. CDNs can therefore be defined as organizations of large distributed systems of servers positioned at the edges of the Internet network in addition to data centers. They are supposed to provide benefits to the three traditional families of actors in the Internet (ISPs, CPs, users). Indeed, thanks to this placement of servers at the edges of the network, that is, closer to users, content can be delivered with higher availability and better performance, meaning a better quality and higher satisfaction for CPs and end users. Also, because the most downloaded content is often chosen to be cached at the edges and is not flowing several times through the whole network, the load on the Internet network is reduced, diminishing the pressure on ISPs' to invest on capacity and infrastructure.

CDNs have become a key element of the value and supply chain of the Internet. According to *ResearchandMarket*,[1] the CDN market is poised to grow by $48.48 billions during 2021–2025. The top CDN providers by customer count are Cloudflare, Amazon Web Services (AWS), Akamai, NetDNA, Fastly, Imperva, Verizon, and Microsoft Azure. Cloudflare provides CDN services to over 1 million

---

[1] See   https://www.researchandmarkets.com/reports/5313658/global-content-delivery-network-cdn-market-2021.

customers in 2020, by far the largest on this count, but Akamai has the largest market share since working more with companies, with between 65 and 70% of the market in terms of revenue, still in 2020. According to what is advertised on its Web site[2] as of May 2021, Akamai spans approximately 300,000 servers in more than 130 countries and within more than 1500 networks around the world.

CDNs impact the way traffic is exchanged between service providers and therefore their economic relationships [89, 153]. It is also often wondered whether CDNs should be seen as competitors of transit providers because of their similar per-volume charging and because in a sense they also provide a connectivity service. With the increasing importance of this activity in the value chain of content delivery, many actors have started developing a CDN activity, including Internet service providers (ISPs), content providers, and equipment vendors [24, 155]. Nothing seems to prevent such CDN activity development, but this "new" activity can be seen as a way to circumvent packet-based neutrality rules. Indeed, what prevents from caching content in edge servers based on money-driven motivations and providing the service to the most offering CP? Packets flowing through the network would then be treated the same, but from an end-to-end point of view, there is service differentiation. If ISPs, the "regular" target of neutrality rules, can develop a CDN activity, it means that they can favor content to bypass the rules; this *vertical integration* of activities will be discussed in Sect. 6.3. Caching is not regulated by legal frameworks that are favorable to net neutrality, such as the Open Internet Order issued by the FCC in 2015. Under neutrality, prioritization of a class of traffic is allowed under very constrained requirements, while with caching, a differentiation is made within the same type of traffic. The issue also leads to the question of what a "fair" or "neutral" strategy in terms of stored content should be. The accepted idea is to store the most frequently downloaded content to reduce as much as possible the charge on the network and to optimize user experience, but this introduces the debatable notion of fairness since CPs could feel they are not being treated similarly. Note finally that CDNs relieve the stress on service delivery platforms, but not on the last mile where congestion occurs predominantly [155].

CDN business activity, its impact on access, content perception, and therefore innovation and economic fairness, brings the question about their inclusion in the network neutrality debate. The next two subsections illustrate how business-driven CDNs impact the Internet and other economics actors, using mathematical models. Other works on CDN modeling and analysis can be found in [36, 73, 74, 119].

6.2.2 Model Illustrating the Impact of CDNs on Competition Between CPs

We summarize here a model from [70, 118] analyzing the impact of a revenue-maximizing CDN on other actors, namely, end users, network providers, and content

---

[2] https://www.akamai.com/.

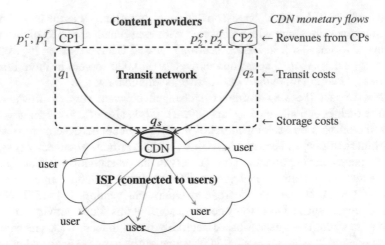

Fig. 6.3 Model representing one CDN, two CPs, and the related economic flows

providers, and comparing it with a neutral behavior (more details and rigorous proofs can be found in the mentioned references). The CDN has to dimension and optimally use its infrastructure, sharing it among its clients (content/service providers) so as to maximize its revenue. Figure 6.3 presents a model with two CPs, both being customers of the CDN. In terms of economic flows, each CP has to pay the CDN for its service. More precisely, we can assume that the CDN charges per unit of data volume delivered to users, with a unit price depending on whether users are served from the cache server (unit price p_i^c for CP i, $i = 1, 2$) or from the CP origin data center, meaning with lower QoS (unit price $p_i^f < p_i^c$ for CP i). In a differentiated case, prices can be different between CPs, while such a differentiation is not allowed in a "neutral" situation. For the CDN, there is a transit cost q_i per unit of volume for sending data from CPs origin servers to users, with a possible different cost due to different paths. On the other hand, from the edge servers (i.e., for content cached close to the users), no cost is assumed to be incurred. We assume these prices and costs fixed and wish to analyze the CDN strategy in terms of cached content selection and its impact on users, CPs, and load on the network. More specifically, we can investigate *(i)* the dimensioning of the storage servers (which has a cost; we aim at looking at the trade-off with the expected gain) and *(ii)* the caching strategy: what content to cache among the two CPs? Note that in any case, among the content from one CP, it is optimal to cache at the edge the most downloaded one (due to more revenue generated from downloads and less frequently incurred transfer costs).

To describe the interest of caching, we need to express the popularity of the content provided by each CP through a function $F_i(x)$, $i = 1, 2$, representing the minimum number of requests per time unit for the x most popular units of content of CP i. Functions F_i are assumed continuous and strictly decreasing; power-law functions of the form $F_i(x) = A_i x^{-\alpha_i}$ (with $A_i, \alpha_i > 0$) are typically used in real life [1], defined for $x \geq x_{i,\min}$ (therefore assuming $F_i(x) = 0$ for $x < x_{i,\min}$).

To simplify notations, define the cumulated user download throughput from requests for the volume y of the most popular content from CP i as:

$$G_i(y) := \int_{x=0}^{y} F_i(x) \, dx = \frac{1}{1-\alpha}(x_{i,\min}^{-\alpha+1} - y^{-\alpha+1})$$

and the total user download throughput of CP i content:

$$\bar{G}_i = G_i(V_i)$$

for $i = 1, 2$, where V_i is the total volume of content proposed by CP i, $i = 1, 2$ and where we assume $C \le \min(V_1, V_2)$ (meaning that the CDN cannot store all the content from any CP).

The income of the CDN depends on the storage capacity C but also the *chosen* capacity C_1 allocated to CP 1 and capacity $C_2 = C - C_1$ allocated to CP 2 content at the edge. From the storage prices described in Fig. 6.3 and download values, the income is:

$$p_1^c G_1(C_1) + p_1^f(\bar{G}_1 - G_1(C_1)) + p_2^c G_2(C - C_1) + p_2^f(\bar{G}_2 - G_2(C - C_1))$$
$$= p_1^f \bar{G}_1 + (p_1^c - p_1^f)G_1(C_1) + p_2^f \bar{G}_2 + (p_2^c - p_2^f)G_2(C - C_1)$$

multiplying prices by volumes downloaded from the different locations.

In terms of costs, assuming the CDN cannot cache all the content from any CP, that is, $C \le \min(V_1, V_2)$, the storage cost is $q_s C$. For the transit costs, we neglect the one-shot costs for the content stored in the CDN cache: therefore, transit costs only correspond to the content that is not in the cache, and for each CP, they are proportional to the aggregated download rate for that content. The total transit costs therefore equal:

$$q_1(\bar{G}_1 - G_1(C_1)) + q_2(\bar{G}_2 - G_2(C - C_1)).$$

It leads to a CDN revenue (or utility):

$$R(C, C_1) = r_1^f \bar{G}_1 + (p_1^c - r_1^f)G_1(C_1) + r_2^f \bar{G}_2 + (p_2^c - r_2^f)G_2(C - C_1) - q_s C, \tag{6.1}$$

with $r_i^f := p_i^f - q_i$ for $i = 1, 2$.

Define the quality experienced by users as Q_c for the cached content and $Q_{f,1}$, $Q_{f,2}$ for content for SP 1 and SP 2, respectively, with $Q_{f,i} < Q_c$. The aggregated quality experienced by users is:

$$Q_c(G_1(C_1) + G_2(C - C_1)) + Q_{f,1}(\bar{G}_1 - G_1(C_1)) + Q_{f,2}(\bar{G}_2 - G_2(C - C_1)).$$

The average user experienced quality is then:

$$Q^{\text{tot}} = \frac{1}{\bar{G}_1 + \bar{G}_2} \sum_{i=1}^{2} \left(Q_c(G_i(C_i) + Q_{f,1}(\bar{G}_i - G_i(C_i))) \right).$$

A revenue-driven CDN has to decide the total storage capacity C as well as the amount C_1 allocated to CP 1. We are going to investigate, for a given C, the optimal C_1; optimizing the full storage capacity is also possible; see [70].

Let the total storage capacity C be fixed. We have the following result: There exists a unique optimal value C_1^{opt} of C_1 maximizing the net revenue of the CDN:

- $C_1^{\text{opt}} = C$ if $(p_1^c - r_1^f)F_1(C) \geq (p_2^c - r_2^f)F_2(0)$
- $C_1^{\text{opt}} = 0$ if $(p_1^c - r_1^f)F_1(0) \leq (p_2^c - r_2^f)F_2(C)$
- C_1^{opt} is the unique solution in $(0, C)$ of

$$\frac{F_1(x)}{F_2(C - x)} = \frac{p_2^c - r_2^f}{p_1^c - r_1^f} \qquad \text{otherwise.} \tag{6.2}$$

With power laws F_i (of the form $F_i(x) = A_i x^{-\alpha} \mathbb{1}_{\{x \geq x_{i,\min}\}}$), with $x_{i,\min}$ small enough to end up within $(0, C)$, Equation (6.2) becomes:

$$\frac{x}{C - x} = \left(\frac{A_1}{A_2} \frac{p_1^c + q_1 - p_1^f}{p_2^c + q_2 - p_2^f} \right)^{1/\alpha},$$

giving:

$$C_1^{\text{opt}} = \frac{C}{1 + \left(\frac{A_2}{A_1} \frac{p_2^c + q_2 - p_2^f}{p_1^c + q_1 - p_1^f} \right)^{1/\alpha}}. \tag{6.3}$$

Indeed, from (6.1), given that each function G_i $(i = 1, 2)$ is continuously differentiable with derivative F_i, strictly increasing and strictly concave on $[0, V_i]$, we have that $R(C, C_1)$ is a strictly concave function of C_1 for C fixed, leading to a unique solution C_1^{opt}. Differentiating $R(C, C_1)$ with respect to C_1 yields:

$$\frac{\partial R(C, C_1)}{\partial C_1} = (p_1^c - r_1^f)F_1(C_1) - (p_2^c - r_2^f)F_2(C - C_1),$$

giving the result stated above (either there is a unique solution for which the derivative is equal to 0 or it is always of the same sign).

This choice C_1^{opt} should be compared with that in "neutral" situations. But what do "neutral" or "fair" mean here? We can actually think of several relevant definitions for what might be considered a neutral CDN.

- A CDN treating content in a way independent of the origin, choosing C_i such that $F_1(C_1) = F_2(C_2)$, i.e., caching the most popular content whatever the origin; that behavior corresponds to what is typically expected.
- A CDN allocating the same amount $C/2$ to both CPs, i.e., treating them in an equal way whatever their content.
- A CDN providing the same average user QoE to all CPs, i.e., choosing C_i such that for all i, j:

$$Q_c \frac{G_i(C_i)}{\bar{G}_i} + Q_{f,i}\left(1 - \frac{G_i(C_i)}{\bar{G}_i}\right)$$

$$= Q_c \frac{G_j(C_j)}{\bar{G}_j} + Q_{f,j}\left(1 - \frac{G_j(C_i)}{\bar{G}_j}\right). \tag{6.4}$$

- A CDN ensuring the same *hit-ratio* to all CPs, i.e., choosing C_i such that:

$$\frac{G_i(C_i)}{\bar{G}_i} = \frac{G_j(C_j)}{\bar{G}_j}.$$

That alternative is actually a special case of (6.4), obtained when $Q_{f,i} = Q_{f,j}$ for all i, j.

The four above notions of a fair treatment illustrate how complicated it can be to define what neutral should be, since all of them seem to make sense.

Let us now illustrate numerically the impact of a revenue-driven CDN and compare with the two first above notions of fairness. Figures 6.4 and 6.5 display the frequency of cached content $F_i(C_i^{\text{opt}})$ for CP 1 and CP 2 and all caching strategies in terms of α and p_1^c, respectively, when the other parameters are fixed to $C = 1$, $\alpha = 2$, $A_1 = 1$, $A_2 = 2$, $p_2^c = 1.1$, $q_2 = 0.7$, $p_2^f = 0.8$, $p_1^c = 1$, $q_1 = 0.5$, and $p_1^f = 0.7$. Sensible differences may mean an unfair treatment between CPs. Figure 6.4 suggests that the value α does not seem to have an important impact on "fairness" (which could be seen as similar values of frequencies whatever the parameter value), even if some variations are observed. The larger α though, the larger the difference between CPs but also between policies. Unsurprisingly, the policy such that $F_1(C_1) = F_2(C_2)$ is the middle curve, but assigning the same amount of cache to both CPs is here less "fair" than the revenue-maximizing policy. Other parameters such as prices in Fig. 6.5 have on the other hand a major impact. The difference can be significant.

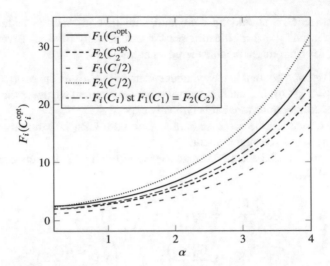

Fig. 6.4 $F_i(C_i^{\mathrm{opt}})$ in terms of α

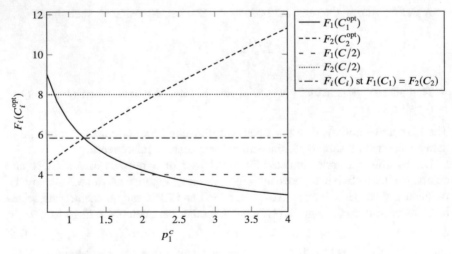

Fig. 6.5 $F_i(C_i^{\mathrm{opt}})$ in terms of p_1^c

Let us now investigate the impact of the CDN strategy on users. We consider three representative scenarios, where in each case the transit costs are the same:

(i) Both service providers pay the same price for the CDN service. In this *regular* scenario, the main question is whether the dominance of the incumbent prevents the growth of the challenger.

(ii) The incumbent player deploys an aggressive strategy where it pays ten times what its competitors pays for the CDN service. It is one of the most critical

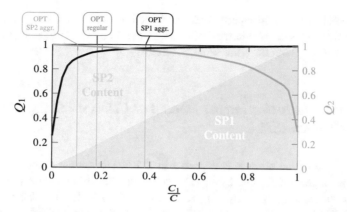

Fig. 6.6 Normalized quality of experience for both service providers CP1 and CP2 according to the ratio of the cache filled with content from CP1

questions in the net neutrality debate: Can a well-established player prevent one competitor from growing?

(iii) Finally, the challenger is now the one that is aggressive.

Regarding the parameters adopted in the scenarios, we extracted from traffic traces the information about the videos, meaning V_i, G_i, and $\bar{G}_i$. More specifically, our measurement dataset,[3] collected in 2014, includes two video-streaming CPs: *(i)* an *incumbent*, namely, *justin.tv* (now replaced with Twitch), then a well-established service, and *(ii)* a *challenger*, namely, YouTube Live, with a smaller population of streamers. In the following, CP2 refers to justin.tv, while CP1 is YouTube Live.

Based on CDNs and Amazon pricing,[4] the remaining parameters we considered are as follows: $p_i^f = 0.005$, $p_i^c = 0.5$, $q_s = 0.0000053$, $q_i = 0.94$, $Q_c = 2$, $Q_{f,i} = 0.5$, and $C = 50$. For scenarios *(ii)* and *(iii)*, we defined $p_1^c = 5$ and $p_2^c = 5$, respectively. We show in Fig. 6.6 the QoE experienced by the end users of both service providers with regard to the evolution of the ratio of the cache that is filled with CP1 content (recall that CP1 is the challenger YouTube). The QoE of CP1 users is represented by Q_1 (black line) and that of CP2 users by Q_2 (gray line). We show with thin vertical lines the optimal values of $\dfrac{C_1}{C}$ for the three considered scenarios. Our main observation is that, due to the heterogeneity of video popularity, the impact of aggressive strategies is limited in all cases. By choosing to maximize its revenues, the CDN serves more content from CP2 in the regular scenario, which in turn leads to a better overall QoE for users of CP2. But the QoE remains excellent for CP1 as well (more than 0.9 of the best possible). More interestingly, both aggressive policies are not worth the price. In both cases, the CDN adjusts the ratio $\dfrac{C_1}{C}$ accordingly to maximize its revenues, but in both

---

[3] Dataset available at http://is.gd/tM6xmH.

[4] https://is.gd/CArKkn, http://aws.amazon.com/s3/pricing/.

cases, its QoE is not significantly affected. Note however that the incumbent acting aggressively affects the challenger's QoE (we observe a 10% QoE reduction), while the challenger does not have the same possibility.

6.2.3   Model Illustrating the Impact of CDNs on Competition Between ISPs

Following one of the situations depicted in [120], let us now show that revenue-oriented management policies by a CDN can impact the competition among network access providers in favor of the largest one. In this sense, it may also be seen as a non-neutral behavior. We consider a CDN in charge of storing and delivering content on behalf of a number n of CPs. The CDN manages an *intermediate* or *regional server* (denoted by R), which is shared by all CPs, and optionally an *edge server* in each **ISP!** (**ISP!**). Figure 6.7 depicts the situation where an edge server is placed at ISP A, while none is placed at ISP B. Indeed, CDNs may or may not dispose of edge servers in ISPs' networks depending on bilateral agreements. While there are several possibilities, such as when the CDN sometimes has to pay a fee to the ISP for the rental of a rack in an ISP's colocation center [37], we consider in this section the case where the CDN pays the ISP for the rental of storage resources in privileged network locations [147].

As in the previous section, we assume that each piece of content may have a different popularity (number of requests). This popularity may also be different for users of ISP A or ISP B, with respective values given by x_A and x_B. Indeed, different countries, for instance, have different interests even if there usually is some correlation. The CDN is charging CPs a higher price p_A when their content is

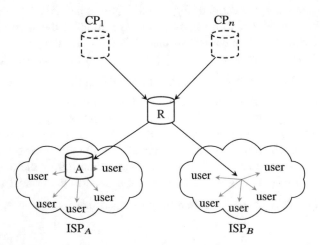

Fig. 6.7 CDN caching with a regional server and when only ISP A include an edge server

Table 6.1 Marginal differences in the revenue depending on the decisions for a piece of content with popularity $x = (x_A, x_B)$ (*Reference case: the content is not stored close to end-users*)

Where to store	Marginal objective variation
nowhere	0
in R only	$(x_A + x_B)r_R - \lambda_R$
in A only	$x_A r_A - \lambda_A$
in R and A	$x_A r_A + x_B r_R - \lambda_R - \lambda_A$

downloaded from the edge server in ISP A, since producing a better QoE for users, while it is p_R (with $p_R < p_A$) when downloaded for the regional server. There are on the other hand transit costs per content unit for the CDN to download content from the origin server to the regional server (denoted by q_R) or to the server in ISP A (denoted by q_A). Those transit costs are borne by the CDN, hence an incentive to cache popular content to avoid undergoing those costs for each download. Based on those values, we express the extra revenue for the CDN per unit of content served from the regional cache or the one within ISP A, that we, respectively, denote by r_R and r_A, compared with a CDN cache miss (service from the origin server). In addition to the received payment p_j, the CDN also saves q_j in transit costs; hence, $r_j = p_j + q_j$ for $j \in \{R, A\}$. In addition, there are storage costs, λ_R and λ_A, for the marginal prices (per time unit) for storage: those values appear when maximizing the CDN revenue under the capacity constraints. We assume here that costs are linear, with marginal prices λ_R and λ_A fixed and known, but these values can also be interpreted as Lagrangian multipliers in the case of capacity constraints in R and A (see [120] for details if needed; note that in this case, there are unknowns, which complicates a bit the analysis).

The CDN has four ways to store a given piece of content: in none of the edge servers (*i.e.*, in the origin server), in R only, in A only, or in both R and A. The four storing options are given in Table 6.1, with the corresponding marginal variations in the revenue optimization problem. The table indicates where to store each piece of content, since the principle for a revenue-maximizing CDN is to choose the option with the largest marginal objective variation.

Figure 6.8 summarizes the one-to-one comparisons of Table 6.1 and illustrates the best caching decisions as a function of the content popularity (x_A, x_B), for given values of λ_I and λ_A.

The figure highlights the impact that the edge server A can have on the QoE of customers of ISP$_B$. More precisely, consider some content with a given popularity x_B, and assume that $x_B \in \left(\dfrac{\lambda_R}{r_R} - \dfrac{\lambda_A}{r_A}, \dfrac{\lambda_R}{r_R} \right)$. In that case, the quality perceived by population B for that content depends on the content popularity among population A:

- If $x_A < \dfrac{\lambda_R}{r_R} - x_B$, the content is not cached at all, and users in population B get basic quality.

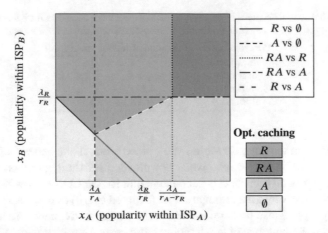

Fig. 6.8 Optimal caching decisions when there is no cache in B ($\lambda_R = 1.5, \lambda_A = 2, r_R = 1,$ $r_A = 2$)

- If $x_A \in [\dfrac{\lambda_R}{r_r} - x_B, \tilde{x}_A)$ with $\tilde{x}_A = \dfrac{\lambda_A}{r_R} + (x_B - \dfrac{\lambda_R}{r_R})(\dfrac{r_A}{r_R} - 1)$, the content is stored in the intermediate cache R; therefore, users in both populations get better (say, medium) quality.
- If $x_A > \tilde{x}_A$, the content is kept in cache A; hence, users in population A get top quality, while those in population B only get basic quality.

The same type of analysis shows that the quality perceived by population A for some content depends on the popularity of that content in population from ISP B: some content that is popular in ISP_B can be cached in R instead of A, which can thus slightly degrade the QoE of users in ISP A.

6.3   Issues Related to Vertical Integration

6.3.1   Vertical Integration and the Internet Ecosystem

Another issue becoming prevalent in the network neutrality debate is related to so-called vertical integration.

In the complex supply "chain" of content delivery to end users, as depicted in Fig. 6.1, actors may be interested in controlling several steps of the chain. Owning different steps is called vertical integration and is known to present several advantages and increase benefits for the tenant, even increase efficiency for customers/users. But vertical integration can also "kill" competition and hence harm innovation. Rules determining whether vertical integration is good or bad are often derived from the theory developed by the Chicago school of antitrust analysis. The rules are followed and used in the guidelines "Vertical Merger Guidelines" promulgated in 1984 in the USA. Basically, preconditions for vertical integration to be harmful are:

1. The integrated actor has a powerful position in a concentrated market.
2. The "secondary" market in which the provider will be integrated must be concentrated and protected by barriers to entry.

This topic has to be monitored in the digital economy because the telecommunication industry, at the origin of the Internet, used to be highly integrated. Indeed, in the twentieth century, telephony was a monopoly in many countries and almost fully integrated, in the sense that companies were detaining almost all the different steps of the supply chain, from device building to network infrastructure installation and maintenance and even the different types of services offering. But in order to introduce competition, many companies were forced to split their services, obeying antitrust regulation. Typical examples are AT&T in the USA or British Telecom in 1984 or France Telecom in France. Even if with the Internet the market has been expanded in terms of actor types and numbers of players at each level, there is still some concern about attempts to vertically integrate services and how they may impact the network neutrality debate (see also [96]), especially when it comes to major actors like the GAFAMs (for Google, Apple, Facebook, Amazon, and Microsoft). Examples of vertical integration of services in the Internet, and sometimes related complains, include:

- ISPs typically proposing portals with news and other applications. That way, they are favoring their own services, or services paying to be partners. Portals are also a way to earn additional money, thanks to displayed advertisements.
- Vertical integration from the merging of major actors, such as the failed tentative between AOL (an ISP) and Time Warner (a media and entertainment leader) in 2000 for a venture worth $350 billion or in 2011 the merger between Comcast (ISP and TV operator) and NBC-Universal (TV program maker).
- The GAFAMs, with their increasing share of the economy, being under scrutiny of the antitrust rules because of their vertically integrated business. For example, Google started with a search engine activity but now integrates services (YouTube, the Chrome browser, etc.), an application store (PlayStore), an operating system (Android), a service of advertisement management (Google Ads), and cloud services (Google Cloud Platform) and builds its own smartphones and televisions and many other things. Google even manages its own networking infrastructure and free in-home wireless broadband service.[5] The same type of service expansion analysis can be obtained for the other GAFAMs: Microsoft expanding from an operating system development company to software development (including the Windows Office suite) and creating the Xbox game console, the Surface Tablet and other hardware devices, the Bing search engine and its related sponsored ad revenues, some cloud services, etc.; Apple now combining

---

[5] See http://www.google.com/tisp/.

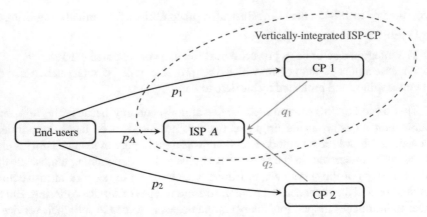

Fig. 6.9 Charging interactions between stakeholders with two CPs and one ISP, one CP 1 being vertically integrated with the ISP

hardware (computers, iPods, iPhones, or iPads) and software services (its own operating systems, iTunes, and Apple Store taxing revenues from application developers); and Amazon creating the AWS cloud services, its own content platform, etc. Those companies face antitrust procedures, the most notable example being the action against Microsoft in 2001, initially sentenced to be dismantled after forcing by default its own Web browser, Internet Explorer, into its operating system.

- Spotify accusing Apple in 2021 of unfair competition by benefiting from the vertical integration of Apple Music, exonerated from the 30% of commission fee applied to its store [7];[6] the European Union is following Spotify on this argument.

6.3.2   Illustration of Vertical Integration on Our Basic Model

To better illustrate the impact of vertical integration, let us come back to the model detailed in Section 4.3 made of one ISP and two CPs in competition, but where we assume here that one CP is vertically integrated with the ISP, say, without loss of generality, CP 1. Figure 6.9 is just a "modification" of Fig. 4.5 by regrouping ISP A and CP 1 into a single entity. Recall that there are subscription prices for users, p_A, p_1, and p_2 to, respectively, ISP A, CP 1, and CP 2. Side payments q_1 and q_2 are, respectively, charged to CP 1 and CP 2 by the ISP, but since ISP A and CP 1 are integrated, q_1 will not be perceived by the "federation." Note that because of that, non-neutrality and weak neutrality (imposing the same side payment to both

---

[6] See also https://ec.europa.eu/commission/presscorner/detail/en/IP_21_2061.

CPs) will not make any difference here. Recall also the options (and their labels) for users:

- Option 1: Subscription to ISP A and CP 1, with total price $p_A + p_1$;
- Option 2: Subscription to ISP A and CP 2, at price $p_A + \beta p_2$;
- Option A: Subscription to ISP A only, with perceived price $p = kp_A$ with $k > 1$ increased perception of price for not CPs' services;
- Option 0: No subscription at all: cost p_0.

With the same developments as in Section 4.3, we obtain the following market shares (restricting ourselves to $\alpha = 2$):

$$\sigma_1 = \frac{(p_A + p_1)^{-2}}{(p_A + p_1)^{-2} + (p_A + \beta p_2)^{-2} + (kp_A)^{-2} + p_0^{-2}}$$

$$\sigma_2 = \frac{(p_A + \beta p_2)^{-2}}{(p_A + p_1)^{-2} + (p_A + \beta p_2)^{-2} + (kp_A)^{-2} + p_0^{-2}}$$

$$\sigma_A = \frac{(kp_A)^{-2}}{(p_A + p_1)^{-2} + (p_A + \beta p_2)^{-2} + (kp_A)^{-2} + p_0^{-2}}$$

$$\sigma_0 = \frac{p_0^{-2}}{(p_A + p_1)^{-2} + (p_A + \beta p_2)^{-2} + (kp_A)^{-2} + p_0^{-2}}.$$

Summing the utilities/revenues of the ISP and CP 1 yields the revenue of the vertically integrated ISP-CP:

$$U_{\text{Vert}} = (p_A + p_1)\sigma_1 + (p_A + q_2)\sigma_2 + p_A\sigma_A. \tag{6.5}$$

The revenue of CP 2, user, and social welfare are still (see Section 4.3):

$$U_2 = (p_2 - q_2)\sigma_2$$

$$\text{UW} = p_0 \left(\frac{p_0}{kp_A}\right)^2 + p_0 \left(\frac{p_0}{p_A + p_1}\right)^2 + p_0 \left(\frac{p_0}{p_A + \beta p_2}\right)^2$$

$$\text{SW} = \text{UW} + U_{\text{Vert}} + U_2$$

$$= p_0 \left(\frac{p_0}{kp_A}\right)^2 + p_0 \left(\frac{p_0}{p_A + p_1}\right)^2 + p_0 \left(\frac{p_0}{p_A + \beta p_2}\right)^2 +$$

$$\frac{p_A}{1 + \left(\frac{kp_A}{p_A + p_1}\right)^2 + \left(\frac{kp_A}{p_A + \beta p_2}\right)^2 + \left(\frac{kp_A}{p_0}\right)^2}$$

$$+ \frac{p_A + p_1}{1 + \left(\frac{p_A+p_1}{kp_A}\right)^2 + \left(\frac{p_A+p_1}{p_0}\right)^2 + \left(\frac{p_A+p_1}{p_A+\beta p_2}\right)^2}$$

$$+ \frac{p_A + p_2}{1 + \left(\frac{p_A+\beta p_2}{kp_A}\right)^2 + \left(\frac{p_A+\beta p_2}{p_0}\right)^2 + \left(\frac{p_A+\beta p_2}{p_A+p_1}\right)^2}.$$

Again, decisions are taken at different time scales. First, ISP A chooses q_2 (only in the non-neutral case) and p_A, then, charges imposed by the ISP being fixed, there is a game between CPs on subscription prices p_1 and p_2, to attract users and maximize their revenues, and finally users decide whether and which providers to subscribe to, depending on the prices. As we did already several times in this book, the analysis of decisions is realized by *backward induction*.

Following the analysis in Sect. 4.3.5 with $p_0 = 0.1$, $\beta = 1.5$, and $k = 2$, the outputs of the neutral scenario ($q_2 = 0$) and non-neutral scenario (q_2 determined by the vertically integrated ISP-CP) are displayed in Table 6.2. Note that it may be optimal for the ISP/CP 1 to set $p_1 < 0$, but we limit for now ourselves to $p_1 \geq 0$ to avoid a visible anticompetitive behavior. In this case, the vertically integrated ISP-CP imposes no side payment to the competitive CP ($q_2 = 0$) exactly as in the fully neutral case, somehow contrary to what intuition could be.

If on the other hand we do not limit prices to be non-negative, the outputs are provided in Table 6.3. Again, allowing side payments does not lead the integrated ISP-CP to impose any side payment ($q_2 = 0$), leading to a neutral case. But it is then optimal for the integrated ISP-CP to *pay* users for access to CP 1 ($p_1 < 0$). It leads to an increased subscription price to ISP A, from 0.122 to 0.129, and a slightly increased revenue for the integrated ISP-CP, but a slightly reduced CP 2 revenue, user, and social welfare. Allowing negative prices is therefore not "recommended" from a regulator point of view.

It may also be interesting to compare the outputs of Tables 6.2 and 6.3 with that of Table 4.4 in the *non-integrated* case. Integrating services increases the subscription

Table 6.2 Comparison of neutral and non-neutral scenarios with a vertically integrated CP when $p_0 = 0.1$, $\beta = 1.5$, and $k = 2$, under constraint $p_1 \geq 0$

Scenario	Fully-neutral	Non-neutral
q_2	0	0
p_A	0.122	0.122
p_1	0	0
p_2	0.09503	0.09503
σ_A	0.08471	0.08471
σ_1	0.3389	0.3389
σ_2	0.07207	0.07207
U_{Vert}	0.06047	0.06047
U_2	0.006849	0.006849
UW	0.09827	0.09827
SW	0.1656	0.1656

Table 6.3 Comparison of neutral and non-neutral scenarios with a vertically integrated CP when $p_0 = 0.1$, $\beta = 1.5$, and $k = 2$ when $p_1 < 0$ is allowed

Scenario	Fully-neutral	Non-neutral
q_2	0	0
p_A	0.129	0.129
p_1	-0.008001	-0.008001
p_2	0.09910	0.09910
σ_A	0.07653	0.07653
σ_1	0.3480	0.3480
σ_2	0.06608	0.06608
U_{Vert}	0.06050	0.06050
U_2	0.006549	0.006549
UW	0.09630	0.09630
SW	0.1633	0.1633

price of ISP A (from 0.8–0.9 to 0.121–0.129), and the sum of revenues of ISP A and CP 1 is significantly increased, thanks to integration, at the expense of CP 2, which may be seen as anticompetitive. But integrating services increases user and social welfare.

6.3.3   Other Illustrations and Results from Models

In the literature, the impact of vertical integration is often shown to be non-negligible. Still about integrating a CP and an ISP, it is argued in [40, 54], as shown with our model in the previous subsection, that setting high side payments will limit profits from competitive CPs. This is in line with the general result that vertical integration changes the nature of competition [72]. In [66], with a model including congestion analysis, vertical integration is similarly to our model shown to benefit the vertically integrated components *and also* users; there are even (high-congestion) conditions under which it even benefits non-integrated CPs. Note that depending on the model, there is no absolute consensus since, for example, [35] claims, using a different model, that vertical integration has no impact on resource allocation and as a consequence that no concern has to come from a vertical merging between an ISP and a CP.

As illustrated above, there are also many situations of vertical integration of other types of actors that could lead to unfair competition and threaten to breach innovation and access, two of the main motivations of setting network neutrality rules. Such situations can concern ISPs who could use integration to circumvent neutrality rules, but also other types of actors.

Consider CDNs, for example. We have described in Sect. 6.2 the particular and important role of CDNs in the delivery chain of content to users. All actors, not only ISPs, may be interested in embracing this type of activity. That includes major transit network operators, with as an illustration the provider Level 3 which has shifted a fraction of its activities to CDN. Hardware builders such as Alcatel-Lucent and Cisco also leverage their activity to develop CDN services, since easily developing the required infrastructure. Major CPs such as Google, Netflix, and Dailymotion also deploy their own CDN infrastructure to be closer to users and not depend on traditional CDN actors. Particularly for ISPs, the regular target of neutrality, it may make sense to vertically integrate a CDN, with an impact that requires to be investigated. A model in [122] is devoted to this question, with the possibility for the vertically integrated ISP to *partially* offer CDN services to competitors in order to optimize the trade-off between CDN revenue (if fully offered) and competitive advantage on subscriptions at the ISP level (if not offered to competitors). Somewhat surprisingly, it is shown in [122] that an ISP may prefer an independent CDN over controlling (integrating) a CDN, while on the other hand, users prefer a vertical integration to an independent CDN. These two outputs are counterintuitive and may be of interest for a regulator. Similarly, using a type of model close to the ones presented in this section, it has been shown in [105] that vertically integrating a CDN can help ISPs to charge CPs but that this results in an outcome that is socially much better in terms of user quality and innovation fostering than having separate actors providing the access and CDN services. Indeed, in the latter case, double marginalization, consisting of both ISP and CDN trying to get some value from the supply chain, leads to suboptimal investments in CDN storage capacities and higher prices for CPs and results in reduced innovation.

6.4   Device Neutrality

Putting Internet actors other than ISPs under scrutiny due to threats to an open Internet is therefore of increasing concern from regulators' point of view. Another illustration regards the choice of the terminal to access the Internet, and its consequences, leading to the question about the *neutrality of the terminal*, or *device neutrality*. For example, ARCEP, the French regulator, is wondering in its 2020 report on the state of the Internet [7] about OS (operating system) neutrality with respect to developers. A recent typical issue was on the limitations imposed to the French state when aiming at developing its own StopCovid application to trace infected contacts during the pandemic, while OS companies were developing their own tools. Other relevant examples already mentioned in previous chapters are Apple threatening to remove Spotify in 2016 and the Fornite game in 2020 for trying to generate revenue without following the App Store rules.

The issue of the browser choice depending on the device is still of major concern, and has not stopped with the action against Microsoft when the company was pre-installing its own browser, Internet Explorer. According again to [7], in France, less than 20% of smartphone owners use a browser different from the pre-installed one, and two thirds have not even ever tested another one; but a majority change if they test. Terminal builders/OS developers can then incentivize to use some applications or direct to some content at the expense of others, in contradiction with the neutrality spirit.

A definition of terminal/device neutrality has been imagined by analogy with the network neutrality for ISPs; here is the Wikipedia definition:[7]

> Device neutrality is the principle that in order to ensure freedom of choice and freedom of communication for users of network-connected devices, it is not sufficient that network operators do not interfere with their choices and activities; users must be free to use applications of their choice and hence remove the applications they do not want.

Several regulators are trying to pass bills to impose device/terminal neutrality, and in December 2020, the European Union included device neutrality in the final draft of the Digital Markets Act.

6.5   Neutrality of Structuring Platforms

Structuring platforms, also often named *gatekeepers*, are usually defined as the largest digital platforms detaining a very significant and lasting market power. Among examples, we can cite the GAFAM (Google, Apple, Facebook, Amazon, Microsoft), but the notion more generally involves *(i)* marketplaces (Amazon, eBay, or marketplaces specific to hotel booking such as Expedia, Booking.com, ebookers, and Hotels.com), *(ii)* community-based platforms (Airbnb, BlaBlaCar), *(iii)* application stores (App Store for Apple on iOS, Play Store for Google on Android, Windows Phone Store for Microsoft, Huawei AppGallery for Huawei), and *(iv)* social networks (Facebook, YouTube, Twitter).

These platforms can use their dominant position to create barriers to entry for competitors, control the supply chain, and cannibalize the market.

There is a strong willingness to put structuring platforms under scrutiny, particularly in Europe, in line with the neutrality spirit. But how to define rules to assert whether a company is a structuring platform? The German Competition Act[8] lists as criteria:

- Massive network effects as well as economies of scale, meaning gaining a huge value from their number of users; criteria in terms of turnover or audience are under investigation.
- A market power restricting competition on the market, inducing an economic dependence of "users" (which can be end users or companies wishing to sell products in a two-sided market). Criteria of evaluation could deal with switching/migrating costs when willing to access the service differently.

---

[7] See https://en.wikipedia.org/wiki/Device_neutrality.

[8] https://www.gesetze-im-internet.de/englisch_gwb/.

- Innovation-driven competitive pressure, which can result from vertical integration, a quasi-monopoly of access to service or to strategical data (see next sections), etc.

This issue is connected with the next section and the *transparency of algorithms* issue we will develop in Chap. 8.

6.6   Also Toward Data Neutrality?

One of the main aspect of structuring platforms is that their "power" relies on the massive amount of data they can exploit, and that gives them a competitive advantage over potential innovative competitors. Platforms have a transparency obligation, a requirement to inform their users and business partners about the data they gather and to let the possibility to verify and control the collected data. This aspect will be also further developed in Chap. 8, on the transparency of algorithms.

Regulators are currently wondering about several possible data neutrality requirements:

- Access to data for users as already required by law, but also for competitors since data access can constitute a barrier to entry in some markets. A typical example is Amazon Marketplace Web Service (Amazon MWS) giving access to some API to sellers, on inventory and sale payment, but does not necessarily give access to data such as buyers' full identity and address, or data on clicks over the platform, which could be useful to better address needs. Therefore, Amazon MWS is the inescapable actor if you want to sell, as the largest selling place but also because it keeps most useful information private. This may lead to a too powerful actor with an anticompetitive behavior and harm innovation.
- Service interoperability, to ensure a decentralized management of data and allow the transmission to (other) service providers if users are asking for it. This would significantly ease the migration from an ecosystem to another.

Chapter 7
Search Neutrality

As developed in Chap. 3, the arguments about neutrality revolve around high-level principles like freedom, user welfare, or innovation. While historically the focus in the debate has been on network operators' behavior—hence the initial neutrality definitions focusing on traffic treatment—Chap. 6 has highlighted that several other actors can also play a role related to the principles that net neutrality proponents and opponents intend to defend, in many cases without violating the operator-targeting neutrality policies that could be defined. In short, any actor whose decisions artificially distort the user quality of experience for some services, and might monetize or get any advantage from that power, should be considered within the neutrality debate.

In the case of network operators, their role as an intermediary in the data supply chain from the content provider to the user justifies them being seen as *gatekeepers*, and with that position comes the power of differentiating, which is the main concern of this book. But *search engines*, which we all use daily to find information regarding products and services, have a somewhat similar position. Indeed, while not being physically intermediaries between users and contents, they are definitely gatekeepers as well, since they can decide in which position, and even whether at all, a user will see (and therefore possibly access) some specific piece of content. So in the process leading to a user accessing content, search engines hold a key position, with enormous economical power. Hence, the behavior of search engines has been under scrutiny by government and regulators, including the US Senate [151], the Federal Trade Commission [27], and the European Union.

While we are stepping slightly aside from the initial *net* neutrality debate, the tenets of neutrality still apply here, and gave rise to a new debate, around *search neutrality*. Indeed, the gatekeeper position of search engines raises the same questions as that of ISPs, regarding the impact on investments, innovation, and in general on ensuring a level playing field in the digital ecosystem.

The search neutrality debate can lead to significant regulatory decisions regarding the ICT ecosystem. Here, a counterpart to the "all packets should be treated the same, without any economic considerations" motto could be "all web pages should be ranked only according to their relevance to the user query, without any economic considerations." But a difficulty with such a statement is that its core notion is difficult to define and evaluate properly: what is *relevance*, and how can we check whether a search engine follows neutrality principles?

This chapter is devoted to search engines as economic actors and their likely dilemmas and stances regarding search neutrality. First, in Sect. 7.1, we investigate their business model and what aspects may drive their decisions when having to display an ordered list in response to a user query. For that, we build and analyze a model where it is in the search engine's interest to display relevant results because that will earn it more visits from users, but some economic components (the search engine getting some value for some specific pages being visited) may also be taken into account to maximize revenue. The section formalizes the trade-offs between those two nonaligned objectives—relevance and revenue—and establishes the form of an optimal ranking strategy. More specifically, we show that to maximize long-term revenue, i.e., display some revenue-yielding pages but also attract users with relevant results, a search engine should rank the candidate results in decreasing order of their weighted sum of estimated relevance and estimated gain (with carefully tuned weights). As the theoretical results of Sect. 7.1 establish that search engines are not incentivized to display the most relevant results and some other (economic) considerations might introduce some biases, we adopt in Sect. 7.2 a more pragmatic approach, in order to design a model and procedure to detect such biases, without knowing the actual relevance values considered by search engines. The methodology relies on detecting discrepancies between the result rankings of several search engines, for the same requests. The comparison is based on an interpretation of search engines' allocating slots to Web pages as giving them *visibility*, and the goal is to highlight outliers, for example, search engines giving some Web pages an abnormally high (or low) visibility. Finally, that interpretation can be used to define a new ranking aggregating those from several search engines, hence building a meta-search engine that would be less prone to biases than each individual one. The objective there is to find the most appropriate way to aggregate several rankings into one, to reduce biases to a minimum and approximate what a "neutral" search engine would look like.

7.1 Is It in Search Engines' Interest to Be Neutral?

The initial business model of search engines like Google consisted in attracting visitor by providing them with highly relevant results related to their queries, for free. The revenues then came by selling advertisement slots located near those so-called "organic" results, through auctions implemented for each search term [172]. Generally, the search engine collects a payment each time one such ad is clicked.

How those two types of results—organic and sponsored—are presented to the user has been the subject of a kind of cat-and-mouse game between the search engine trying to blend them as much as possible to attract clicks on ads and regulators aiming at protecting users from confusing both types of results. As a consequence, over time, sponsored links have been displayed either on the right-hand side of the organic results, on top of them, or interlaced with (subtle) distinctive signs like a "sponsored" annotation or a pastel-colored background.

But search engines can also have other economic interests linked to organic results, which are less obvious than selling advertisement slots: even if we forbid advertisers from directly paying search engines to appear among the organic results, there can be indirect incentives for the search engine to show some pages rather than others. This is especially true if the search engine belongs to an entity offering several types of services: there, the search engine can be used to boost the umbrella entity's other services and/or hurt the competing alternatives. As an illustration, the start of the search neutrality debate is often associated with a 2009 complaint from Adam Raff, a co-founder of Foundem, a "vertical search" service whose goal is to help consumers by offering a comparison of several online offers: Raff accused Google of having penalized Foundem in its rankings since 2006, which can be seen as Google hindering competition of its own similar service, Google Shopping. As a side note, Google favoring Google Shopping over its competitors has been recognized by the European Commission years later and sanctioned with a record €2.4 billion fine in 2017 [55]. Another common situation where Google, the most-used search engine worldwide, can be suspected of favoring its own content is video streaming: In terms of financial gains, it is clear that Google has a strong incentive to drive users toward videos provided by YouTube rather than another provider, because of the corresponding ad revenues on YouTube.

In this section, we intend to model rigorously such incentives for a search engine, focusing on organic results only: Advertisement slots are allocated according to an auction scheme with predefined rules [116] and generate some revenue that we will treat here as exogenous and proportional to the number of visits (search requests) to the search engine.

The key trade-off that we consider when ranking organic results is between the quality/usefulness to the user (in the hope of attracting more visits, hence making more revenue through ads or through indirect gains) and the immediate (though indirect) gains from showing suboptimal but more profitable Web pages. To address those non-aligned objectives, the natural metric would be the overall expected revenue per time unit, which will depend on the expected quality of the displayed rankings (through the number of visits) and on the profitability of the Web pages that are shown.

7.1.1 Modeling the Long-Term vs. Short-Term Gains Trade-Off

Let us formalize mathematically the two effects that the search engine (SE) should be sensitive to when trying to maximize revenue, as initially proposed in [93]:

- A short-time vision would focus on the gains associated with each specific visit: apart from those from advertisements (that we consider fixed), maximizing those gains would consist in showing the links that yield the highest revenue to the SE—typically those controlled by the same entity as the SE or by some actor who paid to be highly ranked. That will be covered in our model by associating with each page a corresponding *gain* for the SE, and a (short-term) revenue-maximizing ranking would just consist in showing the pages in decreasing order of that gain.
- But a longer-time consideration should take into account that such a greedy behavior is likely to repel users, whose frequency of visit to the SE will decrease if they do not find the displayed results relevant enough to their needs: they might then switch to a competing SE, or just perform less queries. To represent that effect, we will assume that the total number of visits (per time unit) to the SE depends on the *average relevance* of the returned rankings, which we will quantify by attaching to each page a *relevance* value to the user's query.

The definition of relevance itself would deserve to be discussed, as it can be a complex notion. We will treat it here as a given value that the SE is able to compute for each (*search term, Web page*) pair, but that computation can involve a lot of machinery and parametrization; for example, Google's ranking algorithm is constantly evolving to improve its estimation of relevance toward users' queries while adapting to the maneuvers of spammers and search engine optimization tools [99]. There has been quite some academic research on the topic of relevance-based ranking (see [10, 12] and references therein). Google's ability to provide quick and relevant results has been the key of its success since its appearance in the end of the last century, earning and maintaining a dominating position: with a worldwide market share higher than 90% for each month of 2021 while the first competitor, Bing, never reached 3%,[1] it is often the only search engine that people know of. But that might change if the quality of the results decreases and alternative SEs get gradually preferred.

7.1.1.1 Modeling Requests as Random Pairs of Vectors

There is a very large number of possible search terms. To account for that heterogeneity, we will treat the search term(s) for a given request as a random variable, drawn from a distribution known to the SE: the SE can indeed estimate

---

[1] Source: https://gs.statcounter.com/search-engine-market-share.

it just by observing what terms were searched. For the time scale considered here, the distribution will be assumed constant, but in practice, it can be updated, and our reasoning remains valid.

Let us denote by $\mathcal{W}$ the set of all Web pages that are indexed (thus, potentially ranked) by the SE; we will refer to an individual page using an index $i = 1, \ldots, |\mathcal{W}|$. With respect to a given search term, we assume that each Web page $i \in \mathcal{W}$ has a relevance value R_i and a gain value G_i corresponding to the expected revenue the SE gets if the page gets clicked on (e.g., through ads on the target page).

With those notations, a request to the SE can be seen as a random pair of vectors $Y = ((R_i)_{i \in \mathcal{W}}, (G_i)_{i \in \mathcal{W}})$, drawn from a given joint distribution. The dilemma for the SE therefore consists, for each request Y, in deciding how to rank those pages, balancing relevance and gain values. The ranking is denoted by a permutation π on $\mathcal{W}$, with $\pi_i(Y)$ the position given to Page i for the search Y.

7.1.1.2   Click-Through-Rate: Impact of Position and Relevance

Consider a request Y. The Click-Through-Rate (CTR) for a page $i \in \mathcal{W}$ is the probability that it gets clicked by the user who performed the search. We model that probability as the product of two probabilities:

- A probability $\theta_{\pi_i(Y)}$, depending of the position $\pi_i(Y)$ of the page
- One denoted by $\psi(R_i(Y))$, depending on the relevance of the page to the query

A possible interpretation is that the user *sees* the result at position k with probability θ_k and, if they see a result with relevance x there, *clicks on it* with probability $\psi(x)$ representing whether it is relevant enough to the search. Summarizing, a page i ranked at position $\pi_i(Y)$ gets a click with probability $\theta_{\pi_i(Y)}\psi(R_i(Y))$, in which case it yields the SE an expected gain of $G_i(Y)$. Those assumptions are standard [170] and discussed in more detail in [93].

Without loss of generality, we index positions in decreasing order of visibilities, i.e., $\theta_1 \geq \theta_2 \geq \ldots$, so that position number 1 is the "best" (most visible) one. More specifically, in the numerical studies, we will only consider the first 10 positions in the result ranking (further positions having a very low visibility), with values $(\theta_k)_{k=1,\ldots,10}$ given in Table 7.1.

To slightly simplify notations and highlight the visibility effect of ranking positions, we can define $\tilde{R}_i := \psi(R_i)R_i$ and $\tilde{G}_i := \psi(R_i)G_i$ as the respective "when-seen" expected relevance (for the user) and gain (for the SE) for a page i once it is seen by a user, i.e., including the probability of a click $\psi(R_i)$. Once the SE has selected its ranking policy π, the *expected* (over the distribution of requests,

Table 7.1 Position-related values (visibilities) used in the simulations, taken from [44]

θ_1	θ_2	θ_3	θ_4	θ_5	θ_6	θ_7	θ_8	θ_9	θ_{10}
0.364	0.125	0.095	0.079	0.061	0.041	0.038	0.035	0.03	0.022

with expected value denoted by $\mathbb{E}_Y$) relevance of clicked links can be expressed as:

$$r := \mathbb{E}_Y \left[\sum_{i \in W} \theta_{\pi_i(Y)} \tilde{R}_i \right].$$

Similarly, since revenues stem from clicks, the expected revenue per request for the SE is:

$$g := \mathbb{E}_Y \left[\sum_{i \in W} \theta_{\pi_i(Y)} \tilde{G}_i \right].$$

7.1.1.3   Frequency of Requests and SE Objective Function

To reflect users being sensitive to getting relevant results, we assume the average number of requests to the SE per unit of time is a non-negative increasing function λ of the average experienced relevance r expressed above.

For each request, we denote by β the expected revenue that the SE gets through *sponsored results*, i.e., advertisement slots sold (generally through auctions).

Summarizing, for a given request, the SE makes on average β through sponsored links and g from pages ranked within organic results. Multiplying by the request frequency, the objective function of the SE we consider is its average overall revenue per time unit, that is:

$$\lambda(r)(g + \beta).$$

The problem faced by an SE wanting to maximize revenue is summarized in Fig. 7.1, where we highlight the feedback loop of relevance impacting the number of visits.

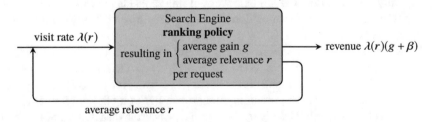

Fig. 7.1   The SE optimization problem: finding a ranking policy to maximize revenue

7.1.1.4   How Would a Neutral SE Work?

Applying neutrality principles in this context, a "neutral" SE would not be considering any criterion other than relevance when ranking results, i.e., it would simply order the pages in decreasing order of their relevance, which maximizes the average relevance r, or equivalently the product $\lambda(r)\beta$, which corresponds to the revenues from sponsored link slots. For our model, that can simply be attained by setting all gain values $(G_i)_{i \in \mathcal{W}}$ to 0.

7.1.2   The Revenue-Maximizing Ranking Policy: An (Almost) Explicit Trade-Off Between Relevance and Gains

Under the model developed in this subsection, it has been shown in [93] that when Y has a continuous distribution, a revenue-maximizing ranking policy consists, for each request Y, in simply ranking pages $i \in \mathcal{W}$ in decreasing value of their weighted sum $\tilde{R}_i + \rho \tilde{G}_i$, where $\rho \geq 0$ is a constant (the same for all requests) whose optimal value ρ^* can be computed as a fixed point, for example, by simulating requests (more details can be found in [93]).

So our a priori very complex problem, with a large decision space (a permutation for each request) and a not-so-simple objective function (the average revenue $\lambda(r)(g + \beta)$), turns out to have a very simple solution, which can be summarized by the factor ρ^* and implemented very fast once ρ^* is known. That factor can be interpreted as encoding the trade-off between relevance (long-term effect) and gains (short-term effect) that the SE should implement to maximize revenue. Note that forcing ρ to 0 would again lead to considering only relevance, i.e., a neutral ranking.

7.1.3   Neutral vs. Non-neutral Search Engine: What Are the Differences?

As pointed out above, the sole difference between neutral and non-neutral rankings resides in the value of ρ used to compare pages: both can be thought of as showing pages in decreasing order of $\tilde{R}_i + \rho \tilde{G}_i$, but a neutral SE would take $\rho = 0$, while a non-neutral would use $\rho = \rho^* > 0$, i.e., give some weight to gains.

But what is the impact of that difference? Would users really perceive a decrease in the quality of their result if the SE is non-neutral rather than neutral? And for companies whose viability depends on their visibility, can a non-neutral SE distort so much the legitimate visibilities that it makes or breaks them? Since our model involves many parameters, we cannot give universal responses, but we provide some elements in the remainder of this section, through simple illustrative scenarios.

7.1.3.1   A Simple Example with 10 Actors

Let us consider a simplistic case, developed in [93] involving only 10 different actors
that we will call content providers (CPs). This situation can be thought of as a focus
on a specific category of requests, for which a limited number of content providers
can offer their services, like finance data, weather forecasts, flight information, or
news.

We make the following assumptions:

- For each request (in that category), we model the **relevance values** $(R_i)_{i=1,\dots,10}$
  of all CPs as independent uniformly distributed random variables over the
  interval [0, 1].
- Only CP 1 is controlled by the SE, and the **gain value** G_1 also follows a uniform
  distribution $\mathcal{U}(0, 1)$, independent of all relevance values. All other CPs have no
  agreement that would benefit the SE; hence, $G_i = 0$ for $i = 2, \dots, 10$ for each
  request.
- The expected revenue β per request from ad slots (non-organic results) equals 1,
  unless specified otherwise.
- The visibilities of the positions within the organic results are those of Table 7.1.
- We take $\lambda(x) = x$ for all x (i.e., the frequency of visits equals the average
  relevance) and $\psi(\cdot) = 1$ (i.e., users cannot estimate the relevance of a result
  before clicking on it).

In that model, all CPs perform the same (in terms of relevance), and only one (CP
1) may be favored by a non-neutral SE. We use it to quantify the a priori positive
impact of non-neutrality on the favored CP and the negative impact on the other CPs
and on users.

To illustrate the impact of the parameter ρ used in the ranking (recall that the SE
will rank page with respect to the values of $R_i + \rho G_i$), we display in Fig. 7.2 several
metrics (visit rates, relevance, SE revenue) when ρ varies. As expected, when the
weight ρ given to gains over relevance increases, the average gain g per search of

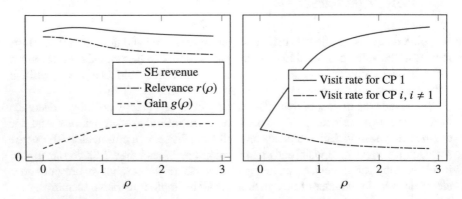

Fig. 7.2 Performance measures as a function of ρ (simulation results) [93]

the ranking policy increases, and the average relevance r decreases, since the SE favors gain over relevance. The visit rates of non-favored CPs also decrease (recall the SE visit rate is $\lambda(r) = r$ in this model), due to two cumulative effects: the visit rate to the SE decreases, and those CPs are ranked worse.

The less obvious impacts regard the overall revenue and the visit rate for CP 1, since there are two opposite effects at play. In terms of CP 1 visibility, note that even though the overall visit rate to the SE decreases, the visibility effect dominates here so that the visit rate to CP 1 keeps increasing over the considered range for ρ. Finally, as regards SE revenue, there is an optimal value ρ^* slightly above 0.5, after which the negative impact of the SE visit rate decreasing overcomes the gain from favoring the revenue-yielding pages of CP 1 over more relevant pages. The revenue-maximizing ranking will consist in applying that value ρ^*.

7.1.3.2 Ad Revenues Are Good for Result Quality!

A simple observation that we can make is that letting SEs sell advertisement slots displayed next to the organic results is actually good for the quality of those organic results. The intuition is as follows: if there is a lot of revenue stemming from those ad slots for each visit to the SE, then the goal of the SE will be to attract as many visits as possible and therefore to maximize the average relevance of the organic results (provided of course that displaying too many ads is not "polluting" the page and deterring users from choosing the considered SE).

For our model, that corresponds to the parameter β (the per-visit revenue from ad slots) being large with respect to the possible gains from pages shown in the organic results (the values $(\tilde{G}_i)_{i \in \mathcal{W}}$). In that case, the term $(g + \beta)$ almost equals β for any ranking policy, so that maximizing the overall revenue $\lambda(r)(g + \beta)$ is equivalent to maximizing $\lambda(r)\beta$, i.e., maximizing r since λ is increasing. This is then easily attained, by just ranking results in terms of relevance for each request, or in other words, by being neutral.

Hence, revenues from ad slots drive SEs toward a more neutral behavior, and the parameter β is therefore a key to determine "how neutral" a revenue-maximizing SE may be. Figure 7.3 illustrates that fact, by showing how β influences the value ρ^*: as β increases, the weight given to gains over relevance decreases, meaning the ranking is closer to a neutral one.

7.1.3.3 Should Users Care Whether Their SE Is Neutral?

To investigate the impact of non-neutrality perceived by users, the most natural metric within our model would be the quality of the results, measured here through the average relevance r.

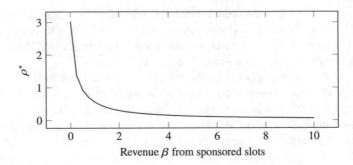

Fig. 7.3 Value of ρ^* (optimal weight given to gains in the ranking) as a function of β [93]

For the example scenario treated in this subsection (with $\beta = 1$), the relevance $r(\rho^*)$ when the SE applies the revenue-maximizing ranking is 0.618, while a neutral ranking would lead to $r(0) = 0.635$, hence a 3% reduction in quality, which may not be perceivable by users. But that observation is only valid for our very specific example, with the parameters we took: if the request rate $\lambda(r)$ varies less with r (we took $\lambda(r) = r$, but with a function with less variations, the SE could increase its short-term gain with a smaller long-term impact), or if β is smaller, or if the relevance and gain distributions change, the impact on the relevance perceived by users can be much larger.

7.1.3.4   Quantifying How Non-neutrality Distorts Competition Among CPs

Again, the observations given here only hold for our scenario but highlight some tendencies. Let us now have a look at the survivability of some CPs that would not be favored by the SE (CPs labeled from 2 to 10): To model their gains and be consistent with our model so far, we assume that for each request the gain for each CP follows a uniform distribution $\mathcal{U}(0, 1)$, independently of everything else. Note that we made the exact same assumption for CP 1, except that the gain was perceived by the SE: for CPs 2 to 10, the gain is only for themselves.

To show the sensitivity to the sponsored slot revenues β, we compare in Table 7.2 several possible values, giving in each case the average relevance perceived by users, and the visit rates and revenues of both types of CPs (the favored one and the non-favored ones). We also indicate the variations with respect to a neutral ranking (with $\rho = 0$). We observe again that smaller values of β lead to less-neutral rankings; however, the degradation of the average relevance r remains below 11%. On the other hand, the impact on the CP ecosystem is significant: for example, if $\beta = 0.25$, a non-neutral ranking more than triples the visit rate for the favored CP, at the expense of the other CPs who see a 32% decrease with respect to a neutral ranking. In terms of CP revenues, the same orders of magnitude are observed, with a 177% increase for the favored CP and an 32% decrease for the others. Such values

Table 7.2 Impacts of a non-neutral ranking for our specific scenario [93]

	Relevance	CP 1 revenue	other CP revenue	CP 1 visit rate	other CP visit rate
Neutral, $\rho = 0$ (reference case, optimal for $\beta \to \infty$)	0.635	0.0283	0.0283	0.057	0.057
Non-neutral, $\rho = 0.559$ (optimal for $\beta = 1$)	0.618 (-3%)	0.066 (+136%)	0.0243 (-14%)	0.112 (+96%)	0.049 (-14%)
Non-neutral, $\rho = 0.924$ (optimal for $\beta = .5$)	0.592 (-7%)	0.084 (+200%)	0.0215 (-24%)	0.140 (+146%)	0.043 (-25%)
Non-neutral, $\rho = 1.374$ (optimal for $\beta = .25$)	0.568 (-11%)	0.093 (+232%)	0.0193 (-32%)	0.158 (+177%)	0.039 (-32%)

certainly do not constitute a level playing field among CPs, pleading in favor of search neutrality defendants.

7.1.3.5 Impact of Search (Non-)Neutrality on Innovation

We close this subsection by investigating an argument often raised by net neutrality advocates, regarding non-neutrality hindering innovation: Would that argument still hold in the context of the search neutrality debate?

To get some insight on that question, we develop further our simple scenario, by considering that one of the non-favored CPs (say, CP 2) makes an investment effort to improve the relevance of its content. To set a model, let us say that an innovation effort of z has the consequence that R_2 follows a uniform distribution $\mathcal{U}(0, 1 + z)$ instead of $\mathcal{U}(0, 1)$, which remains the case for all other CPs. How would such innovation efforts be rewarded/incentivized in neutral and non-neutral situations?

Figure 7.4 shows how the investment level z influences the SE revenue and the relevance experienced by users, both in neutral ($\rho = 0$) and non-neutral (ρ set to maximize SE revenue) contexts. For the non-neutral setting, the optimal weight ρ^* given to short-term revenue over relevance in the ranking is also displayed. All the curves follow the same increasing trend: as CP 2 improves the quality of its content, the SE becomes less and less neutral (ρ^* increases), and the effort leads to a higher overall relevance (with a **larger relevance increase in the neutral case**) and a higher SE revenue (with a **larger SE revenue increase in the non-neutral case**).

Now, to investigate the consequences for CPs, we plot in Fig. 7.5 the revenues and visit rates of the three types of CPs (CP 1, whose gains go to the SE, CP 2 that invests in content quality, and the other eight CPs), in neutral and non-neutral cases, when CP 2 effort z varies. Note that in the neutral case, CP 1 is treated exactly like the other CPs; hence, the curves coincide. To compute CP 2 revenue, we have assumed a fixed monetary cost per unit of innovation effort, here set to 0.4: an effort z costs $0.4z$ to CP 2.

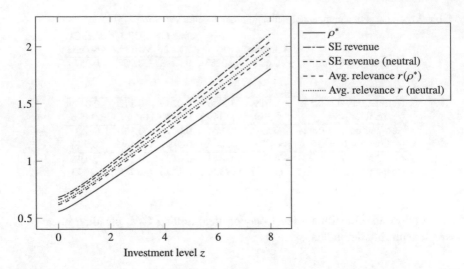

Fig. 7.4 Optimal (non-neutral) weight ρ^* and relevance and SE revenue in neutral and non-neutral cases, as functions of CP 2 effort, when $\beta = 1$ [94]

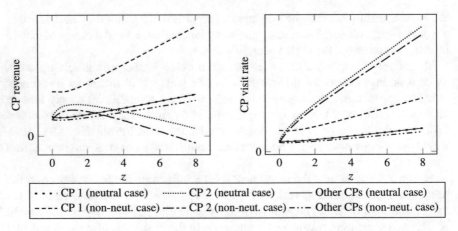

Fig. 7.5 CP net revenues (including quality investment, at unit cost 0.4) (*left*) and visit rates to various CPs (*right*) as a function of the investment z from CP 2

As expected, because of the improved overall relevance, CP 1 benefits from CP 2's effort in both situations, with higher gains in the non-neutral case due to the SE being "less neutral" (ρ^* increases). CP 2 would of course prefer the neutral situation: the difference in revenue increases with CP 2's effort z, again because the ranking is less neutral. As the overall relevance—and thus the visit rate—increases, the revenue of the other CPs increases with z when the effort is large enough, but an opposite effect comes from those CPs being less often among the most relevant ones, hence a lower visibility.

Finally, if we consider that CP 2 would choose an optimal investment effort, we observe that in a neutral situation, CP 2 should set $z = 1.25$ (yielding a net profit of 0.046), while in a non-neutral situation, the optimal effort is $z = 1.05$ (with a net profit of 0.038). Summarizing, in our scenario, non-neutrality would lead CP 2 to invest 16% less and to lose 26% in revenue when compared to a neutral setting. As regards users, the perceived relevance would decrease by 4% (from 0.773 to 0.7395).

This example supports the claim that search neutrality helps level the playing field among CPs and stimulates innovation.

7.2 Detecting Bias and Trying to Build a "Neutral" Search Engine

The previous section has established in what regards it may not be in the interest of an SE to base its ranking decisions only on the relevance of the result pages. We saw that even when taking into account user demand depending on the result page quality, the SE will still tend to favor short-term revenues, to an extent that depends on user demand sensitivity. We have also illustrated via simple examples why regulators may want to protect search neutrality, mostly for reasons similar to protecting net neutrality, namely, ensuring fair competition among CPs, stimulating innovation, or keeping the Internet open and accessible to all.

In this section, we focus on the more pragmatic questions for a regulator wanting to enforce a neutral behavior of SEs: how can one verify that an SE behaves in a "neutral" manner, i.e., ranks CPs according to *relevance* only, without any economic motivation? We develop here a simple framework that can be applied in practice, without knowing the underlying "objective relevance" (a quite elusive notion) value of Web pages: instead, the method relies on comparing the results of several search engines.

We design some statistical tests to detect potential biases (Web pages unfairly hidden or highlighted, SEs behaving very differently than the others) and introduce two meta engines aiming at reducing bias.

7.2.1 A Look At Related Contributions

A key motivation for neutrality, whether in networks or other contexts, is the notion of *fairness*. For search engines, the question of how to ensure some fairness or equity through rankings has been studied in [21], but without our interpretation of visibility. An approach closer to the one presented here is taken in [51], but the focus there is more on aggregating ranking to satisfy certain properties than on detecting potentially biased behaviors.

A simple way to analyze self-favoring bias was used in [177], by comparing how frequently SEs like Bing or Google tend to show their own content in the top positions, while other SEs do not; that method has highlighted some consistent biases, but we aim here for more general approaches.

Other works address the question of search neutrality. For example, in [129], Mowshowitz and Kawaguchi define a measure of similarity among SE rankings and highlight some differences among SE that occur consistently on some domains of search terms. Those authors were interested in detecting bias in search engines as early as 2002 [128], through a dissimilarity measure that we think is harder to interpret than the visibility-based tests we design here. Research works like [171] have focused on identifying some differences among SEs, and understanding their causes. Again, the difficulty is to compare ranked lists of partially overlapping sets of elements [144, 175].

On a related topic, the influence of SE results in elections has been investigated [90, 150], the goal being to distinguish between different potential causes for bias (e.g., from the users, or from the ranking algorithm itself). Finally, note that our framework can be used to evaluate the performance of SEs, an approach also taken in [97] using "jurors" to estimate the relevance of Web pages to queries. Here our method assumes that on average SEs tend to collectively highlight the most relevant pages, so that it requires no human intervention.

7.2.2   An Estimation of Page Relevance: Average Page Visibility

The approach we present here has first been introduced in [81]. We will rely on the results provided by a number n of SEs: as in the previous section, we will denote by y a search term (a request, but we will not be using the notions of gain and intrinsic relevance here) and by $\mathcal{W}$ the set of candidate Web pages indexed by at least one SE.

We focus on the a top-ranked organic results by each SE; typically, $a = 10$ if we consider the first page (that attracts almost all the user clicks upon a request).

For a search term y, the key metric we associate with each displayed result page is its average visibility over all n SEs, which we will call its *score* for the search term. To compute it, we need to know some visibility values for each position $1, \ldots, a$ and each SE. Those values can be estimated through surveys; for simplicity, here we will assume that they are the same on all SEs and vary only with the position, which is realistic if all SEs result page layouts are similar.[2] Keeping the same notation and values as in the previous section, the visibility given by an SE to a result at position k is denoted by θ_k (with $\theta_1 \geq \theta_2 \geq \ldots \geq \theta_a$), and for the experiments, we use $a = 10$ and the visibility values in Table 7.1.

---

[2] If SE differs in the layout of their result pages, then the visibility values may differ, which can easily be incorporated in the model.

Formally, the score of a page $i \in \mathcal{W}$ for a search term y is then defined as:

$$R_{i,y} := \frac{1}{n} \sum_{j=1}^{n} \theta_{\pi_j(i,y)}, \tag{7.1}$$

with $\pi_j(i, y)$ the position in which SE j displays page i for search term y (pages that are not displayed by an SE are given a visibility 0 by it).

That score metric will tend to reduce biases from some SEs by averaging them out; hence, it makes sense (for a lack of a better way) to treat $R_{i,y}$ as a reasonable estimation of the actual relevance of page i to search term y.

7.2.3   Quantifying How "Consensual" a Search Engine Is: The SE Score

Once the page scores are computed, we can use the position visibility values again to define a metric at the SE level, measuring whether a given SE tends to give a high visibility to high-score pages, i.e., to the most visible pages among all SEs. That SE score, which we denote by $S_{j,y}$ for SE j and search term y, is simply the weighted sum of the displayed page scores, with weights equal to the visibility values $(\theta_k)_{k=1,...,a}$:

$$S_{j,y} := \sum_{\text{page } i \in \mathcal{W}} \theta_{\pi_j(i,y)} R_{i,y},$$

with again $\theta_{\pi_j(i,y)} = 0$ if page i is not shown among the top a results.

If page scores are interpreted as approximating the actual page relevances, then the SE score can be thought of as measuring the relevance "seen" by users with that SE.

Finally, one can again aggregate those SE scores over a set $\mathcal{Y}$ of search terms and compute the expected value $S_j := \mathbb{E}_Y[S_{j,Y}]$ for a random request Y as $\sum_{y \in \mathcal{Y}} p_y S_{j,y}$, where p_y is the probability that the search term be $Y = y$ (relative frequency of search term y over $\mathcal{Y}$). That metric S_j then corresponds to the expected score of SE j if a term randomly chosen in $\mathcal{Y}$ is searched.

7.2.4   Pointing Out Possible Bias: Statistical Tests

One reason for considering several SEs is the possibility it gives to *compare* their results. Here, we want the comparison to be run automatically and detect abnormalities; this can be done by designing statistical tests, aimed at estimating whether the observed values can reasonably be obtained with neutral rankings or at the contrary are likely due to some bias.

To be reliable, tests generally need a large sample size, a luxury we cannot afford here because of the limited number of existing SEs. Few methods exist for limited sample sizes; we suggest here to use one for detecting *outliers* in a limited-size sample of numerical values, first introduced by Dixon [43, 49]. Simply said, the test is fed with a list of numerical values and tells us whether the largest (or smallest) values are too extreme and should be considered outliers in the list.

Some statistical libraries implement that test (in R, e.g., through the function `dixon.test`), named the Dixon Q-test. More details can be found in [43, 49, 123], but mostly one must keep in mind that the mathematical analysis of the test relies on assumptions that are not satisfied here: the "non-outlier" values in the sample are assumed to be independent identically distributed random variables with a Gaussian distribution, which is far from being the case in our context. So for us, one should remain cautious and not immediately accuse an SE of bias if the test detects an outlier; rather, the test should be used as a tool to identify *potential* bias instances deserving further consideration.

We list below four different ways to use Dixon's Q-test in the search neutrality context we have described so far, to answer four different types of questions each time a request is performed:

- **Does a SE particularly disagree with the others?** Here the list of values is the list of SE scores $(S_{j,y})_{j=1,...,n}$, and we focus on the lowest value(s).
- **Is a SE showing at the top position a "bad" Web page?** To answer that question, the Q-test can be applied to the list of values $(R_{t(j),y})_{j=1,...,n}$, with $t_{(j)}$ the page shown in first position by SE j (omitting y for notational simplicity). Again we are wondering whether the lowest value is an outlier.
- **Is an SE showing at the top position a Web page not shown by the others?** This question is very close to the previous one, but here, instead of comparing the scores of all top-ranked pages (only one test), we perform one test for each SE j, by considering the list of values $(\theta_{\pi_{\bar{j}}(t(j),y)})_{\bar{j}=1,...,n}$, i.e., the visibility individually given by each SE to the top-ranked page of SE j.
- **Is an SE disregarding the "best" page?** For that fourth question, we look at the "best" page $\bar{i}$ according to the consensus, and the list of values is the list of visibilities $(\theta_{\pi_j(\bar{i},y)})_{j=1,...,n}$ given by SEs to that page.

Note that all those tests, as well as the meta-rankings proposed in the next subsection, have been implemented in a publicly available tool, which the reader can experiment with at:

$$\text{https//snide.irisa.fr.}$$

7.2.5 Aggregating Results from SEs to Create Meta-SEs

With the hope that potential biases will get averaged out over the considered SEs, we suggest here two possible simple ways of taking into account the variety of rankings proposed by all SEs for a given search y, to form a new ranking, thereby creating a meta-SE.

7.2.5.1 The Consensus Ranking

The Consensus ranking, initially introduced in [81], simply ranks pages in W according to the average visibility they are given over all SEs for search term y, i.e., to their scores $R_{i,y}$ as computed in (7.1).

That new ranking can be seen as following a Borda rule [42, 182] and will of course maximize the weighted sum of page visibilities (SE score) introduced in Sect. 7.2.3.

7.2.5.2 The Majority Judgment Ranking

The Consensus ranking can still be sensitive to biases, since one single SE showing a page in the first position already gives it quite some visibility, and that contribution to the page score is likely to be sufficient for the page to appear among the top 10.

To avoid that effect, we consider another meta-SE alternative, which would rank pages not in terms of the sums of the visibilities they are given by SEs, but in terms of their *median* visibility over all SEs (the highest visibility given by at least half of the SEs). In case of equality between two pages, the comparison is repeated after removing one SE "vote" with that median value. The ranking can be thought of as an application of the Majority Judgment method, suggested for election management, which has some desirable properties [15, 16].

7.2.5.3 Robustness to Bias: Consensus Ranking *vs* Majority Judgment

The intuition when introducing the Majority Judgment ranking is that it would be less sensitive to bias than the (Borda) Consensus ranking. We use here an artificial but simple model, presented in [114], to quantity that effect.

Consider 15 SEs, out of which 14 are "neutral," with a small set W of 20 Web pages to rank. For each possible search y, each page has an intrinsic relevance value $r(y)$ that we simulate as a random variable uniformly distributed on the interval [0, 1]. The neutral SEs rank pages according to their *estimated* relevance: we assume that for each page and each SE, there is some Gaussian-distributed estimation noise, with variance σ^2, which is added to $r(y)$, so that even among neutral SEs, the observed ranking can differ, not due to voluntary biases but to (honest) estimation errors.

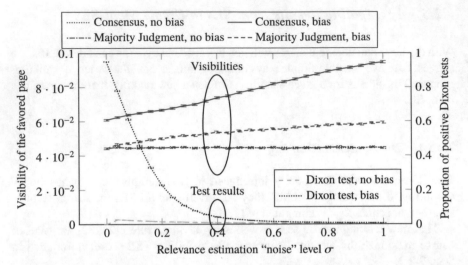

Fig. 7.6 Visibilities with the two meta-SEs, with and without bias introduced by one SE (favoring one page), and corresponding proportion of Dixon test detections for that SE (Dixon test on the SE score being abnormally low). Average values over 10^5 simulations, with 95% confidence intervals [114]

The behavior of the sole non-neutral SE is simple: it favors one page, which it always displays at the top position. The other pages are ranked "neutrally," i.e., according to the estimated relevance. For comparison purposes, we also simulate what happens when all SEs are neutral.

Figure 7.6 displays how our meta-ranking methods behave in that context, when the "estimation noise" σ varies. Specifically, the average visibility of the favored page increases with σ, as that page benefits from there being less agreement among the other SEs to push the most relevant pages. In addition, the figure clearly shows how the Consensus ranking remains affected by the non-neutrality of only one SE (the visibility of the favored page is larger than that of the other pages), in much larger proportions than the Majority Judgment ranking.

The figure also displays how frequently a Dixon test has detected the score of the non-neutral SE as abnormally low, highlighting another consequence of the estimation noise σ: as neutral SEs agree less because of discrepant relevance estimations, it is harder to detect anomalies.

7.2.6   A Few Observations from a Campaign on 1000 Search Terms

In the summer of 2020, we have run a campaign on the 1000 most searched terms at the time (according to mondovo.com/keywords) and performed the statistical tests

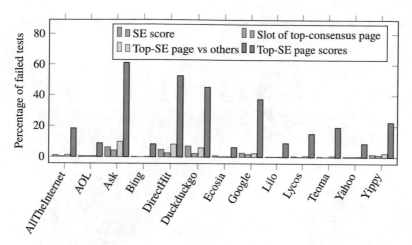

Fig. 7.7 Proportion of failed tests (Dixon tests presented in Sect. 7.2.4) at risk level 1% for each SE [114]

described previously, with 13 SEs. To account for the popularity of each search term, the results have been weighted by their number of requests, an information also available at mondovo.com/keywords. The results are detailed in [114]; we just summarize here a few of the conclusions.

First, we display in Fig. 7.7 how each SE performs with regard to the four tests designed in Sect. 7.2.4. The figure may highlight some SEs performing "better" than others, by failing less frequently on the tests. But that may be an artefact of the SEs in our panel not being completely independent, and of our tests relying on outlier detection: if several SEs are affected by the same bias, it will be harder for our test to detect it. To further look into that idea, we can compute a distance measure among all pairs of SE rankings (defined as the minimal "mass of visibility" to shift from one ranking to obtain the other, see [114]). The average values of those pairwise distances are given in Table 7.3 and indeed show that some SEs are very similar, like AOL and Yahoo, as well as the triplet Bing/Lilo/Lycos, so biases by those actors may be underestimated.

Another type of analysis that can be made from the survey consists in aggregating, over all search terms (weighted by their popularities), the visibilities of pages in the same domain. This way we can see whether an SE tends to show one domain more than the others do. Figure 7.8 summarizes our findings, by displaying the differences for each SE with the overall average visibility of the most shown domains (normalized with the standard deviation). Unsurprisingly, the domains wikipedia.com and wikipedia.fr are the most visible (the survey was run from an Inria server located in France), and the figure can highlight which SEs tend to favor the French-speaking over the English-speaking version, their algorithm likely giving a higher weight on the location of the user.

Table 7.3 Average distances between SEs (darker cells indicate a higher similarity) [114]

	Majority	AllTheInternet	AOL	Ask	Bing	DirectHit	Duckduckgo	Ecosia	Google	Lilo	Lycos	Teoma	Yahoo	Yippy
Consensus	0.3	0.55	0.49	0.7	0.49	0.69	0.67	0.52	0.64	0.49	0.49	0.52	0.49	0.54
Majority		0.56	0.46	0.77	0.5	0.75	0.69	0.55	0.67	0.48	0.49	0.53	0.46	0.54
AllTheInternet			0.63	0.85	0.81	0.5	0.7	0.81	0.8	0.81	0.81	0.44	0.63	0.67
AOL				0.9	0.72	0.8	0.73	0.75	0.87	0.71	0.7	0.69	0.03	0.38
Ask					0.8	0.44	0.9	0.8	0.56	0.8	0.8	0.76	0.9	0.9
Bing						0.9	0.84	0.42	0.66	0.28	0.32	0.75	0.72	0.76
DirectHit							0.84	0.89	0.87	0.9	0.89	0.65	0.8	0.81
Duckduckgo								0.86	0.85	0.85	0.83	0.7	0.73	0.77
Ecosia									0.71	0.34	0.44	0.75	0.75	0.76
Google										0.67	0.68	0.67	0.87	0.88
Lilo											0.34	0.76	0.71	0.73
Lycos												0.74	0.68	0.72
Teoma													0.69	0.73
Yahoo														0.38

A surprising observation in Fig. 7.8 regards Google, which appears to be the SE showing YouTube the least frequently, despite both being controlled by the same entity. That observation is probably misleading, and due to the fact that Google has a specific way of displaying video results on its result page, our tool did not identify as organic results.

7.2.6.1   The "Chrome" Search Term

Let us conclude this section with the specific example of the search term "chrome," that we think is worth a closer look. For that search term, our two meta-search engines give the rankings below.

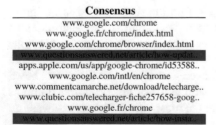

Consensus	**Majority judgment**
www.google.com/chrome	www.google.fr/chrome/index.html
www.google.fr/chrome/index.html	www.google.com/chrome/browser/index.html
www.google.com/chrome/browser/index.html	apps.apple.com/us/app/google-chrome/id53588..
www.questionsanswered.net/article/how-updat..	www.google.com/chrome
apps.apple.com/us/app/google-chrome/id53588..	support.google.com/chrome/answer/95346?co=G..
www.google.com/intl/en/chrome	play.google.com/store/apps/details?id=com.a..
www.commentcamarche.net/download/telecharge..	www.commentcamarche.net/download/telecharge..
www.clubic.com/telecharger-fiche257658-goog..	support.google.com/chrome/?hl=en
www.google.fr/chrome	www.clubic.com/telecharger-fiche257658-goog..
www.questionsanswered.net/article/how-insta..	chrome.google.com/webstore

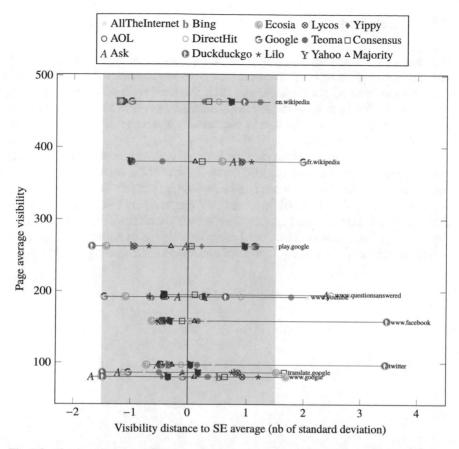

Fig. 7.8 Distance between visibilities of domains for the most-shown domains. Each line is a domain, the line height is the domain average visibility, and each dot represents a specific SE (the abscissa of the dot is the difference between the domain visibility for that SE to the mean domain visibility, normalized with the standard deviation among SEs). The gray zone indicates the interval with semi-width 1.5 standard deviation [114]

A few remarks can be made:

- The SEs Ask and DirectHit gave the same top three results, all from "question-sanswered.net," while no other SE showed a page from that domain.
- But because those two SEs agreed, no outlier has been detected by our test regarding the visibility that each SE's top page has among others. However, both SEs are detected by the test that compares the visibility score of SE top results.
- The Consensus ranking is significantly affected by those two SEs because of the large visibility weight of top positions, as it shows two pages from the domain "questionsanswered.net". On the other hand, as observed previously with our synthetic model, the Majority Judgment ranking is more robust to such possible biases, and does not display any page from that domain.

7.3   Conclusion

It is undeniable that search engines, and in particular the overwhelmingly most used one Google, have a considerable impact on e-commerce actors and the digital ecosystem in general. As discussed in [121], the antitrust legal arsenal does not seem to be sufficient to solve the issues generated by possible biases. Due to their gatekeeper position, some think it is paramount to include SE behavior in the discussions around neutrality.

The approach developed in the previous section is of course not the only one that can be applied to check and analyze differences between SEs; we mostly intended to show examples of methods that can be used, what types of results they can lead to, and their limitations. In a digital landscape evolving at a very fast pace, monitoring those key actors (that can very rapidly change their algorithms or just the layout of their result pages) is a very delicate and complex task, but an immensely important one to protect the Internet as a fair place of innovation and economic opportunity.

Chapter 8
Algorithmic Transparency

The two previous chapters advocated for the extension of the neutrality debate to a class of actors of the digital economy broader than just ISPs, since service discrimination could be applied at other steps of the supply chain between content and users. We particularly discussed the cases of major intermediaries such as CDNs, search engines, structuring platforms, or terminal builders. A common factor for all actors, but not the only one involved in the debate, is the use of algorithms to implement their service according to a strategy. That is typically the case for structuring platforms such as search engines implementing an algorithm to select and sort links or marketplace platforms sorting objects to be sold, etc. ISPs too can be categorized that way, with protocols implementing packet routing at routers and congestion control techniques. Therefore, algorithms in the broad sense have an impact on how we use and interact through the Internet, and many questions are popping up on the role and actions and regulation of algorithms, leading to the debate on *algorithmic transparency*. The term *algorithmic transparency* was probably coined for the first time in the 2017 publication [46] when dealing with the decision on the displayed content in news media, even if questioning automated decisions by algorithms has been discussed for about 50 years.

But first, what is an algorithm? Actually, quite surprisingly, there is no clear definition. Basically an algorithm is usually defined as below [140]:

> An algorithm is an unambiguous, precise, list of simple operations applied mechanically and systematically to a set of tokens or objects (e.g., configurations of chess pieces, numbers, cake ingredients, etc.). The initial state of the tokens is the input; the final state is the output.

Algorithms are omnipresent in our daily life with the advent of computers but were already present before computers. Indeed, going as far as before Christ, there were already algorithms existing for mathematical factorization to find the square root of a number, or in everyday life to describe cooking recipes. Now, with the omnipresence of computing systems, algorithms are "everywhere" and influence the way we behave and interact, while we may not be aware of their impact.

Algorithms are also implemented in all the areas of the economy, from finance (to exercise options, etc.) to transportation and so on. A popular and representative illustration of algorithms' economic benefit is the success of revenue management techniques and dynamic pricing implemented first in the airline industry: it was credited to American Airlines in the early 1980s to cope with the deregulation of the US airline industry, with ticket prices made dependent on many parameters (time-of-week trip, remaining availability, service options, etc.) and often seen as obscure by travelers, but proved to yield an efficient output with more revenue for the airline and an increased social welfare. Algorithms have also many (potentially) positive impacts on society. An illustrative example is when a data-driven approach is used to detect patterns of criminal behavior (like the National Data Analytics Solution (NDAS) in the UK, or *paved* in France) or of a potential hotspot (predpol tool[1]).

For what concerns "neutrality" in a broad sense, the topic of this book, what algorithms are we interested in? We actually think of all algorithms that are part of the *digital economy*, in particular those used by structuring platforms. We have already discussed in details the ranking algorithms and optimal strategies of search engines in Chap. 7, but all marketplaces, the main example being Amazon, are also concerned: what algorithm is used to rank items proposed to clients? What notion of relevance is used, if any, and isn't there any other unknown component included? The same questions apply to hotel and travel booking Web sites; to YouTube, Netflix, and other such video streaming sites for their video recommendation algorithms; and to newsfeeds for Facebook or Twitter, or all the news aggregators which can influence populations' beliefs, an important and sensitive question in our societies. Why and how do they choose the first displayed items? People do not particularly know why something is proposed to them in priority and tend to trust the platform.

The questions people and regulators could legitimately ask are: Are all the algorithms loyal to the users, displaying the most "relevant" content, or instead something that is in the interest of the platform, such as financially or even ideologically, by biasing content toward a given set of opinions? Are they also loyal to vendors for double-sided platforms such as Amazon or accommodation platforms, or do they again prefer vendors leading to a larger revenue? Then what should really be expected from platforms? It may be hard to obtain "neutrality" especially given that the meaning of this notion is not totally clear, particularly in this context: should we want all content to be equally proposed? Or selected and ranked according to some measure of relevance? Is there some economic component involved? Do we by the way really want an unbiased ranking? Those are very sensitive questions. For marketplaces, there is often the possibility to rank items from the cheapest to the most expensive or the other way around, but the default setting is according to an obscure supposed relevance we have to trust. A proposition gaining interest as an intermediary "solution" is, at least for some actors, to enforce some *algorithmic transparency* to let the user be informed and able to switch (if possible).

---

[1] https://www.predpol.com/.

What exactly does algorithmic transparency mean? A definition on Wikipedia is:[2]

> Algorithmic transparency is the principle that the factors that influence the decisions made by algorithms should be visible, or transparent, to the people who use, regulate, and are affected by systems that employ those algorithms.

Typically, it is not requiring to totally disclose the algorithms, applications, and software in an open-source format but to clearly reveal the components and factors that enter into the process. Then, it is up to users and regulators to ensure that the algorithms are following the rules (but one might ask the platforms to prove they are indeed processing as declared).

As it can be seen in the previous paragraphs, we are asking more questions than providing answers, but our purpose is rather to inform the reader about the existing issues so that they can make their own opinion. In any case, we often face strong views on this type of topic—it is somewhat similar to politics—and it is probably illusory to convert someone.

The issue of algorithmic transparency involves and/or can be decomposed into several concepts, among which:

1. *Awareness.* All actors have to be aware of the existence and consequences of algorithms in the digital economy: where algorithms are applied, their implementation, as well as the potential dangers and harm they can produce. It is often claimed that there is in general a low level of awareness about the use of algorithms, particularly among individuals.
2. *(Limited) Asymmetry.* Asymmetry typically occurs when data-driven companies collect data, even more than the user or involved partner is aware of or can oversee. GDPR (General Data Protection Regulation) policies have been introduced to limit this type of asymmetry.
3. *Accountability and responsibility.* Entities using algorithms must be accountable for the decisions determined by those algorithms, even though those decisions are being made by a machine. Accountability, or responsibility, is the ability to define the role of each involved stakeholder in decisions and identify errors or unexpected results. The institutions should be held responsible for the decisions resulting from their algorithms. In other words, they should not be able to hide behind a "blackbox."
4. *Loyalty.* A platform should provide information to any user on the behavior of the(ir) algorithm and use of data that is truthful with respect to what is implemented. Typically, for search engines, any contractual relationship leading to goods or links being put forward should be explicitly stipulated.
5. *Non-discrimination.* The use of algorithms (and the usual associated search for "optimization") can lead to discrimination that could be tacit, it is indeed not necessarily explicit. That is even more possible with the growing use of AI and

---

[2] https://en.wikipedia.org/wiki/Algorithmic_transparency.

data-driven innovations. Transparency as to how algorithms operate is therefore essential.

6. *Fairness.* Fairness is related to the notions of loyalty and nondiscrimination. However, not everyone agrees on what a fair algorithm is, and it is not commonly admitted that algorithms have to be fair in the sense that all users are treated the same in terms of decisions, independently of the knowledge the algorithm has about them. In most cases, algorithm fairness is about removing biases caused by data usage.

7. *Intelligibility.* Intelligibility is the quality of being possible to understand. It is admitted that the most accurate AI algorithms, such as those based on deep learning, are not very intelligible, while the most intelligible models, such as those based on regression, are often less accurate.

8. *Explainability.* Explainability is the principle that the algorithm, no matter how complex, should be explained and expressed in human terms. It encompasses the explanation in human terms of how data are collected and used.

9. *Traceability.* Traceability means the possibility to recover all steps and provenance of data at the different steps of the execution of an algorithm. It is considered a key requirement for trustworthy AI. Data provenance has to be described, meaning how the training data was collected, with all the associated privacy concerns.

10. *Auditability.* Algorithms and data, as well as the associated decisions should be recorded so that they can be audited to verify that they conform to rules and regulations, in particular when harm is suspected. Indeed, and this is particularly the case for "blackbox" AI, monitoring and testing algorithms throughout their entire life cycle is required.

11. *Proof and certification.* The institutions and companies implementing algorithms should provide rigorous methods (with appropriate descriptions) to validate their models and perform tests to ensure that their algorithms do not generate harm.

12. *Performance.* The performance of algorithmic transparency tools should be reported, for example, through statistics. An illustration is for content moderation programs.

13. *Ethics.* Algorithms create several issues related to ethics. They may be related to (implicit) discriminatory behaviors, such as when prediction algorithms managing the health data in the USA exacerbate racial discrimination with white patients given better care than black patients [166]. Ethical issues are either epistemic through inconclusive, inscrutable, or misguided evidence or normative through unfair outcomes and transformative effects [166].

The USACM (US Association for Computing Machinery) describes the principles for algorithmic transparency as the decomposition into awareness, access and redress, accountability, explanation, data provenance, auditability, and validation and testing (equivalent to proof and certification)[168].

The next sections detail some of the issues. Section 8.1 lists and details the threats brought by the algorithms used by structuring platforms. Section 8.2 has a more particular focus on worries around artificial intelligence algorithms, their understanding, and control. Section 8.3 provides some hints about how algorithmic transparency is or can be addressed. Finally, Sect. 8.4 discusses an important and related topic: the manipulation of opinions through platforms, social networks, and the associated control of hateful content and fake news.

8.1 Algorithmic Transparency and Structuring Platforms: Why Introduce Scrutiny?

Both the use of big data (in particular all data about Internet users collected by applications or Web sites) and the use of algorithms to optimize prices lead to improved commercial efficiency for companies of all kinds. But as a consequence, they impact society [140] and therefore require scrutiny. As pointed out in the introduction of this chapter, customers/users of structuring platforms may wonder about the choice of what is proposed/displayed to them and how it is ranked. Similarly, in a double-sided market, vendors on online marketplaces may have several concerns, most of them related to some potential neutrality principles not being satisfied. Here is a list, probably non-exhaustive, of such concerns brought by structuring platforms:

1. *Truthfulness to users.* This corresponds to the issue raised in the previous chapter for search engines (the search neutrality debate). The problem also arises with the (equivalent) type of list displayed as a response to a request, provided by marketplaces, that strongly influence users' behavior as they are more likely to follow or choose (depending on context) the advised items. It is not always clear what drives platforms to provide the proposed list: Is it really the expected relevance with respect to the request? It is actually believed that this is not always the case and that instead some marketplaces may favor in their ranking the items, vendors, or sites yielding a larger commission to the platform.
2. *Anticompetitive behaviors and vertical integration.* We already discussed the case of search engines, with the shopping comparison site Foundem launching complaints against Google at the European Commission and US FCC, accusing Google of "threat to competition and innovation" because its site was ranked low with respect to the similar Google Shopping service, hence limiting (in a way claimed abusive) Foundem's visibility and therefore its business opportunities. This potential anticompetitive behavior is due to vertical integration and the possibility and willingness to put forward one's own products. Similarly, in 2012, TripAdvisor and Expedia filed complaints to Europe's competition regulators about Google putting forward its competing services, claiming that "anticompetitive and unfair practices by Google" harm the marketplace and consumer welfare. This type of behavior may affect and concern all types of integrated services. In 2017, the European Commission fined Google 2.42 billion euros for abusing of their dominance position as a search engine by giving illegal

advantage to their own comparison shopping service,[3] systematically giving it a prominent placement when a related request is placed. The examples we just provided are similar to Microsoft abusing its dominant position by tying its Web browser to its operating system, but here concerning the behavior of algorithms. Can algorithmic transparency "solve" the issue?

3. *Anticompetitive behaviors and abuse of dominant position.* In 2019, a complaint was filled against Expedia and Booking.com by Danish hotel booking platform Nustay, a competitor but small actor in the field. Nustay was accusing Expedia and Booking.com of using their dominant position by punishing hotels commercially if they exercised their right to sell accommodation at lower prices to competitors. It was also claimed that the dominant platforms were seeking to blacklist Nustay. Similarly, Expedia was accused in 2011 of blacklisting non-member hotels and lying on "regular" hotel rates to display larger savings through their platforms than the actual ones.[4] This concern is in line with the issue mentioned in the previous item, but here the context is a threat by using a dominant position as a competitive advantage against competitors, not putting forward an integrated service. Another example is the online advertising sector, generating a significant part of revenues in the digital economy (indeed estimated at around 78 billion US dollars in 2020 and believed to reach 646 billion US dollars by 2024[5]). Google and Facebook have a dominant position in this industry (Google accounted for 30% in the USA in 2020, Facebook 25%, and Amazon 10%[6]). But Google was accused of abusing its market dominance by imposing a number of restrictive clauses to contracts with third-party Web sites, which prevented Google's rivals from placing their adverts on those Web sites. In 2019, the European Commission fined Google 1.49 billion euros for breaching EU antitrust rules in this context. In the USA, ten states accused Google in 2020 of overcharging for the ads it showed; they also claimed that Google had reached an agreement with Facebook to limit the social network's own efforts to compete with Google. The Fortnite/Apple argument we discussed in the previous chapters also enters this abuse of dominant position category. Those examples do not *directly* relate to the application of algorithms but to the use of powerful algorithms to twist the market. If rules/decision components were disclosed, could such behaviors be limited?

4. *Collusion.* A different question and concern is: Can algorithms make tacit collusion easier? From [140], "algorithms might facilitate tacit co-ordination, a market outcome that is not covered by competition law, by providing companies with automated mechanisms to signal, implement common policies, as well as

---

[3] https://ec.europa.eu/commission/presscorner/detail/en/MEMO_17_1785.

[4] https://hospitality-on.com/en/online-distribution-travel/expedia-accused-unfair-business-practice-france.

[5] https://www.statista.com/statistics/237974/online-advertising-spending-worldwide/.

[6] https://www.statista.com/statistics/242549/digital-ad-market-share-of-major-ad-selling-companies-in-the-us-by-revenue/.

monitor and punish deviations." Tacit collusion is defined as a collusion between competitors, which do not explicitly exchange information and achieving an agreement about coordination of conduct, in contrast with explicit collusion. That situation typically occurs in marketplaces and e-commerce where search and pricing policies can be automatically adapted from the strategies of competitors, thanks to monitoring algorithms. If all actors use this principle, the actions are repeated as if directly communicated to competitors on purpose (even if not in reality), and we are dealing with tacit collusion without any contact. Actually, learning and tacitly collude are often considered as among the most efficient individual behaviors. Algorithms, by their adaptability, can increase tacit collusion, inducing worries from authorities due to its induced impact on competition and society. In this particular context, note the difference of vision between law institutions and regulators: while the *means* used by algorithms is of more interest to legal authorities, regulators are usually more interested in the *outcomes*, when trying to design appropriate rules, if needed. Algorithms are expected to expand the gray area between unlawful explicit collusion and lawful tacit collusion, hence the increased scrutiny about potential rules to be applied. According to EU Commissioner for Competition Margrethe Vestager, "[...] competition enforcers[...] need to make it very clear that companies can't escape responsibility for collusion by hiding behind a computer program."

5. *Data-driven barriers to entry.* Data accumulated by major actors and not shared can be detrimental to competition. While that situation happens in all areas of the economy, it is exacerbated in the more dynamic and algorithm-driven digital economy. The expected and main goal of using data is to propose the most appropriate services to users. The revenue of many major companies in the digital economy comes from business models based on the collection and commercial use of data on their users, sometimes in a quasi-monopolistic situation leading to limited possibilities for new entrants to prosper. Google's search engine and Facebook's social network are typical examples. In 2016, French and German authorities released together a report [11] studying the impact of data on competition and identifying some actions that could lead to exclusion of competition in a data-related business: *(i)* mergers, acquisition of newcomers, and vertical integration to access new data resulting in differentiated data access; *(ii)* deprivation or refusal of the access to data to some competitors, which can reduce competition; a refusal can prevent the emergence of a new product. For example, in France, Cegedim, the owner of the main medical information databases, did not want to sell its main database to competitors, something seen as prejudicial by the French authority; *(iii)* exclusive agreement excluding rivals; *(iv)* tied sales and cross-usage of datasets when data from given market is used to increase market power on another market in an anticompetitive way; and *(v)* data as a vehicle for discriminatory pricing relying on a better knowledge of users' willingness to pay. There is actually no reason why that question about the use of data should be limited to telecommunications and the digital economy, but the technological novelties of the digital world have accelerated data collection possibilities.

6. There are also concerns about *privacy and the use of personal data without consent*. This worry has led to several requests from authorities to reveal rules and use of personal data. For instance, Facebook now offers the possibility to click on a "why do I see this advertisement" button. Similarly, Web sites have to get the consent of visitors to use cookies. But much has still to be done toward a full disclosure of the use of personal data.

7. *Fake e-commerce goods*. Even if not exactly the topic of this book, we cannot pass on another threat related to the online economy: the question of fake e-commerce goods that users are buying but do not exist or of goods not corresponding exactly to what was claimed or being defective. These swindles are increasingly present and represent for some persons a major reason not to fully use Internet services. The liability of online marketplaces in those cases is the topic of many trials: for example, now that Amazon allows third-party sellers to operate on its platform, Amazon is related to the transactions, particularly given that the marketplace earns a commission with each sale. But laws are not crystal clear with that respect, and usually depend on the country, with issues arising in particular when vendors and platforms are not located in the same country. With a clear description of transparency about the used algorithms, customers would more easily understand what the risks are.

8. *Vendors' lack of information*. Vendors on marketplaces, hotels on accommodation platforms, advertisers on Web pages and social media, etc. complain not to have a complete access to data and performance of the product they sell. In the advertising sector, despite tools such as Google AdWords and Google AdSense, several advertisers do not feel that they have a full control on data related to their ads. In early 2021, there was a class action against Google alleging that company overcharged pay-per-click advertisers (how to be sure that the charged price corresponds to the expected generalized second-price auction [115] and that the involved click-through-rate for the ad is not overestimated, increasing the price?). Similarly, the hotels referenced on accommodation platforms wish to have a larger access to data on who is looking at their description, etc.

9. *Filter bubbles*. According to the Oxford dictionary (2019), the term refers to "a situation in which an internet user encounters only information and opinions that conform to and reinforce their own beliefs, caused by algorithms that personalize an individual's online experience." Typically, thanks to data and personalization, an individual could only face newsfeeds, products, or opinions that are in line with what they are pleased to see, i.e., find themselves in what is called an echo chamber. This lack of diversity may be considered as a danger since the individual could miss information and have a misrepresentation of the world, or considering the other potential "items" as minor ones, without clearly understanding the origins of such biases. That issue will be discussed more in Sect. 8.4, since it is related to the principles of opinion orientation or confirmation bias.

8.2   Worries About the Transparency of Artificial Intelligence Algorithms

Artificial intelligence (AI) algorithms form a special class of algorithms "able to carry out tasks of significant difficulty in a way that is perceived as intelligent" [140], for example, by learning from data and/or experience (so-called machine learning), or thanks to the enhanced *deep learning* techniques where the identification of relevant features are automated. Why do we isolate this subclass of algorithms in a specific section? Actually due to their learning and adaptive functioning, their output is less easy to understand, which induces concerns since they can surpass human brain performance (this was crystallized when in 2015 the AlphaGo algorithm was the first computer program to defeat a professional human Go player, and even the Go world champion Lee Sedol in 2016). The worries were exacerbated when Professor Stephen Hawking, one of Britain's popular and highly touted scientists, told to the BBC in 2014 "the development of full artificial intelligence could spell the end of the human race," claiming that efforts to create thinking machines pose a threat to mankind.

AI algorithms have been productive worldwide and pushed by countries and companies since constituting one of the "technologies" expected to yield a significant competitive advantage. Major investments are involved in the area, with a strong competition worldwide. For example, it is reported that the AI Chinese industry is generating around $59 billion annually [33]. Some companies are dominating the market, buying start-ups, with antitrust issues that might pop up. In 2020, North America was leading the AI market with over 40% share of global revenue. According to Analytics Insight,[7] the five main AI actors in 2019 were IBM (10.3% of the market share), Google (8.2%), Microsoft (7.6%), Amazon (7.1%), and Facebook (6.6%).

What particularly scares people about AI algorithms is that they are autonomous, seen as "black boxes" where what happens inside is hard to understand, and even computer scientists cannot always explain the output produced by algorithms. Their adaptability and learning process to improve their performance create a worry that they can be used as a malicious tool by companies or governments and hard to control if their actions are not understood. Worries are even more present with deep learning algorithms where the neural network features are learned (and somewhat felt as even less controlled by humans). Afraid of the impact of AI on our society, several scientists signed in 2015 an open letter asking for more investigation on this topic.[8]

To better account for the understanding/transparency of algorithms, the notion of *algorithmic explainability* has been introduced. The principle is to take raw information about the algorithm functioning and make it understandable to humans.

---

[7] https://www.analyticsinsight.net/top-5-artificial-intelligence-companies-with-market-share.

[8] https://futureoflife.org/ai-open-letter/.

Indeed, in the case of AI, explanations may be needed regarding the learning algorithm, including information on how the training data is collected and used.

8.3   How to Proceed?

Algorithmic transparency is therefore an important issue under the radar of regulators and lawyers to "ensure" neutrality of algorithms or at least to keep the users informed about what is proposed to them. As described in [64], algorithmic transparency can be described in different ways. As a basic principle, it could mean explaining (publishing) the key criteria that led to a result in the case of ranking, recommendation, advertising, or why something is not posted, that might be considered sufficient for individuals or non-experts. That is typically what Facebook is doing when displaying an advertisement: you can click on a "why do I see this ad" button to be given the reasons why you were targeted from the data collected from you and the criteria used by the advertiser. But there are cases where asking for more details should be allowed. By a company for example, such as hotels with respect to accommodation platforms, or vendors on e-commerce platforms. Indeed, from a more expert perspective, that is, a regulator or a company/business owner whose activity is laying on the use of algorithms from intermediaries, more information or verification is required. This means both more explanations about the way the algorithm works and uses data and measurements of algorithms' performance to check the conformity with the claimed behavior. As an example, a hotel on an accommodation platform is interested in measuring false-positive or false-negative rates in moderation, or vendors on selling platforms are interested in understanding their ranking for given keywords.

A theoretically simpler solution would be to ask for *full transparency*: companies totally disclosing the code of their algorithms. Following this principle, it was publicly asked in 2016 by the German Chancellor Angela Merkel that major companies such as Facebook and Google disclose their proprietary algorithms. This "extreme" solution, while attractive to solve all issues related to algorithmic transparency, leads to proprietary issues: Is it fair to require to disclose technological secrets acquired from research and development investments? Again, similarly to the basic ISP neutrality issue, very few (if none) other economic sector would face this type of constraint. It is even claimed that it could be a disincentive to innovation. As another limit, enforcing full transparency could ease the manipulation of the weaknesses of algorithms by other actors, creating worse and unexpected effects with respect to the nontransparent situation. Indeed, we have to be cautious that any regulatory intervention might lead to negative impacts that could outweigh its potential benefits.

Since data is a key element from privacy (from the user point of view) to proprietary (for algorithm owners) concerns, DGE (*Direction Générale des Entreprises*, part of the Ministry of Economy) in France proposes to separate three types of algorithms:

- Those not using user data (e.g., ranking by Rakuten); they could be required to provide the list of considered parameters for the algorithm.
- Algorithms using data from users. Their operators could be asked to signal such algorithms and their impact; the goal would be for regulators to check the compliance to the declaration.
- Algorithms crossing data from users; more complicated and needing specific methods.

Ensuring transparency means needing to monitor the activity of algorithms. It is for example the case for algorithm builders, regulators, and users to verify a valid behavior. This will be described more in the next chapter, and involves two main aspects: *(i)* verifying how the algorithms proceed and if they conform to what they claim; this can be done by using APIs (Application Programming Interfaces, which are applications used to access data and interact with external software components) or scraping (using bots to extract content and data). Of course, this has to be limited to avoid overloading the target of supervision. *(ii)* A clear description of the used data, use which can also be verified.

8.4 Fake News, Manipulation of Opinions, Hatred, and Fact Checking

Neutrality and transparency of algorithms and the digital economy as a whole face new challenges when it comes to information. The key issue is to allow all users to be informed and to discuss with other persons, but could organizations, states, or companies "bias" toward some news and influence opinions? Should some messages of hatred and violence be allowed? If forbidding some news, aren't we going against neutrality and freedom, one of its often claimed most important component? Addressing that question is the purpose of this section.

The most striking illustration of this new type of problem is due to the advent of social networks. Social networks have revolutionized the media and communication industry. Thanks to social networks, often with just a (free) account, but that is not even compulsory, you can communicate with others and express your opinion. The most well-known social networking tools are Facebook, YouTube, Twitter, Snapchat, and TikTok but also all discussion forums on news Web sites, blogs, etc. According to [64], one third of French people and half of 18- to 24-year-olds obtain their information from social networks.

The positive impact of social networks was emphasized during the Arab Spring, a series of pro-democracy uprisings that started in several largely Muslim countries (Tunisia, Morocco, Syria, Libya, Egypt, and Bahrain) in the Spring of 2011. Social networks, hard to control, led movements to be relayed and publicized. At the time, the events emphasized their ability to promote freedom of speech, connectivity, and democracy; this was highlighted by Mark Zuckerberg (CEO of Facebook) and Eric Schmidt (executive director of Google) as a reason for not regulating the Internet.[9] But more recently, the Internet and social networks have been more perceived as a means to promote hatred and *fake news*, defined on Wikipedia as "a type of yellow journalism or propaganda that consists of deliberate misinformation or hoaxes spread via traditional print and broadcast news media or online social media." Indeed, we see an important number of hatred messages on forums and social networks. Or political groups or alien countries are often organizing false information dissemination to bias mass opinions. Terrorists are even said to use social media for radicalization, recruitment, funding, planning, and execution of terror activities.[10]

Without any control, internal or external, social media can manipulate opinion by showing content optimally selected for that purpose. This has been exacerbated by the Cambridge Analytica scandal: In the 2010s, the firm Cambridge Analytica collected data of up to 87 millions of Facebook subscribers *without their consent* and used them for political advertising, data being helpful to infer the political opinions of users. This was known to be used as an assistance in the 2016 presidential campaign of Donald Trump by targeted advertisements depending on the user's personality: depending on pre-existing knowledge, the most adapted message is sent for better persuasion and larger impact. The use of those data was leaked in 2018, and Facebook had to apologize; its CEO Mark Zuckerberg even had to testify in front of the UQA Congress, and a $5 billion fine was issued by the FTC for privacy violations. That scandal highlights how algorithms in social media can influence opinions. Similarly, forums, news Web pages, news aggregators, and social media select the order in which they display information, leading to biased "important" news since items displayed first are much more likely to be seen. The order is even often personalized, leading to a *bias of confirmation* (providing links to articles in the same vein of what you have already read and very probably would like to read) but barring you from a diversity of views. An important example is about politics, with a resulting politically oriented bias in the presented information. Search platforms such as Google were also accused of manipulating elections through the presented links: Republicans during hearings in the Congress in 2018 complained about political bias, claiming that conservative voices were suppressed; CNBC on the other hand claimed that Google search displayed more negative links on Democrats and positive ones on Republicans.

It has been shown that a false story disseminates six times faster than a factual one, particularly when bots are used to further automate the propagation of fake news.[11] So what responsibility should be engaged for social media? Should they be regulated? But if so, what regulation can be implemented without leading to an infringement of the freedom of speech? Another relevant question is: What is the

---

[9] https://www.theguardian.com/technology/2011/may/26/facebook-google-internet-regulation-g8.

[10] https://www.interpol.int/Crimes/Terrorism/Analysing-social-media.

[11] https://www.state.gov/wp-content/uploads/2019/05/Weapons-of-Mass-Distraction-Foreign-State-Sponsored-Disinformation-in-the-Digital-Age.pdf.

difference with "regular" newspaper, radio, or television media? That question is similar to the neutrality issue of ISPs, which is something strongly supported while there is no such strong feeling in other key "access" types where it is applied, such as transportation (with tool freeways) or mail (with faster but more expensive UPS) among examples. Should social media be regulated more than regular media, which in most cases also have an opinion biased toward a political side (it is known that some media are more left- or right-wing oriented) or even sport media which has a national/chauvinism bias without being asked to reveal the "algorithm" driving their choice of priorities? The enhanced question in digital media probably comes from the "filter bubble" issue being exacerbated on the Internet due to algorithms. There is actually an increased risk of false information spreading on the Internet and an uncertainty from non-reviewed published articles, something not (or less) expected on traditional media, even if it could be increasingly counter-exampled. The public debate is thus currently more on social media and on the control of posted "information" which could be unethical and wrong: Are forum owners and social media responsible for what is posted? Social media actors generally claim that they are platforms not creating their own content, so they should not be held responsible for libel and defamation or be subject to other laws and regulations governing regular media; new and specific regulation rules may have to be applied.

To cope with the negative view created by fake news and inappropriate messages, moderation tools are put in place. We can refer to comments or content being reviewed *before* being posted on forums or selling platforms (such as leboncoin in France), or removed ex-post if signaled by other participants to forums or social networks. The latter decentralized solution, while simple, could nevertheless lead to "valid," say ethical, content being removed when signaled by others just not liking what was posted; this may happen on forums or on social networks when users are signaled by ideological opponents and banned by the social network for a period of time. Issues with signaling are also observed when realized through AI algorithms, another solution recently adopted by major social media platforms. It was reported in 2020 that Facebook posts, pictures, and videos have been flagged by AI or reported by users about 3 million times a day,[12] among which about 10% can be considered mistakes. Regularly advertised examples include pictures of pieces of art rejected for nudity reasons. In 2021, in order to limit false information spreading during the coronavirus crisis, Facebook was also displaying fake news alerts when vaccine-related messages were posted. Following the same line, still in 2021, Twitter removed over 20,000 QAnon (a powerful pro-conspiracy movement)-related accounts, and both Twitter and Facebook even closed Donald Trump's account still while he was the US president, due to all the fake news and aggressive posted messages. Many Trump partisans then moved to Parler, an alternative social media platform.

---

[12] https://issuu.com/nyusterncenterforbusinessandhumanri/docs/nyu_content_moderation_report_final_version.

But isn't moderating content an attempt to freedom of speech? How to define and identify fake news? How to exactly define violent or even terrorist content? Some governments close accounts or remove content from organizations or opponents declared terrorist but not considered as such in other countries. Some content is considered subversive in some places but without any problem in others; this shows we have a gray area with a border difficult to define.

How to define regulation on this matter? A French attempt is made in [64] where it is said that regulation could be based on five pillars:

1. *A public regulatory policy guaranteeing individual freedoms and platforms' entrepreneurial freedom.*
2. *A prescriptive regulation focusing on the accountability of social networks, implemented by an independent administrative authority and based on three obligations for the platforms: (i)* Obligation of transparency of the function of ordering content; *(ii)* Obligation of transparency of the function which implements the Terms of Service and the moderation of content; *(iii)* Obligation to defend the integrity of its users.
3. *Informed political dialogue between the operators, the government, the legislature and civil society.*
4. *An independent administrative authority, acting in partnership with other branches of the state, and open to civil society.*
5. *A European cooperation, reinforcing Member States' capacity to act against global platforms and reducing the risks related to implementation in each Member State.*

French Ministry of Economy and Finance, 2019 [64]

The first pillar is about freedom of speech, the second about transparency of the post choices and moderation, and the last three about the way to define limits for bans and moderation. The application of those principles is undermined by the limited access to information that regulators have, often reduced to what platforms communicate. The trade-off between freedom of speech and limitation of fake news still is to be clearly defined and publicly advertised.

In [64], it is also advocated that what should be implemented, progressively and pragmatically according to the size of the operators and their services, is that:

[...] the social network platform incorporates public interest objectives, modifies its organization, adapts itself to this "social" objective and acts either upstream at the design stage, to prevent difficulties, abuses and other misuse of its service, or downstream, to address unacceptable behavior by its users.

8.5   Conclusion on Transparency and Neutrality

As a conclusion, even if the debates on network neutrality and algorithmic transparency are usually disjoint in the media and by regulators, we feel that there are actually close connections in the spirit of what should be implemented and that the borders between the two is not well-defined if we want to address all aspects of the net neutrality issue.

Chapter 9
Tools to Monitor Neutrality

9.1 Why Are Specific Tools Needed?

Neutrality is regulated in a variety of regions and ways, as we have seen in the previous chapters. Laws are passed worldwide, with levels of enforcement varying according to the countries. But however strict laws are, as soon as rules are imposed, it is necessary to design procedures to monitor whether the targeted actors respect those rules. Without any such procedure, nothing prevents the actors from differentiating services since there would be no tool to detect inappropriate behaviors and above all to *prove* them, which is compulsory if we wish to impose sanctions in court.

Designing tools is thus required to monitor in particular the activity of ISPs, the initial and main target of the debate, and detect potential infringements to neutrality regulations. But tools also have to deal with all actors of the digital economy we have discussed in previous chapters: how to know whether a CDN is behaving in a way to favor not the most downloaded content but rather some "relative" content or content paying more for that? How to detect a biased behavior from a search engine or an e-commerce platform ranking some pieces of content abusively high? Since those behaviors also mean a differentiation impacting society, designing monitoring procedures is needed: detecting and analyzing the consequences of an inappropriate behavior is important even if no rule is already passed, just to understand if regulation may become necessary.

As another perspective of the problem, not only regulators and institutions need tools, but users and content providers may too. Indeed, these other categories of actors need to trust service providers and be convinced that they are not fooled with respect to what they believe to be provided, sometimes from an economic contract. Tools *not* provided by the service providers themselves are needed toward this goal. This concerns of course content providers expecting to check if they are not served with a lower priority by ISPs, but also, for example, hotel managers on accommodation platforms wishing to control if their ranking on platforms is fair,

© The Author(s), under exclusive license to Springer Nature Switzerland AG 2022
P. Maillé, B. Tuffin, *From Net Neutrality to ICT Neutrality*,
https://doi.org/10.1007/978-3-031-06271-1_9

content providers making use of CDNs wanting to check if their files are served at the edge with the same criteria as competitors, etc. To highlight this need from a legal point of view, if citizens of Canada believe that their Internet traffic is being throttled, they need to file formal complaints, meaning that practical measurements need to be realized. Indeed, how to ask for reparation if no practical *and reliable* arguments are given?

If no tool is available, it is hard and maybe even impossible to act. Currently, asking for a compliant behavior is often done *ex post*, with tools built after a problem is identified, taking sometimes a long period before identification, then another period to design the specific tools, and then often years of legal procedures before making a stance. Over these cumulated periods of time, harm can be made, hence the need to design general monitoring tools in order to act quicker, ideally proactively, that is, *ex ante*, in the definition of rules.

The purpose of this chapter is to review existing tools, their limits, and shortages, illustrating that very little actually exists as concerns neutrality issues. We will start in Sect. 9.2 with tools for monitoring ISPs in the network neutrality debate context. Section 9.3 discusses monitoring tools for other actors in the digital economy, focusing on CDNs and search engines as the main other intermediaries between content and users, in relation to the issues raised in Chaps. 6 and 7. Section 9.4 deals with tools for algorithmic transparency, and Sect. 9.5 is about fact-checking tools, echoing the questions raised in Chap. 8.

9.2   Tools for the Monitoring of ISPs

9.2.1   Potential Infringements

The network neutrality debate came from a list of experienced and/or potential service differentiation practices, limiting the access to or the quality of service of some types of traffic. The most-raised technical ways that limitations are realized are the following: (see also [143])

- *Blocking of port, protocol, source, destination traffic using DPI (Deep Packet Inspection).* There are several ways to apply blocking: you can just drop any packet of the targeted traffic or terminate the TCP connections related to that traffic with RST (i.e., reset) packets. Identifying the traffic is usually fairly easy with DPI, through the IP address of the source or destination, through the port number often characteristic of the service type, or, thanks to a signature in the packet payload, as a keyword in a search engine query, or from the flow shape [20, 83]. P2P traffic has, for example, historically been a specific target of ISPs for traffic blocking, as illustrated in the first chapters of this book.
- *Throttling of some traffic.* Degrading the quality of some traffic, while not completely blocking it, may be another (subtler) option. It may be more interesting for ISPs willing to limit a targeted traffic but without forbidding it:

It may indeed be perceived better to keep authorizing the traffic while offering more bandwidth to other and "friendly" flows or to voluntarily deteriorate traffic and try to evade detection from regulators or user associations. Here, too, the first chapters are full of illustrations of traffic throttling. Another example of specific and technical limitation with the purpose of dealing with congestion is that of the ISP Cogent, limiting in 2016 "big" TCP connections with respect to small ones to restrict big file transfers,[1] which is another typical traffic management procedure.

- *Denial of service by domain name system (DNS) manipulation* is another possibility, rendering some domains non-accessible.

The list above illustrates the range of potential targets and means. As there are many and very different possibilities to differentiate or block traffic, monitoring all possible scenarios is often considered infeasible: it would mean knowing all possible technical ways to limit traffic—a quite strong assumption—while new ideas could pop up and fly under the radar. Another possibility is to look at the output, that is, just look whether some traffic is differentiated in terms of offered quality without initially looking at how this traffic is served. But then this could be due to technical and networking reasons independent of any willingness to differentiate from ISPs. For example, in 2013, the low quality in France of YouTube on ISP Free was due to peering issues, not to traffic management.[2] For this reason, regulators often rely on alerts from users or service providers before investigating a particular infringement to the rules.

9.2.2 Available Tools

In accordance with the above arguments, the French regulator ARCEP also believes that a regulator needs tools to monitor ISP activity, the claimed goals being to verify the compliance of ISPs with imposed neutrality principles and to inform users, associations, and regulators about their traffic management practices [6, 145]. ARCEP recommends a kind of "roundtable" between user associations, ISPs, and other actors to point out the relevant QoS parameters for Internet access (and neutrality) and the corresponding indicators. The underlying idea is that, thanks to well-defined and measured relevant indicators, users can make an informed choice between available service offers, and insufficient QoS levels can be pointed out.

There exist several network neutrality monitoring tools in the research and development literature. Each currently existing tool as of 2021 actually focuses on specific service-based traffic differentiation; there is to our knowledge no comprehensive tool encompassing the monitoring of all known infringements. In

---

[1] https://lafibre.info/transit-ip/qos-cogent/ (in French).

[2] https://www.phonandroid.com/free-youtube-problemes-debit.html (in French).

general, the focus is either on a specific protocol (HTTP, TCP, FTP, etc.), on the service type (historically in most cases BitTorrent since historically the most differentiated type of traffic, but it also often concerns video streaming, video gaming, file transfer, etc.), or on the specific application (the main targets being YouTube, DOOM, Facebook, etc.).

Monitoring is performed through measurements, which are separated into two classes: *active* measurements and *passive* measurements, even if a combination of both is always possible. The principle of active measurement methods is to inject traffic into the network in order to investigate its performance and compute performance metrics, for example, end-to-end delay of packets, throughput of a flow, loss rate, etc. The generated traffic has to perfectly mimic the targeted one to ensure a real performance replication. Among criticisms though, active measurements induce an increased network load, meaning that it has to be implemented with parsimony to limit the additional congestion, and it could also induce increased fees for mobile users, for instance, since often included in their data plans. Passive measurements on the other hand monitor existing user traffic without the cost of introducing additional artificial traffic; the analysis of existing and "real" traffic may however be more tricky and limited than with controlled traffic that is injected for the specific purpose of performance evaluation.

We now list and provide a brief description of some existing tools, in line with what was published in [31]; see also [145] for a list provided by Ofcom.

- A first deployed tool is *Switzerland* [53] that was released in 2008. Its goal is to detect packet manipulation between two nodes of the network. To realize this objective, the targeted packets are hashed to investigate if new packets are injected or if the sent ones are dropped or modified. More precisely, a modified traffic is detected from different hashes, dropped packets detected, thanks to received hash from the sender only (i.e., not found on the receiver side), and new injected traffic is detected if a hash appears on the receiver only. To compare hashes at origin and destination, the first n bits of these hashes are sent with a timestamp to a server. Therefore, even if no extra traffic is generated from source to destination, a traffic containing those hashes is generated from source and destination to a verification server, meaning that the measures can be considered as "semi-passive." This method is considered costly since requiring to carry out hashing and communication to the server; it also suffers from a lack of anonymity.
- *NetPolice* [183] addresses a specific issue through measurements at the edge: it looks if traffic type, origin, or destination influences routing, which as a consequence also means a difference in terms of performance. Measurements are made by sending packets with an adjusted Time-To-Live (TTL) field: a packet is dropped when its TTL reaches 0, and a notification is sent to the sender, while no notification occurs when differentiation is applied. Furthermore, thanks to tomography theory, it is possible to detect when a potential differentiation is carried out by sending probes for various (source, destination) pairs.

- *NANO* [22] is one of the few tools using passive measurement techniques. It seeks to point out differentiation due to factors such as operating system, geographical location, source and destination addresses, time of the day, type of physical link, etc. The measurements are sent to a server analyzing the results, thanks to the declared above characteristics, and statistically compared.
- *Glasnost* [47] and its mobile terminal variant *BonaFide* [17] are active measurement tools sending a specific traffic (peer-to-peer, Web, mail, and SSH) through the network and resending it by just changing one of its characteristics suspected to be a cause of differentiation, such as port number. Non-neutrality is investigated by comparing the results.
- *DiffProbe* [82] is another (active measurement) tool, making the assumption that a non-neutral ISP separates the traffic into two classes: one with high priority and the other with low priority. By sending an original flow and a probing flow simultaneously, a performance comparison is carried out.
- Similarly to DiffProbe, *POPI* [98] is an active measurement tool aiming at detecting prioritization between traffic through active measurements. For the various types of traffic, packets are sent by bursts, and losses are detected and compared.
- *Packsen* [176] also enters the category of priority detection tools. It singles out the characteristic suspected to create differentiation (such as port number or time of day), and then two flows are sent, the original and the one without the characteristic, and their performance compared.
- *OONIProbe* [135], still an active measurement tool, is tackling a different issue: the blocking of Web pages, instant messaging applications, or overlay network traffic. It compares the connectivity results obtained through a DNS resolution from an ISP and an assumed-neutral reference from Google DNS servers (which could be subject to discussion).
- *Wehe* [127] is a tool co-developed by a regulator, ARCEP, and academia, here Boston's Northeastern University. It is to our knowledge the first publicly available tool co-designed by a regulator even if limited in terms on non-compliance detection. It is an active measurement tool primarily aimed at mobile terminals, since wireless networks are suspected to be where most net neutrality infringements are experienced (which makes a lot of sense due to the scarcity of radio resources). The general idea is to send two versions of a pre-recorded and often targeted traffic (some available ones on the application are flows for Hangouts, Netflix, Skype, Spotify, Viber, and YouTube) and to statistically test if there are significant differences in terms of throughput between those two sent versions: the original one and an encrypted one that an ISP could not identify (and therefore discriminate). France has been the European country which has been tested the most by Wehe. According to preliminary results, no infringement has yet been detected by users, but this was not the case in its western European neighbors Germany, Ireland, Spain, and especially the UK.

Table 9.1 Summary and comparison of developed net neutrality tools

Tool	Traffic	Metrics	Measure	Test
Switzerland	any	packet hash	semi-passive	hash comparison
NetPolice	HTTP, BitTorrent, SMTP, PPLive, VoIP	packet loss rate	active	Kolmogorov-Smirnov (KS) with Jackknife
NANO	any	throughput	passive	causal inference
Glasnost	BitTorrent (can add others)	throughput	active	max. throughput comparison
DiffProbe	Skype, Vonage	packet loss rate, delay	active	Kullback-Leibler divergence
POPI	ICMP, FTP, Telnet, POP3, BGP, HTTPS, Fasttrack, Donkey, Gnutella, BitTorrent	packet loss rate	active	ranking, averaging and clustering
Packsen	BitTorrent	inter-arrival packet time	active	Mann-Whitney U
OONIProbe	web, DNS, Tor, messaging apps	DNS resolution, connection success	active	comparison
ChkDiff	any	packet loss rate, delay	active	Kolmogorov-Smirnov
CONNEcT	any	packet loss rate	passive	no analysis
Wehe	any	packet loss rate, throughput, delay	active	KS-inspired
nntool	any	port blocking, proxy detection or DNS manipulation	active	no analysis

- *nntool*. BEREC is following the ARCEP view and is defining a network neutrality[3] tool available starting in December 2019 for iOS, Android, browser, and desktop, with usage indicators on Web browsing or video streaming quality and net neutrality investigations about port blocking, proxy detection, or DNS manipulation.
- *CONNEcT* [124] is a tool claimed to be specifically designed to escape ISP oversight trying to bypass measurements from traditional neutrality tools: ISPs trying, for example, to detect uncommon TTL values by NetPolice (common values are 64 or 128). When an ISP detects a measurement campaign, it can indeed momentarily suspend its differentiation procedures. CONNEcT aims at avoiding tool detection by making use of a meta-communication called a covered channel: a hidden synchronization allows two machines to insert messages into the legit traffic data with an offset only known by both of them. This hidden data contains measures concerning the previous packet such as a timestamp, a packet pseudo-hash, etc.

The characteristics of the above tools are summarized in Table 9.1.

9.2.3   The Limits of the Existing Tools

As seen in the previous subsection, several tools exist to monitor ISP activity, with the purpose of detecting violations of neutrality principles. But all tools suffer from some deficiencies, as pointed out in the conclusions of Ofcom in 2015 about tools [145]. Note also that a "'positive" detection does not necessarily mean a deliberate intent to introduce bias: some technical reasons may be the origin. This complicates the work from regulators who have to process official complaints (sometimes in

---

[3] https://github.com/net-neutrality-tools/nntool.

court). The issues/defaults of existing detection tools can be regrouped in the following categories:

1. *Sustainability*. Most of the tools described above are actually academic tools developed during research projects. Maintenance, duration of life, and even availability are major issues when the projects are terminated. Among the above tools, Switzerland, Glasnost, DiffProbe, and BonaFide are not maintained anymore. In addition, some tools were not released for public usage, but instead only designed with a purpose limited to the contour and illustration within a research project; this is the case of NetPolice, NANO, POPI, Packsen, or ChkDiff. For a tool such as CONNEcT, no implementation has been developed to our knowledge, the tool being actually just a proof of concept. Designing sustainable tools is therefore a major challenge, and initiatives launched by regulators or government-related institutions (like Wehe, co-developed by ARCEP and nntool, supported by BEREC) or user associations (OONIProbe) who have an interest in maintaining such tools are probably the direction to be encouraged.

2. *Span of monitored infringements*. One limitation of the tools is that they usually target a specific net neutrality violation: traffic blocking; throughput limitation, for example; and/or a specific class of traffic such as peer-to-peer, YouTube, any video streaming, or HTML. But ideally a tool should be comprehensive in terms of testing hindrances and ideally even be pro-active by anticipating or investigating new infringements. This is unlikely though in a near future.

3. *Resource consuming*. To be accurate, tools need to perform tests that can be consuming from the end user side in terms of power, battery, bandwidth, CPU, data storage, or even data plans for active measurements; this may deter users from participating in the required periodic campaigns of tests. Simplicity of usage is also a key factor to keep people motivated by a regular and even occasional use. Users' involvement has probably to be as limited as possible to ensure success, which means campaigns using resources servers or terminals managed from regulators or user associations. Some such factors were hinted in the use of the tools described above. It was, for example, highlighted by Glasnost developers that when performing tests, half of the users were abandoning before the end since wanting to get a quicker result than what the tool was able to provide [47]. To solve storage issues, crowd-sensing procedures can be used to gather a huge amount of measures [126], introducing issues related to data anonymity, big data processing, citizen participation and incentives, etc.

4. *Mathematical rigor*. Finally, one of the limits of the tools is the lack of theoretical grounds for the statistical tests they implement. Tools such as NetPolice or ChkDiff use a Kolmogorov-Smirnov test, the most well-known statistical test to point out a difference in the distributions of two sets of samples, here to determine whether a traffic is differentiated with respect to another. The test involves very few assumptions but requires the independence of values within a sample set, which is hardly verified since successive sampled values of throughput, for example, are dependent due to a common backlog to be treated. Packsen uses another test, the Mann-Whitney U test, which looks at the difference between the median of inter-arrival times of two flows and is therefore much more

limited than the Kolmogorov-Smirnov test in terms of distribution comparison but anyway keeps the independence issue within sample sets. Other tools use customized metrics and make use of heuristic rules without theoretical ground to decide if differences are significant. A typical example is Glasnost, which evaluates an external noise as $(\text{bitrate}_{max} - \text{bitrate}_{mean})/\text{bitrate}_{max}$ and does not proceed to analysis if it exceeds 20%; otherwise, it quite arbitrarily decides that differentiation takes place if the difference between flow rates is larger than 50% of the maximum flow rate. DiffProbe uses the Kullback-Leibler divergence metric, known in the statistics literature, but no valid test exists using that metric, and heuristics are used to consider the divergence as representative or not of a service differentiation. Wehe also makes use of a customized Kolmogorov-Smirnov test (computing not the max difference between distributions but its "average" value) for which no statistical theory exists either. This illustrates that much more can be done to provide valid statistical tests for network neutrality measurement tools. Since the implemented tests are based on heuristics or do not verify required assumptions, they may be subject to complaints from ISPs and invalidated in court. They are therefore in general very conservative to limit false positives, which may leave some room for ISPs to implement (a limited) differentiation and still evade detection [32].

9.3   Monitoring Other Actors

Even if ISPs are at the center of the network neutrality debate, we have highlighted in the previous chapters that numerous other economic actors of the digital economy may behave non-neutrally and therefore need to be monitored. But are there available tools for that? We discuss below the case of two important other intermediaries, CDNs and search engines, and see that very little is existing.

9.3.1   Monitoring CDNs

The important role of CDNs, choosing which content to cache closer to users, therefore improving the quality of this specific content with respect to others, means that differentiation can lead to an "unfair" treatment based on commercial contracts or to advantage some partners (see Chap. 6). To our knowledge, regulators have not yet developed tools to ensure a "proper" behavior by CDNs, basically because the question has only recently been introduced or is even eluded by most regulators (see Chap. 2). Even the academic literature is quite slim on monitoring CDN activity. We can, for instance, cite [57] and the references therein which deal with identifying the location of caches from content requests. The purpose was to investigate performance from the user and content provider point of view, to understand where content is stored (namely, in which countries), which may create legal/privacy issues that are interesting from a regulator point of view. However, nothing is really related to the neutrality/fairness of the content cached.

CDNs themselves provide tools to assess their performance. It is typically what Amazon is doing[4] to monitor their service if you are a content provider and want to check whether the various downloads have been from the servers at the edge or not. Most if not all CDNs apply such technologies to improve understanding and reputation; Akamai is doing the same with Akamai mPulse.[5]

But are there independent tools able to monitor CDNs without having to blindly trust them? Very few public or commercial tools exist to measure CDN performance. ThousandEyes[6] and Splunk[7] are commercial tools for network performance monitoring in general, able among other things when looking at CDNs to compute their performance in terms of latency and fetch time and compare between edge and origin servers.

In this domain, a lot remains therefore to be done to monitor neutrality-related behaviors.

9.3.2 Monitoring Search Engines

Chapter 7 was mentioning bias potentially introduced by search engines to favor their own content or content from economic partners; this means putting forward some content, which is then more visible and therefore more often accessed, and downgrading other by placing it lower in the rankings. Here, too, very little software is known to help users and regulators to detect a non-neutral behavior from a search engine. There are research papers developing methodologies such as [128, 144, 171, 175, 177], but they are usually not accompanied with a usable and publicly available tool. We can mention the publicly available platform/Web page

https://snide.irisa.fr/

on which a keyword can be composed and the corresponding results from 15 engines are analyzed and compared, trying to point out outliers in the different rankings of the search engines that can be symptomatic of intentional bias (positive bias when putting forward a "'friend', or negative when forgetting a relevant but 'foe' link"). The methodology is described in Chap. 7 following [123], with statistical tests based on Dixon's Q test being performed. Since we are performing a statistical test, more specifically a test to reject a hypothesis, failing a test does not necessarily mean

---

[4] See   https://aws.amazon.com/fr/cloudfront/reporting/   or   https://docs.aws.amazon.com/AmazonCloudFront/latest/DeveloperGuide/monitoring-using-cloudwatch.html.

[5] https://developer.akamai.com/akamai-mpulse-real-user-monitoring-solution.

[6] https://www.thousandeyes.com/lps/network-monitoring/,   see   also   https://fr.slideshare.net/ThousandEyes/monitoring-cdn-performance about CDN monitoring for this tool.

[7] https://www.splunk.com/; see https://rigor.com/blog/monitor-optimize-your-cdn/ about CDNs.

Fig. 9.1 Home page of the Web site https://snide.irisa.fr/ *(left)* and for multiple searches *(right)* when clicking on "advanced"

intentional bias; it could be the result of statistical bad luck. It could additionally be for another reason, from using a different notion of relevance from the other engines when a given keyword is requested, which may be fully legitimate and even expected. But failing a test points out that scrutiny may be needed and a deeper investigation carried out.

The tool https://snide.irisa.fr/ is designed to work for single searches, showing the outputs of search engines, results of statistical tests, and even two meta-engines (aggregating all results and reducing biases) corresponding to a keyword. But it also offers the possibility to collect simultaneously the results (mostly for research purposes) for several searches when given a list of search terms, to analyze more generally if a search engine is regularly different from competitors. The home page for single and multiple searches is displayed in Fig. 9.1. An interested reader is advised to look at [123] for a more detailed description.

The outputs from the following 15 search engines are collected using a Web crawler written in Python:

- AllTheInternet
- AOL
- Ask
- Bing
- DirectHit
- Duckduckgo
- Ecosia
- Google
- Latlas
- Lilo
- Lycos
- Qwant
- Startpage
- Yahoo
- Yandex.

An example of result for a single search term, here "search neutrality," is presented in Fig. 9.2 (the ten first results of each search engine can also be displayed by clicking on the arrow button next to the search engine name). On the right of the figure, the results of the statistical tests described in Chap. 7 are provided. For the particular case displayed in Fig. 9.2, we note that no search engine can be pointed to have a score abnormally low (i.e., displaying different results from the others); among the top-ranked linked, the one with the lowest visibility (according to all engines) does not seem ranked too low by others; for the third test, the top-ranked links of some engines, here Ask, DirectHit, and Latlas, do not have a similar visibility by other engines (basically meaning that those links *may* be abusively ranked high); for the fourth test, the most visible link among all engines is not ranked abnormally low on any particular SE.

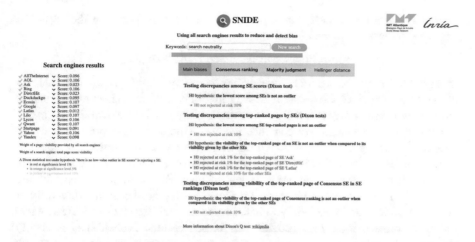

Fig. 9.2 Example of results for a simple search: here "search neutrality" in September 2021

9.4   Tools and Algorithmic Transparency

Even for the transparency of algorithms, there is very probably a need for tools. Here too, we are at the infancy of designing specific softwares, and to our knowledge, no public tool exists as of 2021. Knowing that fact, regulators are trying to establish guidelines toward the goal of defining and monitoring algorithmic transparency.

It is probably and notably why ARCEP in its 2019 report [64] raised specific issues related to algorithmic transparency requiring monitoring:

- About the collected data when relevant, particularly in the case of artificial intelligence: it should be made clear which data is used to train the algorithm, and the privacy issue should be clearly solved. Determining bias in the data is also considered an important aspect to be investigated and controlled, since impacting the output of the algorithm.
- About the algorithm flow of decision and the used algorithmic components which should be explained, as well as the level of personalization.
- About the metrics to report the algorithm performance, which have to be known and which can be monitored.

In summary, it is expected that decision-makers be provided with the tools to be able to understand the effects and consequences of algorithmic systems.

9.5   Fact-Checking Tools

Fact-checking tools are much more developed than algorithmic transparency described in the previous section, probably since it is an issue that has been raised in society for a longer period of time. Many tools are available on the Web. For example, at least 15 are mentioned on:

https://libguides.valenciacollege.edu/c.php,

probably the most famous ones being FactCheck.org, PolitiFact, or FullFact. As of 2021, the Duke Reporters' Lab already identified 305 fact-checking initiatives worldwide (human-driven mostly),[8] illustrating the need in a world where disinformation is spreading. We can mention that Google is also proposing a fact checker,[9] working a bit like a search engine, where you can compose a claim to check whether the assertion is true. As we mentioned, fact checkers are still mostly human-driven and themselves very subject to bias. For example, newspapers are often politically oriented and may distort fact-checking information, voluntarily or not. Even if it is believed that automated tools are not expected in a foreseeable future, automated tools may provide less biased results, even if bias is clearly still possible, and at a lesser cost. For this reason, there is an initiated research activity around deep learning AI algorithms for the veracity of claims. This typically involves several tasks such as collecting related information from a broad range of sources, understanding the stance and reputation/reliability of all the considered sources with respect to the claim, and finally deriving the truthfulness of the claim [50, 132]. Of course, automated tools do not solve the difficult question of defining *relevance* [100]. Also, interestingly, these tools are themselves subject to the neutrality and algorithmic transparency issues raised in the previous chapter.

---

[8] http://reporterslab.org/fact-checking/.

[9] https://toolbox.google.com/factcheck/explorer.

Chapter 10
Conclusions

This book had several purposes. First, to recall historical milestones and reasons why the network neutrality debate came up and became so vivid in our digital society: the Internet is perceived, rightfully or not, as a common good, and it is expected to be fairly shared; any attempt to block or even limit access to a digital service is perceived as a threat to society. Different views are opposed. Roughly speaking, computer scientists, involved in the creation of the network (even if initially a military network), are in large part strongly supporting neutrality, while economists are rather supporting the possibility of applying differentiation. We have presented in Chap. 2 the various existing definitions and laws passed worldwide, with the corresponding levels of strictness in terms of neutrality principles, and in Chap. 3 the different arguments in favor or against neutrality. As our main objective, we have illustrated, trying to be as neutral as possible with respect to the debate, that having a definitive and extreme answer on the debate may be unwise. This was pointed out through game-theoretic models in Chaps. 4 and 5, showing that counterintuitive outcomes may happen and that any statement has to be addressed with care.

But in the later chapters, we also have hinted that a lot needs to be done, meaning several challenges to solve, summarized below:

- Introducing a more general definition of neutrality to avoid bypasses from ISPs differentiating services through other technologies (e.g., the new gray zone around sponsored data) with an increasingly complex network, to encompass issues related to vertical integration, and to include the numerous other intermediaries between users and content (such as CDNs or search engines). This widening of the debate probably leads to linking the notion of neutrality to the notion of fairness: fairness defined at the packet or flow level is different from fairness at the search engine level for example. Do we need to define fairness each time it becomes necessary, or can we introduce a general definition that will be relevant to all problems?

P. Maillé, B. Tuffin, *From Net Neutrality to ICT Neutrality*,
https://doi.org/10.1007/978-3-031-06271-1_10

- Ideally, in the line of being more general, neutrality should be linked with the increasing algorithm transparency debate that regulators are also addressing.
- Finally, we have highlighted that enforcing neutrality means having at our disposal monitoring tools to check that rules are respected and to detect whether some other unexpected behaviors occur. Very few such tools currently exist, and an important challenge is to fulfill that goal.

Therefore, we believe that the debate is not really ready to be closed and that it may expand to more general issues. We hope that this book has helped the reader grasp the main issues, make their own opinion, and be able to understand, criticize, or even contribute to neutrality-related regulations for the network of the future.

References

1. L.A. Adamic, B.A. Huberman, Zipf's law and the Internet. Glottometrics **3**, 143–150 (2002)
2. K. Agarwal, P. Maillé, B. Tuffin, Impact of heterogeneous neutrality rules with competitive content providers, in *IFIP/IEEE International Symposium on Integrated Network Management*, Bordeaux, France, 17–21 May 2021
3. H. Allcott, M. Gentzkow, Social media and fake news in the 2016 election. J. Econ. Perspect. **31**(2), 211–236 (2017)
4. E. Altman, P. Bernhard, S. Caron, G. Kesidis, J. Rojas-Mora, S. Wong, A study of non-neutral networks with usage-based prices, in *Proceedings of the 3rd ETM Workshop*, Amsterdam (2010)
5. E. Altman, A. Legout, Y. Xu, Network non-neutrality debate: An economic analysis, in *Proceedings of Networking*, Barcelona. LNCS 6641 (Springer, Berlin, 2011), pp. 68–81
6. ARCEP, Internet and network neutrality. proposals and recommendations (2010). Available at https://www.arcep.fr/uploads/tx_gspublication/net-neutralite-orientations-sept2010-eng.pdf
7. ARCEP, L'état d'internet en France (in French). Technical report, ARCEP (2020)
8. R.C.G. Arnold, J. Scott Marcus, M. Waldburger, A. Schneider, B. Morasch, F. Schmid, All but neutral: citizen responses to the European Commission's public consultation on network neutrality, in *Net Neutrality Compendium*, ed. by L. Bellim P. De Filippi (Springer, Berlin, 2016), pp. 199–210
9. Assemblée Nationale, Conclusion des travaux d'une mission d'information sur la neutralité de l'internet et des réseaux (2011). Available at http://www.assemblee-nationale.fr/13/dossiers/neutralite_internet_reseaux.asp
10. D. Austin, How google finds your needle in the web's haystack. Am. Math. Soc. Feat. Column. **10**(12) (2006)
11. Autorité de la concurrence and Bundeskartellamt. Competition law and data (2016)
12. K. Avrachenkov, N. Litvak, Decomposition of the Google PageRank and Optimal Linking Strategy. Rapport de recherche RR-5101, INRIA (2004)
13. J.S. Bain, *Barriers to New Competition* (Harvard University Press, Cambridge, 1956)
14. F. Baker, D.L. Black, K. Nichols, S.L. Blake, Definition of the Differentiated Services Field (DS Field) in the IPv4 and IPv6 Headers. RFC 2474 (1998)
15. M. Balinski, R. Laraki, *Majority Judgment: Measuring Ranking and Electing* (MIT Press, Cambridge, 2010)
16. M. Balinski, R. Laraki, Judge: Don't vote! Oper. Res. **62**(3), 483–511 (2014)
17. V. Bashko, N. Melnikov, A. Sehgal, J. Schönwälder, Bonafide: a traffic shaping detection tool for mobile networks, in *2013 IFIP/IEEE International Symposium on Integrated Network Management* (2013)

© The Author(s), under exclusive license to Springer Nature Switzerland AG 2022   171
P. Maillé, B. Tuffin, *From Net Neutrality to ICT Neutrality*,
https://doi.org/10.1007/978-3-031-06271-1

18. M. Beckmann, C.B. McGuire, C.B. Winsten, *Studies in the Economics of Transportation* (Yale University Press, New Haven, 1956)
19. BEREC, BEREC guidelines on transparency in the scope of net neutrality: best practices and recommended approaches. Document number: BoR (11) 67 (2011). Available at https://berec.europa.eu/eng/document_register/subject_matter/berec/regulatory_best_practices/guidelines/365-berec-guidelines-on-transparency-in-the-scope-of-net-neutrality-best-practices-and-recommended-approaches
20. L. Bernaille, R. Teixeira, I. Akodkenou, A. Soule, K. Salamatian, Traffic classification on the fly. ACM SIGCOMM Comput. Commun. Rev. **36**(2), 23–26 (2006)
21. A.J. Biega, K.P. Gummadi, G. Weikum, Equity of attention: amortizing individual fairness in rankings, in *Proceedings of 41st International ACM SIGIR Conference on Research & Development in Information Retrieval*, New York (2018), pp. 405–414
22. M. Bin Tariq, M. Motiwala, N. Feamster, M. Ammar, Detecting Network Neutrality Violations with Causal Inference, in *CoNEXT '09: Proceedings of the 5th International Conference on Emerging Networking Experiments and Technologies* (2009), pp. 289–300
23. D.L. Black, Z. Wang, M.A. Carlson, W. Weiss, E.D. Davies, S.L. Blake, An Architecture for Differentiated Services. RFC 2475 (1998)
24. V. Bonneau, Evolution of the CDN market, in *CDN World Summit* (2010)
25. F. Boussion, P. Maillé, B. Tuffin, Net neutrality debate: Impact of competition among ISPs, in *Proceedings of the Fourth International Conference on COMmunication Systems and NETworkS (COMSNETS)*, Bangalore (2012)
26. W. Briglauer, C. Cambini, K. Gugler, V. Stocker, Net neutrality and high speed broadband networks: evidence from OECD countries, in *Proceedings of 23rd Biennial Conference of the International Telecommunications Society (ITS)* (2021)
27. J. Brill, Statement of the Commission regarding Google's search practices (2013). http://www.ftc.gov/public-statements/2013/01/statement-commission-regarding-googles-search-practices. Last accessed Nov 2021
28. Canadian Radio-television and Telecommunications Commission. Framework for assessing the differential pricing practices of internet service providers (2017). Available at http://crtc.gc.ca/eng/archive/2017/2017-104.htm
29. M. Candela, V. Luconi, A. Vecchio, Impact of the COVID-19 pandemic on the Internet latency: a large-scale study. Comput. Netw. **182** (2020)
30. S. Caron, E. Altman, G. Kesidis, Application neutrality and a paradox of side payments, in *Proceedings of the Re-Architecting the Internet Workshop* (2010)
31. X. Castoreo, P. Maillé, B. Tuffin, Weaknesses and challenges of network neutrality measurement tools, in *16th International Conference on Network and Service Management (CNSM)*, Bordeaux (2020)
32. X. Castoreo, P. Maillé, B. Tuffin, Analyzing the Wehe network Neutrality Monitoring Tool, in *Proceedings of GECON* (2021)
33. H. Chen, L. Li, Y. Chen, Explore success factors that impact artificial intelligence adoption on telecom industry in china. J. Manage. Anal. **8**(1), 36–68 (2021)
34. M. Cho, M. Choi, Pricing for mobile data services considering service evolution and change of user heterogeneity. IEICE Trans. Commun. **E96-B**(2), 543–552 (2013)
35. J.P. Choi, B.C. Kim, Net neutrality and investment incentives. RAND J. Econ. **41**(3), 446–471 (2010)
36. B.G. Chun, K. Chaudhuri, H. Wee, M. Barreno, C.H. Papadimitriou, J. Kubiatowicz, Selfish caching in distributed systems: A game-theoretic analysis, in *Proceedings of PODC'04* (ACM, New York, 2004), pp. 21–30
37. Cisco, Wholesale Content Delivery Networks: Unlocking New Revenue Streams and Content Relationships. Technical Report 710667, Cisco (2011)
38. P. Coucheney, P. Maillé, B. Tuffin, Impact of reputation-sensitive users and competition between ISPs on the net neutrality debate. IEEE Trans. Netw. Serv. Manag. **10**(4), 425–433 (2013)

39. P. Coucheney, P. Maillé, B. Tuffin, Network neutrality debate and ISP inter-relations: traffic exchange, revenue sharing, and disconnection threat. Netnomics 1(3), 155–182 (2014)
40. P. Crocioni, Net neutrality in Europe: desperately seeking a market failure. Telecommun. Policy 35(1), 1–11 (2011)
41. R. De', N. Pandey, A. Pal, Impact of digital surge during Covid-19 pandemic: a viewpoint on research and practice. Int. J. Inf. Manag. 55 (2020)
42. J.-C. de Borda, Mémoire sur les élections au scrutin, in *Mémoires de l'Académie Royale des Sciences* (1781), pp. 657–664
43. R.B. Dean, W.J. Dixon, Simplified statistics for small numbers of observations. Anal. Chem. 23(4), 636–638 (1951)
44. R. Dejarnette, Click-through rate of top 10 search results in Google (2012). http://www.internetmarketingninjas.com/blog/search-engine-optimization/click-through-rate. Last accessed 8 June 2017
45. X. Deng, Z. Feng, C.H. Papadimitriou, Power-law distributions in a two-sided market and net neutrality, in *Proceedings of 12th Conference on Web and Internet Economics (WINE 2016)*, Montreal (2016), pp. 59–72
46. N. Diakopoulos, M. Koliska, Algorithmic transparency in the news media. Digit. J. 5(7), 809–828 (2017)
47. M. Dischinger, M. Marcon, S. Guha, K.P. Gummadi, R. Mahajan, S. Saroiu, Glasnost: enabling end users to detect traffic differentiation, in *Proceedigs of USENIX Symposium on Networked Systems Design and Implementation* (2010)
48. A. Dixit, A model of duopoly suggesting a theory of entry barriers. Bell J. Econ. 10(1), 20–32 (1979)
49. W.J. Dixon, Processing data for outliers. Biometrics 9(1), 74–89 (1953)
50. C. Dulhanty, J.L. Deglint, I. Ben Daya, A. Wong, Taking a stance on fake news: Towards automatic disinformation assessment via deep bidirectional transformer language models for stance detection (2019)
51. C. Dwork, R. Kumar, M. Naor, D. Sivakumar, Rank aggregation methods for the web, in *Proceedings of 10th International Conference on World Wide Web (WWW)*, Hong Kong (2001), pp. 613–622
52. R. Easley, H. Guo, J. Krämer, From network neutrality to data neutrality: a techno-economic framework and research agenda. Inf. Syst. Res. 29(2), 253–272 (2018)
53. P. Eckersley, Switzerland Design (2008). https://www.eff.org/files/2018/06/21/design.pdf
54. N. Economides, J. Tag, Network neutrality on the internet: a two-sided market analysis. Inf. Econ. Policy 24(2), 91–104 (2012)
55. European Commission, Antitrust: commission fines google €2.42 billion for abusing dominance as search engine by giving illegal advantage to own comparison shopping service (2017). Press release, available at https://ec.europa.eu/commission/presscorner/detail/en/IP_17_1784
56. European Parliament and the Council of the European Union. Regulation (EU) 2015/2120 of the European parliament and of the council (2015). Available at https://eur-lex.europa.eu/legal-content/EN/TXT/HTML/?uri=CELEX:32015R2120&rid=2
57. X. Fan, E. Katz-Bassett, J. Heidemann, Assessing affinity between users and CDN sites, in *7th Workshop on Traffic Monitoring and Analysis (TMA)*, ed. by M. Steiner, P. Barlet-Ros, O. Bonaventure, vol. LNCS-9053. Traffic Monitoring and Analysis, Barcelona (2015), pp. 95–110. Part 3: Web
58. Federal Communications Commission, FCC classifies cable modem service as information service: initiates proceeding to promote broadband deployment and examine regulatory implications of classification (2002). Available at http://transition.fcc.gov/Bureaus/Cable/News_Releases/2002/nrcb0201.html
59. Federal Communications Commission, Appropriate framework for broadband access to the internet over wireline facilities. Policy statement FCC 05-151, CC Docket No. 02-33 (2005)
60. Federal Communications Commission, Preserving the open internet (2010). Available at https://docs.fcc.gov/public/attachments/FCC-10-201A1.pdf

61. Federal Communications Commission, FCC adopts strong, sustainable rules to protect the open internet (2015). Available at https://www.fcc.gov/document/fcc-adopts-strong-sustainable-rules-protect-open-internet

62. Federal Official Gazette, Federal telecommunications and broadcasting law (2017). Available at http://www.ift.org.mx/sites/default/files/contenidogeneral/asuntos-internacionales/federaltelecommunicationsandbroadcastinglawmexico.pdf

63. G. Ford, Covid-19 and broadband speeds: a multi-country analysis. Phoenix Cent. Policy Bull. **49** (2020)

64. French Ministry of Economy and Finance, Creating a French framework to make social media platforms more accountable: Acting in France with a European vision (2019). Available at https://minefi.hosting.augure.com/Augure_Minefi/r/ContenuEnLigne/Download?id=AE5B7ED5-2385-4749-9CE8-E4E1B36873E4&filename=Mission%20Re%CC%81gulation%20des%20re%CC%81seaux%20sociaux%20-ENG.pdf

65. D. Fudenberg, J. Tirole, *Game Theory* (MIT Press, Cambridge, 1991)

66. J. Fudickar, Net neutrality, vertical integration, and competition between content providers. Working Papers 2015014, Berlin Doctoral Program in Economics and Management Science (BDPEMS) (2015)

67. T. Garrett, L.E. Setenareski, L.M. Peres, L.C.E. Bona, E.P. Duarte Jr., Monitoring Network Neutrality: A Survey on Traffic Differentiation Detection. IEEE Commun. Surv. Tutorials **20**(3), 2486–2517 (2018)

68. Gas Telekommunikation Post und Eisenbahnen Bundesnetzagentur für Elektrizität. Net neutrality in Germany, Annual report 2017/2018 (2018). Available at https://www.bundesnetzagentur.de/SharedDocs/Downloads/EN/Areas/Telecommunications/Companies/MarketRegulation/NetNeutrality/NetNeutralityInGermanyAnnualReport2017_2018.pdf

69. A. Gore, Remarks as delivered by vice president Al Gore to the superhighway summit (1994)

70. G. Gourdin, P. Maillé, G. Simon, B. Tuffin, The economics of CDNs and their impact on service fairness. IEEE Trans. Netw. Serv. Manag. **14**(1), 22–33 (2017)

71. J. Groshek, K. Koc-Michalska, Helping populism win? social media use, filter bubbles, and support for populist presidential candidates in the 2016 us election campaign. Inf. Commun. Soc. **20**(9), 1389–1407 (2017)

72. O. Hart, J. Tirole, D.W. Carlton, ,O.E. Williamson, Vertical integration and market foreclosure, in *Brookings Papers on Economic Activity. Microeconomics* (1990), pp. 205–286

73. K. Hosanagar, R. Krishnan, M. Smith, J. Chuang, Optimal pricing of content delivery network (CDN) services, in *Proceedings of the 37th Annual Hawaii International Conference on System Sciences* (2004)

74. K. Hosanagar, J. Chuang, R. Krishnan, M.D. Smith, Service adoption and pricing of content delivery network (CDN) services. Manag. Sci. **54**(9), 1579–1593 (2008)

75. H.L. Hu, The political economy of governing ISPS in china: Perspectives of net neutrality and vertical integration. China Q. **207**, 523–540 (2011)

76. M.A. Jamison, R. Layton, Net Neutrality in the USA during Covid-19, in *Telecommunications Post-Covid (working title)*, ed. by J. Whalley (Forthcoming, 2022)

77. T. Jitsuzumi, Ten years of Japan's net neutrality policy: a review of the past and recommendations for the future, in *The 44th Research Conference on Communication, Information and Internet Policy* (2016)

78. C. Joe-Wong, S. Ha, M. Chiang, Sponsoring mobile data: An economic analysis of the impact on users and content providers, in *Proceedings of INFOCOM*, Hong-Kong (2015)

79. D.W. Jorgenson, K.M. Vu, The ICT revolution, world economic growth, and policy issues. Telecommun. Policy **40**(5), 383–397 (2016)

80. B. Jullien, W. Sand-Zantman, Internet regulation, two-sided pricing, and sponsored data. Int. J. Ind. Organ. **58**, 31–62 (2018)

81. A. Kamoun, Maillé, B. Tuffin, Evaluating the performance and neutrality/bias of search engines, in *Proceedings of 12th EAI International Conference on Performance Evaluation Methodologies and Tools (VALUETOOLS)*, Palma de Mallorca (2019)

82. P. Kanuparthy, C. Dovrolis, Diffprobe: detecting ISP service discrimination, in *Proceedings of IEEE INFOCOM*, San Diego (2010)

83. T. Karagiannis, K. Papagiannaki, M. Faloutsos, BLINC: multilevel traffic classification in the dark. ACM SIGCOMM Comput. Commun. Rev. **35**(4), 229–240 (2005)

84. S. Keshav, *An Engineering Approach to Computer Networking: ATM Networks, the Inteernet and the Telephone Network* (Addison-Wesley, Boston, 1999)

85. A. Kieffer, P. Maillé, B. Tuffin, Non-neutrality with users deciding differentiation: a satisfying option? in *Proceedings of IEEE MASCOTS* (2020)

86. K. Kilkki, *Differentiated Services for the Internet* (Macmillan Technical Publishing, Stuttgart, 1999)

87. S.Y. Kim, S.J. Jeon, H.Y. Kwon, Smart city, net neutrality, and antitrust: findings from Korea, in *21st Annual International Conference on Digital Government Research*, dg.o '20, New York (Association for Computing Machinery, New York, 2020), pp. 90–96

88. J. Kocsis, V.I. Weda, The innovation-enhancing effects of network neutrality. Technical report, SEO Report (2013)

89. A.M. Kovaks, Internet peering and transit. Technical report, Technology Policy Institute (2012)

90. J. Kulshrestha, M. Eslami, J. Messias, M.B. Zafar, S. Ghosh, K.P. Gummadi, K. Karahalios, Quantifying search bias, in *Proceedings of ACM Conference on Computer Supported Cooperative Work and Social Computing*, Portland (2017)

91. S. Kumar, S. Dharmapurikar, F. Yu, P. Crowley, J. Turner, Algorithms to accelerate multiple regular expressions matching for deep packet inspection, in *Proceedings of ACM SIGCOMM* (2006), pp. 339–350

92. R. Layton, Which open Internet framework is best for mobile app innovation? An empirical inquiry of Net neutrality rules around the world. PhD thesis, Technical Faculty of IT and Design, Aalborg University (2017)

93. P. L'Ecuyer, P. Maillé, N. Stier-Moses, B. Tuffin, Revenue-maximizing rankings for online platforms with quality-sensitive consumers. Oper. Res. **65**(2), 408–423 (2017)

94. P. L'Ecuyer, P. Maillé, N. Stier-Moses, B. Tuffin, Non-neutrality of search engines and its impact on innovation. Internet Technol. Lett. **1**(1) (2018)

95. M.A. Lemley, L. Lessig, The end of end-to-end: Preserving the architecture of the internet in the broadband era. UCLA Law Rev. **48**, 925 (2001)

96. T.M. Lenard, R.J. May (eds.) *Net Neutrality or Net Neutering: Should Broadband Internet Services be Regulated* (Springer, Berlin, 2006)

97. D. Lewandowski, Evaluating the retrieval effectiveness of web search engines using a representative query sample. J. Assoc. Inf. Sci. Technol. **66**(9), 1763–1775 (2015)

98. G. Lu, Y. Chen, S. Birrer, F.E. Bustamante, POPI: a user-level tool for inferring router packet forwarding priority. IEEE/ACM Trans. Netw. **18**(1), 1–14 (2010)

99. C.-J. Luh, S.-A. Yang, T.-L.D. Huang, Estimating Google's search engine ranking function from a search engine optimization perspective. Online Inf. Rev. **40**(2), 239–255 (2016)

100. E. Lurie, The challenges of algorithmically assigning fact-checks: a sociotechnical examination of Google's reviewed claims, in *Proceedings of the 10th ACM Conference on Web Science* (2018)

101. R.T.B. Ma, D.-M. Chiu, J.C.S. Lui, V. Misra, D. Rubenstein, Interconnecting eyeballs to content: a Shapley value perspective on ISP peering and settlement, in *Proceedings of International Workshop on Economics of Networked Systems (NetEcon)* (2008), pp. 61–66

102. R.T.B. Ma, D.-M. Chiu, J.C.S. Lui, V. Misra, D. Rubenstein, On cooperative settlement between content, transit and eyeball internet service providers, in *Proceedings of ACM International Conference on Emerging Networking EXperiments and Technologies (CoNEXT)* (2008)

103. R.T.B. Ma, D.M. Chiu, J.C.S. Lui, V. Misra, D. Rubenstein, On cooperative settlement between content, transit, and eyeball internet service providers. IEEE/ACM Trans. Netw. **19**(3), 802–815 (2011)

176 References

104. P. Maillé, B. Tuffin, *Telecommunication Network Economics: From Theory to Applications* (Cambridge University Press, Cambridge, 2014)

105. P. Maillé, B. Tuffin, Impact of Content Delivery Networks on service and content innovation, in *NetEcon 2015: the 10th Workshop on the Economics of Networks, Systems and Computation*, Portland (2015), pp. 1–4

106. P. Maillé, B. Tuffin, Users facing volume-based and flat-rate-based charging schemes at the same time, in *8th Latin American Network Operations and Management Symposium (LANOMS)*, Joao Pessoa (2015), pp. 23–26

107. P. Maillé, B. Tuffin, Non-neutrality pushed by big content providers, in *Proceedings of GECON*, Biarritz (2017)

108. P. Maillé, B. Tuffin, Preventing competition using side payments: when non-neutrality creates barriers to entry. NETNOMICS Eco. Res. Electron. Netw. **18**(1), 3–22 (2017)

109. P. Maillé, B. Tuffin, Analysis of sponsored data in the case of competing wireless service providers, in *NETGCOOP 2018 – 9th International Conference on Network Games, Control and Optimization*, New York City (2018), pp. 1–16

110. P. Maillé, B. Tuffin, Neutral and non-neutral countries in a global internet: what does it imply? in *Proceedings of GECON – 16th International Conference on the Economics of Grids, Clouds, Systems, and Services*, Leeds (Springer, Berlin, 2019)

111. P. Maillé, B. Tuffin, Wireless service providers pricing game in presence of possible sponsored data, in *15th International Conference on Network and Service Management (CNSM)*, Halifax (2019)

112. P. Maillé, B. Tuffin, Wireless service providers pricing game in presence of possible sponsored data, in *Proceedings of 15th IEEE International Conference on Network and Service Management (CNSM)*, Halifax (2019), pp. 1–5

113. P. Maillé, B. Tuffin, Big content providers weighing on non-neutrality? NETNOMICS Econ. Res. Electron. Netw. **22**, 1–26 (2021)

114. P. Maillé, B. Tuffin, Are search engines biased? Detecting and reducing bias using meta search engines. Electron. Commer. Res. Appl (in press). Available online 25 February 2022

115. P. Maillé, E. Markakis, M. Naldi, G. Stamoulis, B. Tuffin, An overview of research on sponsored search auctions. Electron. Commer. Res. J. **12**(3), 265–300 (2012)

116. P. Maillé, E. Markakis, M. Naldi, G. Stamoulis, B. Tuffin, Sponsored search auctions: an overview of research with emphasis on game theoretic aspects. Electron. Commer. Res. J. **12**, 265–300 (2012)

117. P. Maillé, P. Reichl, B. Tuffin, Internet governance and economics of network neutrality, in *Telecommunications Economics – Selected Results of the COST Action IS0605 EconTel*, ed. by A. Hadjiantonis, B. Stiller. Lecture Notes in Computer Science 7216 (Springer, Berlin, 2012), pp. 108–116

118. P. Maillé, K. Pires, G. Simon, B. Tuffin, How neutral is a CDN: an economic approach, in *Proceedings of the 10th International Conference on Network and Service Management (CNSM)* (IEEE, Piscataway, 2014)

119. P. Maillé, B. Tuffin, How do content delivery networks affect the economy of the internet and the network neutrality debate? in *Proceedings of 10th International Conference on Economics of Grids, Clouds, Systems, and Services (GECON)*. LNCS (Lecture Notes in Computer Science) 8914, Cardiff (Springer, Berlin, 2014), pp. 222–230

120. P. Maillé, G. Simon, B. Tuffin, Impact of revenue-driven CDN on the competition among network operators, in *Proceedings of CNSM* (2015)

121. P. Maillé, G. Simon, B. Tuffin, Toward a net neutrality debate that conforms to the 2010s. IEEE Commun. Mag. **54**(3), 94–99 (2016)

122. P. Maillé, G. Simon, B. Tuffin, Vertical integration of CDN and network operator: model and analysis, in *IEEE/ACM International Symposium on Modelling, Analysis and Simulation of Computer and Telecommunication Systems (MASCOTS 2016)*, London (2016)

123. P. Maillé, G. Maudet, M. Simon, B. Tuffin, Are Search Engines Biased? Detecting and Reducing Bias using Meta Search Engines. Working paper or preprint (2021)

124. A. Maltinsky, R. Giladi, Y. Shavitt, On Network Neutrality Measurements. ACM Trans. Intell. Syst. Technol. **8**(4) (2017)
125. J. McNamee, M. Fernandez Perez, Net neutrality: an analysis of the European Union's trialogue compromise, in *Net Neutrality Compendium*, ed. by L. Belli, P. De Filippi (Springer, Berlin, 2016), pp. 183–191
126. D. Miorandi, I. Carreras, E. Gregori, I. Graham, J. Stewart, Measuring net neutrality in mobile internet: towards a crowdsensing-based citizen observatory. *IEEE International Conference on Communications* (2013)
127. A. Molavi Kakhki, A. Razaghpanah, A. Li, H. Koo, R. Golani, D. Choffnes, P. Gill, A. Mislove, Identifying traffic differentiation in mobile networks, in *Proceedings of the 2015 Internet Measurement Conference* (2015), pp. 239–251
128. A. Mowshowitz, A. Kawaguchi, Assessing bias in search engines. Inf. Process. Manag. **38**(1), 141–156 (2002)
129. A. Mowshowitz, A. Kawaguchi, Measuring search engine bias. Inf. Process. Manag. **41**(5), 1193–1205 (2005)
130. J. Musacchio, J. Walrand, G. Schwartz, Network neutrality and provider investment incentives, in *Proceedings of 41st Asilomar Conference on Signals, Systems and Computers (ACSSC)* (2007), pp. 1437–1444
131. J. Musacchio, G. Schwartz, J. Walrand, A two-sided market analysis of provider investment incentives with an application to the net-neutrality issue. Rev. Netw. Eco. **8**(1) (2009)
132. P. Nakov, D. Corney, M. Hasanain, F. Alam, T. Elsayed, A. Barrón-Cedeño, P. Papotti, S. Shaar, G. Da San Martino, Automated fact-checking for assisting human fact-checkers (2021)
133. J.F. Nash, Equilibrium points in *n*-person games, in *Proceedings of NAS*, vol. 36 (1950), pp. 48–49
134. J. Nash, Two-person cooperative games. Econometrica 128–140 (1953)
135. Network Neutrality Squad, Open Observatory of Network Interference. https://www.ooni.org. Accessed 5 Mar 2020
136. M.E.J. Newman, Power laws, Pareto distributions and Zipf's law. Contemp. Phys. **46**(5), 323–351 (2005)
137. V. Nguyen, D. Mohammed, M. Omar, P. Dean, Net neutrality around the globe: a survey, in *2020 3rd International Conference on Information and Computer Technologies (ICICT)* (2020), pp. 480–488
138. P. Njoroge, A. Ozdaglar, N. Stier-Moses, G. Weintraub, Investment in two sided markets and the net neutrality debate. Technical Report DRO-2010-05, Columbia University, Decision, Risk and Operations Working Papers Series (2010)
139. A. Odlyzko, The history of communications and its implications for the Internet. Technical report, AT&T Labs (2000)
140. OECD, Algorithms and collusion: Competition policy in the digital age (2017). http://www.oecd.org/competition/algorithms-collusion-competition-policy-in-the-digital-age.htm
141. M. Osborne, A. Rubinstein, *A Course in Game Theory* (MIT Press, Cambridge, 1994)
142. H. Pang, L. Gao, Q. Ding, L. Sun, When data sponsoring meets edge caching: a game-theoretic analysis. CoRR, abs/1709.00273 (2017)
143. A. Pisantly, Network neutrality under the lens of risk management, in *Net Neutrality Compendium*, ed. by L. Belli, P. De Filippi (Springer, Berlin, 2016), pp. 53–62
144. E. Pitoura, P. Tsaparas, G. Flouris, I. Fundulaki, P. Papadakos, S. Abiteboul, G. Weikum, On Measuring Bias in Online Information. ACM SIGMOD Rec. **46**(4), 16–21 (2018)
145. Predictable Network Solutions Limited, Traffic management detection methods and tools (2015). Available at https://www.ofcom.org.uk/research-and-data/technology/internet-wifi/traffic-management
146. R. Preston Mcafee, H.M. Mialon, M.A. Williams, Economics and antitrust barriers to entry (2003). http://vita.mcafee.cc/PDF/Barriers2Entry.pdf

147. S. Puopolo, M. Latouche, F. Le Faucheur, J. Defour, CDN federations: how SPs can win the battle for content-hungry consumers. Technical report, Cisco (2011). "Point of View" White Paper
148. P. Reichl, R. Schatz, B. Tuffin, Logarithmic laws in service quality perception: where microeconomics meets psychophysics and quality of experience. Telecommun. Syst. **52**(2), 587–600 (2013)
149. G. Robb, R. Hawthorne, Net neutrality and market power: the case of South Africa. Telecommun. Policy **43**(9), 101814 (2019)
150. R.E. Robertson, S. Jiang, K. Joseph, L. Friedland, D. Lazer, C. Wilson, Auditing partisan audience bias within google search, in *Proceedings of the ACM on Human-Computer Interaction*, 2 (CSCW) (2018)
151. D. Rushe, Eric Schmidt Google senate hearing – as it happened (2012). http://www.guardian. co.uk/technology/blog/2011/sep/21/eric-schmidt-google-senate-hearing. Last accessed Nov 2021
152. C.V. Saavedra, Bargaining power and the net neutrality debate (2009). www.sites.google.com/ site/claudiasaavedra/attachments/bargaining_power.pdf
153. H. Saunders, IP interconnection: trends and emerging issues (2012)
154. H. Schulzrinne, Network neutrality is about money, not packets. IEEE Int. Comput. **22**(6), 8–17 (2018)
155. B. Schwarz, Content delivery networks 3.0. Technical report, CTOiC White paper (2013)
156. D. Shin, A comparative analysis of net neutrality: Insights gained by juxtaposing the U.S. and Korea. Telecommun. Policy **38**(11), 1117–1133 (2014)
157. E.-K. Shin, D.-H. Han, How will net neutrality be played out in Korea? Gov. Inf. Q. **29**(2), 243–251 (2012)
158. I. Smirnova, E. Lipenbergs, V. Bobrovs, P. Gavars, G. Ivanovs, Network slicing in the scope of net neutrality rules, in *2019 PhotonIcs Electromagnetics Research Symposium – Spring (PIERS-Spring)* (2019), pp. 1516–1521
159. R. Somogyi, The economics of zero-rating and net neutrality. CORE Discussion Papers 2016047, Université catholique de Louvain, Center for Operations Research and Econometrics (CORE) (2016)
160. F. Sorensen, A Norwegian perspective on European regulation of net neutrality, in *Net Neutrality Compendium*, ed. by L. Belli, P. De Filippi (Springer, Berlin, 2016)
161. F. Sorensen, Specialised services and the net neutrality service model, in *Net Neutrality Compendium*, ed. by L. Belli, P. De Filippi (Springer, Berlin, 2016), pp. 99–107
162. F. Sorensen, COVID-19 and the value of Internet Openness: The European experience, in *The Value of Internet Openness in Time of Crisis, Internet Governance Forum* (2020)
163. F. Sorensen, The Norwegian model for net neutrality. http://is.gd/HtQuuJ
164. E. Stepanova, The role of information communication technologies in the "Arab spring". PONARS Eurasia Policy Memo No. 159 (2011)
165. R.D. Triviño, A.A. Franco, R.L. Ochoa, Internet and net neutrality in the time of covid-19: a global overview, in *2021 Eighth International Conference on eDemocracy eGovernment (ICEDEG)* (2021), pp. 133–138
166. A. Tsamados, N. Aggarwal, J. Cowls, J. Morley, H. Roberts, M. Taddeo, L. Floridi, The ethics of algorithms: key problems and solutions. AI & Soc **37**, 215–230 (2022)
167. B. Tuffin, Side payments as barriers to entry in non-neutral networks, in *Proceedings of IEEE Conference of Telecommunication, Media and Internet Techno-Economics (CTTE)*, Munich (2015)
168. USACM, Statement on algorithmic transparency and accountability. Technical report, US Public Policy Council (2017). http://www.acm.org/binaries/content/assets/public-policy/ 2017_usacm_statement_algorithms.pdf
169. P.A. Vargas-Lopez, Net neutrality: an overview of enacted laws in South America, in *Net Neutrality Compendium*, ed. by L. Belli, P. De Filippi (Springer, Berlin, 2016), pp. 109–126
170. H.R. Varian, Position auctions. Int. J. Ind. Organ. **25**, 1163–1178 (2005)

171. L. Vaughan, M. Thelwall, Search engine coverage bias: evidence and possible causes. Inf. Process. Manag. **40**(4), 693–707 (2004)

172. D. Vise, The Google story. Strateg. Dir. **23**(10) (2007)

173. P. Vyavahare, J. Nair, D. Manjunath, Sponsored data: on the effect of ISP competition on pricing dynamics and content provider market structures, in *MobiHoc'19*, Catania (2019)

174. J. Walrand, P. Varaiya, *High-Performance Communication Networks*, 2nd edn. (Morgan Kaufmann Publishers, Burlington, 2000)

175. W. Webber, A. Moffat, J. Zobel, A similarity measure for indefinite rankings. ACM Trans. Inf. Syst. **28**(4), 20:1–20:38 (2010)

176. U. Weinsberg, A. Soule, L. Massoulie, Inferring traffic shaping and policy parameters using end host measurements, in *Proceedings of IEEE INFOCOM* (2011)

177. J. D. Wright, Defining and measuring search bias: Some preliminary evidence. George Mason Law & Economics Research Paper 12–14, George Mason University School of Law (2012)

178. T. Wu, Network neutrality, broadband discrimination. J. Telecommun. High Technol. **2**(1), 141–176 (2003)

179. T. Wu, L. Lessig, Ex Parte Submission in CS docket No. 02-52 (2003). available at http://www.savetheinternet.com/sites/default/files/resources/wu_lessig_fcc.pdf

180. Z. Xiong, S. Feng, D. Niyato, P. Wang, Y. Zhang, Competition and cooperation analysis for data sponsored market: a network effects model. ArXiv e-prints (2017).

181. C.S. Yoo, J. Lambert, 5G and net neutrality, in *The future of the Internet – Innovation, integration and sustainability*, ed. by G. Knieps, V. Stocker, Nomos (2019)

182. H.P. Young, An axiomatization of Borda's rule. J. Econ. Theory **69**(1), 43–52 (1974)

183. Y. Zhang, Z. Morley Mao, M. Zhang, Detecting traffic differentiation in backbone ISPS with netpolice, in *Proceedings of 9th ACM SIGCOMM conference on Internet measurement (IMC)*, Chicago (2009), pp. 103–115

184. L. Zhang, W. Wu, D. Wang, Sponsored data plan: a two-class service model in wireless data networks. SIGMETRICS Perform. Eval. Rev. **43**(1), 85–96 (2015)

Printed in the United States
by Baker & Taylor Publisher Services